AGAINST THE ODD

Against the Odds?

Social Class and Social Justice in Industrial Societies

GORDON MARSHALL
ADAM SWIFT
and
STEPHEN ROBERTS

CLARENDON PRESS · OXFORD
1997

Oxford University Press, Great Clarendon Street, Oxford OX2 6DP

Oxford New York
Athens Auckland Bangkok Bogota Bombay
Buenos Aires Calcutta Cape Town Dar es Salaam
Delhi Florence Hong Kong Istanbul Karachi
Kuala Lumpur Madras Madrid Melbourne
Mexico City Nairobi Paris Singapore
Taipei Tokyo Toronto
and associated companies in
Berlin Ibadan

Oxford is a trade mark of Oxford University Press

Published in the United States
by Oxford University Press Inc., New York

British Library Cataloguing in Publication Data
Data available

Library of Congress Cataloging in Publication Data
Marshall, Gordon.
Against the odds?: social justice in modern Britain/Gordon
Marshall, Adam Swift, and Stephen Roberts.
Includes bibliographical references and index.
1. Social mobility—Great Britain. 2. Social classes—Great
Britain. 3. Social justice. I. Adam, Swift. II. Roberts,
Stephen, 1950– . III. Title.
HN400.S65M37 1996 305.5'13'0941—dc21—96-40028
ISBN 0–19–829240–6
ISBN 0–19–829239–2 (Pbk.)

Typeset by Best-set Typesetter Ltd., Hong Kong
Printed in Great Britain
on acid-free paper by
Bookcraft (Bath) Ltd
Midsomer Norton, Somerset

PREFACE

This book explores the implications of social class for social justice by studying patterns of social mobility in modern Britain. Class analysts seem to find discussion of justice unhelpfully abstract and akin to splitting philosophical hairs. Political theorists may be oblivious to some of the difficulties involved in conducting empirical investigations of class inequality. The argument that follows is an attempt to link these two traditions of research in a manner that gives due recognition to the complexities of both.

That argument has its origins in a series of conversations between Marshall and Swift. These served to convince us that the hitherto largely separate debates about class and justice converged upon important issues of common interest. An earlier indication of our thinking about these issues, published as an article in a scholarly journal, provoked a certain amount of ill-tempered controversy (compare Marshall and Swift (1993), Saunders (1995), Lampard (1996), and Marshall and Swift (1996)). Perhaps critics will find this new and fuller account more persuasive. We hope at least that it demonstrates the value of cross-disciplinary dialogue to sceptical colleagues in sociology and political theory.

Our evidence relates mainly to Britain, although data from a dozen or so other industrialized societies have also been examined for purposes of comparison, and these are introduced at appropriate points in the analysis. The various sources are outlined briefly in Chapter 1. Full technical details of the relevant data-sets are given in Appendix A.

We owe a substantial debt to the many other researchers originally involved in gathering this material. The data from the International Social Justice Project (ISJP) were provided by Galin Gornev, Pepka Boyadjieva, Petr Matějů, Jan Hartl, Andrus Saar, Bernd Wegener, Stefan Liebig, Tamas Kolosi, Antal Orkeny, Maria Nemenyi, Gyorgy Csepeli, Masaru Miyano, Akihiro Ishikawa, Wil Arts, Piet Hermkens, Witold Morawski, Bogdan Cichomski, Aleksander Borkowski, Ludmilla Khakhulina, Svetlana Sydorenko, Vojko Antoncic, David Mason, James Kluegel, and Duane Alwin. Much of the difficult work involved in merging and standardizing the ISJP surveys was done, under Alwin's direction, by David Klingel and Merilynn Dielman at the Institute for Social Research (University of Michigan, Ann Arbor). Anthony Heath and John Goldthorpe first provided, and then helped guide us through, the various codebooks for the British General Election Surveys and the CASMIN (Comparative Analysis of Social Mobility in Industrial Nations) Project. Jane Roberts extracted the relevant variables from the Essex Class Study, and provided assistance in pooling data-sets held at the archive in the Social Studies Faculty, University of Oxford. Without this collective effort our study would not have been possible.

Thanks are also due to a number of friends and colleagues for the generosity and good humour with which they offered advice and encouragement. In particular, we wish to record our gratitude to Carole Burgoyne, Matthew Clayton, David Cox, Rosemary Crompton, Robert Erikson, David Firth, David Routh, and Andrew Williams. John Goldthorpe and David Miller deserve particular mention for reading an earlier draft of the manuscript and making many helpful suggestions.

Some of the analysis was done during leave granted to Marshall and Swift, generously supported by a British Academy/Leverhulme Trust Senior Research Fellowship and by Balliol College, respectively. Earlier versions of parts of the text have appeared in *The British Journal of Sociology*, *The European Sociological Review*, and *Sociology*.

Finally, since the production of a volume such as this imposes all sorts of unreasonable demands on the time and energy of its authors, we must thank Heather, Greg, Lucy, Danny, and Lillie for their invaluable support.

CONTENTS

THE AUTHORS

GORDON MARSHALL is an Official Fellow of Nuffield College, Oxford, and was formerly Professor of Sociology at the University of Bath.

ADAM SWIFT is Fellow in Politics and Sociology, Balliol College, Oxford.

STEPHEN ROBERTS was formerly a Research Officer at Nuffield College, Oxford.

TABLES

FIGURES

1

Introduction

I

What is the relation between social class and social justice? Few would deny that the distribution of rewards in Britain today is unequal. There is, however, sharp disagreement about whether or not such inequality can be justified.

This is a matter of public as well as academic controversy. The reports of The Commission on Social Justice (1993: 14; 1994: 81–2) argue that, in Britain at least, class is the most important determinant of a person's life-chances and so ranks first among the factors that make ours an unfair society. For example, observing that children of fathers in un-skilled and semi-skilled manual jobs are one-third as likely to enter university as they would be were places allocated at random, the Com-missioners conclude that this demonstrates both that British society is stratified by class and that class differences in access to positions of advantage are unjust. It is clear that, for many on the political left, the connection between social class and social injustice is axiomatic.

Conversely, among those on the political right, inequalities between classes are often attributed to those personal traits that are said to distinguish virtuous from undeserving individuals. For example, one popular interpretation of the high rates of unemployment and poverty among the so-called underclass in Britain is that the dependency of single-parent families on state welfare has created a subculture which devalues work and education, encourages crime, and so perpetuates deprivation. From this point of view, the economic circumstances of the underclass, and its tendency to self-reproduction, are by no means un-just or the result of social barriers to advancement. They derive mainly from the self-defeating attitudes and behaviour of the poor themselves. Here, as elsewhere in market societies, class inequalities reflect the distribution of just rewards to differently deserving households.[1]

Social scientists are no less divided on this issue. On the one hand, and having identified substantial discrepancies in the chances of securing privileged white-collar occupations between children from middle-class and working-class backgrounds, the authors of the well-known Oxford Social Mobility Study maintain that

where inequalities in class chances of this magnitude can be displayed, the presumption must be, we believe, that to a substantial extent they do reflect inequalities of opportunity that are rooted in the class structure, and are not simply the outcome of the differential 'take-up' of opportunities by individuals with differing genetic, moral, or other endowments that do not derive from their class position. (Goldthorpe et al. 1980: 252)

In fact most studies of class routinely deploy a similar language of social injustice or unequal access to positions of advantage.[2]

However, as Peter Saunders (1990: 51, 82–3) and others have argued in reply, 'to show that a society is unequal is by no means the same as showing that it is unfair'. The ideal of equality, at least as Saunders construes it, does not admit of the possibility that talents are unequally distributed, with the most gifted people tending to rise to the highest social positions, and passing on their (perhaps genetic) endowments to their children. In class analysis, innate advantages (notably inherited intelligence) or social perquisites (such as parental support and encouragement) are assumed either not to exist or to be evenly distributed across the different social classes. In the case of the Oxford study, for example, critics have claimed that no justification is given for the presumption of unequal opportunities, and no attempt was made to compare the abilities of people who had been upwardly mobile with those who had not. On this account, inequalities of outcome and of mobility chances may simply be a reflection of the unequal distribution of talents, and entirely compatible with social justice. As Keith Joseph and Jonathan Sumption (1979: 30) state with characteristic bluntness, 'anyone who accepts that all individuals are not capable of the same achievements, must also agree that perfect equality of opportunity will give rise to very striking inequalities of results'.

The purpose of this study is therefore to consider the evidence for and against these radically different interpretations of the relationship between social class, social mobility, and social justice. We seek to do so in a way that gives due recognition to the complexities both of empirical class analysis and of normative political theory. At the same time, we will attempt to make the issues raised by each of these literatures accessible to readers familiar only with discussion in the other, while retaining sufficient detail (sometimes in notes and appendices) to satisfy the specialist. We hope this will encourage our perhaps diverse readership to resist the temptation to skip sections in accordance with disciplinary backgrounds and interests. The argument here presented, if it is to be at all convincing, must draw on political theory and sociological analysis in equal measure.

II

That argument will be constructed in the following way. We begin by reviewing several competing conceptions of social justice—each of which is of possible relevance to the issue of social class. We also contrast inequalities of outcome (or condition) and inequalities of access (or opportunity). This distinction is fundamental to our analysis and explains why issues of social mobility have been placed centre-stage.

In Chapter 3, we describe in some detail the conception of social class that informs our investigation, since this determines the methodology that we adopt in studying patterns of social mobility. More specifically, we explain the theoretical rationale behind the so-called Goldthorpe class schema, and examine the implications of this particular approach to class analysis for the study of issues of social justice.

Chapter 4 then introduces the data on social mobility in advanced societies. These demonstrate the general increase in mobility chances throughout the industrialized world during the course of the twentieth century. They show that, because of the steady expansion of skilled white-collar work, there are more opportunities for mobility now than were available in previous decades. However, the distribution of these enhanced opportunities across classes is quite another matter, and this further consideration focuses attention squarely upon the principle of equality of opportunity and the question of relative mobility chances.

We observe that, of the many possible justifications for class inequality, appeals to equal opportunities—equal access to unequally rewarded positions—are most frequently heard and have been most influential. In democratic capitalist and state-socialist societies alike, this principle has been linked closely to the notion of merit, so that unequal outcomes are seen to be a reflection of the differing abilities of those taking part in the competition to secure the most advantageous class positions. A central theme of our analysis will therefore be the role of education in distributing individuals to the various locations in the class structure.

Of course, to identify merit with educational achievement is somewhat simplistic, but (as we shall see) this is certainly how the meritocratic defence of class inequality has most commonly been constructed, at least by sociologists. Proponents of this argument concede both that origins influence destinations and that people from different class backgrounds tend to perform differently in educational terms. But they also insist that as long as the first of these associations is explained by the second, and the second simply reflects class differences in relevant abilities, then there is nothing here that fails to satisfy the demands of social justice.

Do class inequalities and unequal mobility chances in fact reflect merit rather than inequalities of opportunity? Our own findings, which are reported mainly in Chapters 5 and 6, suggest that, even when educational attainment is held constant, social origins still exert an important influence upon class destinations. Most noticeably, among individuals attaining only modest educational credentials, those from relatively privileged class backgrounds are less likely to arrive at working-class destinations than are similarly qualified men and women from disadvantaged class backgrounds. Moreover, a sex effect is also apparent, since women tend to fare worse than their male class and educational peers. It might be argued, therefore, that class privilege (and being a man) offers a measure of protection against the consequences of educational failure that is inconsistent with meritocratic principles.

Matters are, however, not that straightforward. As we explain in Chapter 7, there are several varying interpretations of merit, with distinctive conceptions tending to be appealed to in different contexts. In a variety of ways these make it illegitimate to draw conclusions about meritocracy from evidence about people's educational achievements. Once complications such as these are acknowledged, the fact that class background affects a person's opportunity to achieve or maintain an advantaged position, over and above its effects on his or her educational attainments, need not undermine the meritocratic defence of existing inequalities and mobility patterns. However, further difficulties do then arise for that defence, once we see that it depends typically upon the claim that people deserve to be rewarded in proportion to their merits. This, we suggest, is problematic, since it is hard to see how one person can deserve greater reward than another, when it is a matter of chance that he or she possesses the merits supposed to justify that greater reward. The normative issues here are complex, and are discussed at some length in Chapter 8.

III

This is but a crude summary of what is to come, since numerous difficulties pertaining to the formulation of concepts and collection of data are also addressed, as the argument unfolds.

Our data comprise a number of large-scale social surveys conducted mainly by sociologists during the past quarter of a century or so. In fact twenty such data-sets were examined in detail. Six of these are taken from prominent studies of modern Britain. However, in order to set the British results in context, we have also consulted similar surveys for a wide variety of industrialized nations. Some basic information about all of these sources is given in Appendix A.

The speed of recent political changes in Europe is such that some of the countries referred to no longer exist as nation-states, although they are treated as such in this volume, mainly for technical reasons. For example, we have found that it is not possible meaningfully to disaggregate our data for Czechoslovakia, or (conversely) to merge those for the former German Federal and Democratic Republics. We do not think that this anomaly undermines our arguments in any way. Moreover, although the surveys span some twenty or more years (the earliest dates from 1970 while the most recent was fielded in 1992), this can be turned to advantage in so far as it facilitates analysis of social change.

Most of these surveys are based on face-to-face interviews with nationally representative random samples of adults. The size of the samples varies greatly. The smallest data-sets comprise fewer than 1,000 respondents whereas the largest contain more than 32,000. Occasionally this has caused problems—though not insurmountable ones—for some of the statistical techniques that we employ. Sociologists may well be familiar with these techniques, but they will probably constitute uncharted territory for political theorists; so we have included some notes about statistics (most of which will be found in Appendix B) for readers who may be uncertain as to how to read the tables. These notes are perhaps more important to the exposition than they might seem, since at least some of the disputes about the relation between class and justice hinge precisely upon the interpretation that is placed upon particular numerical findings, and indeed upon the choice of statistical techniques themselves.

A few of the surveys were focused specifically upon the issues of social class and social mobility. Others merely collected information about social origins and class destinations as part of a wider-ranging study. However, in all cases the information seems to have been gathered by reputable organizations and competent research teams, who provided documentation adequate for the purposes of our own particular project. Crucially, that documentation allowed us to construct social class and educational variables that we believe to be cross-nationally comparable, an important consideration in selecting data-sets for inclusion. Reliable coding of these sorts of data is a sociological mine-field into which several previous studies have sailed and sunk. For that reason, the coding of relevant class and educational variables is explained at some length, mainly in Appendices C and D. By giving careful attention to the standardizing of data we hope to have greatly reduced the incidence of methodological artefacts in our results.

To round off these introductory remarks, we should perhaps underline our view that the relationship between social class, social mobility, and social justice is complex, certainly more so than might be surmised from a reading of much of the current literature. Concepts such as social class and social justice are far from straightforward. Add to these independent complexities the additional difficulty of marrying the two topics (and indeed two distinct disciplines), plus the fact that both class and justice are matters of political as well as academic controversy, and the reader will understand why it is with some hesitation that we approach the task at hand. That said, let us begin our exposition by considering the basic contours of the much discussed but still contested concept of social justice.

NOTES

1. See e.g. Charles Murray's (1990) account of the emerging British underclass. Murray's article was first published in the *Sunday Times Magazine* on 26 Nov. 1989.
2. For example, after surveying the relevant social science literature, Bryan Turner (1986: 31) concludes that there is an obvious clash between the principles of social justice and the facts of social class. Class inequality is fundamental to capitalist societies. But so too is a tendency towards egalitarianism that (according to Turner) originates in the myriad reciprocities of everyday life. It seems clear to him, therefore, that a 'conflict between our sense of fairness and the reality of mundane inequality shapes the elementary forms of our social world'.

2

Social Justice

I

Philosophers and political theorists have articulated many conceptions of social justice and argued for the validity of several different distributive principles. It is not our intention here to defend any particular theory against others. For present purposes it is sufficient simply to note that, among the variety of principles advanced in the literature, those most relevant to the topic of social class would seem to be equality of outcome, equality of opportunity, desert, merit, entitlement, and functional inequality.[1]

These have been combined in complex ways, both in popular ideologies and in the writings of academic political theorists. Socialists are generally thought to place particular emphasis on need and equality of outcome, although it is well known that Marx considered the distributive principle 'to each according to his labour' as appropriate to the first or lower stage of socialism, to be superseded by the maxim 'to each according to his needs' only in a second or higher stage. Liberals tend to endorse the value of equality of opportunity, with inequalities of outcome deemed legitimate if they reflect differences in merit, but cannot agree about the conditions that are necessary to ensure that kind of equality or about what attributes are meritorious. Some liberals hold a more extreme libertarian position (often confused in popular terminology with conservatism), and argue both that people are entitled to do as they choose with whatever resources they have acquired legitimately and that this is more important than equality of opportunity. Old-style conservatives tend simply to regard hierarchy as a good thing, either because inequality is a necessary prerequisite of culture and civilized values, or because they respect tradition and inequality is traditional. From this last point of view, all talk of the 'principles' of social justice, and perhaps even the notion of 'social justice' itself, is inappropriately rationalist in tenor.[2]

Given this complexity, it is wise to eschew labels, since these merely simplify in such a way as to invite confusion. Rather, we will attempt here to identify directly the particular issues that emerge in relating social justice to inequality, as manifest in the form of social class. How might a class structure be defended as just?

II

The existence of a class structure, however this is defined, implies an unequal distribution of power and advantage. Clearly, therefore, any understanding of justice as equality of outcome must rule out the possibility of a just class structure.[3] Other principles of justice, which may be regarded as serving precisely to provide criteria by which we may justify inequalities of outcome, look like more plausible starting-points. We can identify four distinct principles. The unequal distribution of power and advantage embodied in a class structure might be deemed just if it reflected differential desert or merit; represented the distribution of holdings to which people were legitimately entitled; was the outcome that resulted from an initial situation of equality of opportunity; or was functional for all members of the society. Let us consider each of these briefly in turn.

The idea that an unequal distribution might be legitimate because people deserve or merit unequal rewards has a great deal of intuitive appeal. If justice consists in giving people their due, and those dues are different, then justice seems clearly to require unequal outcomes. This approach raises, however, the question of what it is that constitute the bases of desert or merit. Which qualities of individuals would it be just to reward? A central issue here would seem to be the distinction between those attributes for which the individual can claim responsibility and those which are his or hers merely by chance. If it is the case that I possess particular talents or skills, and others do not, purely because I have been lucky in the natural lottery, then it is by no means clear that justice is served by rewarding such possession. On the other hand, if I work hard and choose to attend evening classes to obtain qualifications, then it seems that I am indeed more deserving than someone who does neither. Matters are further complicated if one thinks that the ability to work hard is itself a chance attribute or, as does John Rawls (1971: 310–15), that it is greatly influenced by the possession of other chance attributes.[4] In any case, the point is that the defence of class inequality in terms of the principles of merit or desert would have to show that the class structure reflected morally relevant differences between individuals, not simply any differences whatsoever.

The idea that inequality might be just because people are entitled to unequal amounts of resources must be distinguished from the previous approach, because it is perfectly possible to hold that people are entitled to certain goods without deserving them. Robert Nozick (1974: 160–4, 213–27) most clearly and systematically articulates this view. He maintains that, even if we accept each individual's natural assets to be a matter of luck and conclude from this that they cannot be invoked to justify claims to superior rewards, people are still entitled to the fruits of those assets and to whatever else other people choose freely to give them. Here we see a libertarian emphasis on property rights and freedom of choice that is quite different from the idea that people should get what they deserve. If a millionaire chooses to bequeath money to an untalented layabout, then justice as entitlement demands that he or she be permitted to do so, and forbids taxation of the inheritance, despite the fact that any normal conception of justice as desert or merit is clearly violated. Meritocratic conceptions of justice are, in Nozick's terms, 'patterned', and necessarily conflict with those free exchanges and legitimate transfers that justify people's entitlements to resources.[5]

Many contemporary thinkers of the new right tend to conflate the principles of entitlement and desert. This is most obvious in their defence of the market as a distributive mechanism. On the one hand, the market is praised because people get out what they put in, with hard work, productive ability, and entrepreneurial skill being rewarded. On the other hand, the market is also thought to give people freedom of choice. Quite apart from questions about what exactly it is that the market does reward, and exactly what choices it does leave people free to make, the point here is that these are quite separate defences that are often confused.[6]

Academic political theorists (but not professional politicians) usually acknowledge the ways in which these different principles can conflict. This is true of Nozick (1974: 235 ff.) himself, for example, not only with regard to the difference between entitlement and desert but also in respect of the potential contradiction between entitlement and equality of opportunity. The principle of equality of opportunity is in any case open to a variety of interpretations. Does it demand that, however unequal their abilities, people should be equally empowered to achieve their desired goals? This would imply that the unmusical individual who wants to be a concert pianist should receive a great deal more training than the child prodigy. Should people have equal resources to devote to their life-plans—irrespective of their abilities? Or, less drastically, does the principle require merely that people with the same abilities should have equal opportunities to achieve their desired goals—an interpretation that is consistent with the idea that the talented should have more opportunities than the untalented? Nozick's point is that, however we understand the principle of equality of opportunity, it is clearly at odds with the idea of justice as entitlement. This is most obvious where rights of bequest and inheritance are concerned. Is the class system to be justified as consistent with equality of opportunity or with justice as entitlement?

Friedrich Hayek is another theorist who recognizes the inadequacy of certain contemporary defences of those inequalities produced by the market. His critique points us to our fourth and final justification of inequality. For Hayek, it is clear that one cannot justify market outcomes as in accordance with merit or desert, for luck plays too large a role in determining who gets what.[7] Fortunately, however, the fact that such outcomes are unintended and unforeseen aggregate consequences of individual actions means that they are not the kind of thing that it is appropriate to regard as just or unjust. Indeed, for Hayek, the whole idea of social justice is a 'mirage' which requires us to make the mistake of seeing society as an agent. Interestingly, Hayek (1974: 64, 74) thinks that the defence of market outcomes at the level of the general public rests upon the erroneous belief that such outcomes actually do reward merit, and he suggests that such a belief is necessary if people are to tolerate the inequalities that markets produce. However, his own justification of the market mechanism is quite different, and points instead both to its relation to individual liberty and to its alleged efficiency. If the first strand of this justification is similar to the libertarian position adopted by Nozick, the second holds rather that inequality is justified because it is functional, working to everyone's advantage:

Productivity is high because incomes are unequally divided and thereby the use of scarce resources is directed and limited to where they bring the highest return. Thanks to this unequal distribution the poor get in a competitive market economy more than they would get in a centrally directed system. (Hayek 1978a: 67)

Sociologists will of course be reminded here of functionalist explanations for social stratification in terms of the unintended positive consequences of hierarchy for economic efficiency and social order more generally.[8]

The connections between efficiency and justice (two concepts that may seem antithetical rather than complementary) are best illustrated in the writings of John Rawls. His famous 'difference principle' asserts that inequalities are justified only if they serve to increase the advantage of the worst-off group in society. What makes this a principle of justice is the idea that justice consists in considering society from an impartial standpoint, in Rawls's case from an 'original position' in which agreement is reached by hypothetical people deprived of information about their talents and attributes, behind a 'veil of ignorance'. According to Rawls, people constrained in this way to choose impartially would be concerned to maximize the welfare of the least advantaged members of society, lest they themselves fall into that group. They will agree to permit inequalities—but only if they contribute to the well-being of those who have least. The functional theory of stratification thus becomes a principle of justice via the additional claim that justice requires us to give priority to the least advantaged members of society.

This attempt to reconcile inequality with justice is quite distinct from the others outlined above. There is no suggestion here that people deserve their advantages. Nor are they entitled to whatever resources people choose freely to give them: the restriction on inequalities precisely rules out many of those that Nozick would permit. Its relation to equality of opportunity is, however, more complex, since it is possible to argue for equality of opportunity on the grounds that it is necessary for an efficient allocation of resources, rather than because it rewards merit or gives people what they deserve.

For example, replying to the charge that it is absurd to describe as fair a competition between individuals unequally endowed with those attributes necessary for success, Simon Green (1988: 7) has argued that:

There is nothing unfair about a competition between any number of individuals in which one wins and others lose solely due to the impact of genetically endowed talent *if* (and only *if*) the competition is conceived as a source of information about the respective abilities of each competitor. If that information is subsequently used to the benefit of all competitors then the competition is not only useful, but also justified.

It would be a mistake to regard those who win the competition as more deserving than those who lose, but we are none the less justified in giving them a greater share of resources, because otherwise we run up against the problem of concealment. What incentive will people have to reveal their talents if there is no reward for exercising them? Or, as Green (1988: 9) puts it, 'to induce an individual to reveal his talents it will be necessary to offer incentives which will—in effect—represent rewards for gratuitous endowments'. Equality of opportunity is here deemed important because without it we are deprived of the social

benefits that would result from the exercise of those talents that have
not had equal opportunity to compete.

Green, then, defends the idea that people should have equal opportunities to compete for unequal rewards as being consistent with the view
that we do not deserve our talents or what we get from them. While it
would be possible to reward people for their morally worthy efforts,
rather than their arbitrary abilities, the result, in Green's view, would be
absurdly inefficient. Inequalities are justified, not in the sense that they
are deserved, but because they are necessary to overcome the problem
of concealment, while equality of opportunity is required so as to ensure
that society benefits from the talents of all its members. The goal is
meritocracy, but meritocracy is valued because we all benefit if people
are doing what they are best at, not because meritocracy gives each
person his or her due.[9]

This defence of inequality of outcome with equality of opportunity as
together consistent with social justice raises, in rather sharper form,
some of the same issues as do functionalist explanations of stratification.
One might, for example, ask questions about the theory of motivation
that is presupposed by this account. On the one hand, this is a theory for
those who are motivated by a sense of justice, here understood as a
concern for the fortunes of the least affluent members of society. It is
this concern that justifies otherwise undeserved inequalities on the
grounds of efficiency. On the other, if people are concerned to promote
the welfare of the least advantaged, why do they need incentives to
encourage them to reveal and employ their talents optimally? The logic
is somewhat contradictory, since it is an argument for altruists with a
sense of justice that assumes people to be self-interested.[10] Alternatively, perhaps, we might distinguish between two kinds of inequality
that could be justified in this way: those that are intrinsically necessary
and those that are necessary on motivational grounds. Among the
former might be inequalities of authority, power, and expertise, functional for efficient organization and management. The latter would
comprise those rewards deemed necessary to induce people to take up
such positions. The justification of the latter, but not of the former, is
dependent upon a particular view of human motivation as self-
interested. Distinctive aspects of social class and the class structure
could in this way be differently related to particular conceptions of
justice.

It is not our purpose here, however, to assess the relative merits of
these diverse attempts to reconcile social inequality with social justice.
We would insist only that they are indeed different. For what we find in
most non-philosophical efforts to justify inequality is a combination of

arguments from desert, merit, entitlement, equality of opportunity, and functionality, without any clear recognition that these may involve disparate, and in some cases incompatible, assumptions. On the one hand, there is nothing wrong with people climbing the social ladder as long as it is through their own efforts, while on the other they are entitled to pass on their advantage to their children. Unequal outcomes are justified both on the grounds that they are needed to give people incentives, and so contribute to social justice by helping the poor, and because they give individuals what they deserve. Clearly, conceptions of justice that validate some forms of inequality may undermine the legitimation of others, and those writers (particularly critics of class analysis) who quite correctly point out that justice does not necessarily require equality of outcome should not be allowed themselves to blur these important distinctions.[11]

III

Given this range of arguments, how can we best bring empirical data to bear on the question of social class, and its relation to social justice? To explain our strategy in the remainder of this book, let us take a step back from the detailed exposition of the previous section, in order to introduce a relatively straightforward distinction between two kinds of inequality. On the one hand, there is what might be called inequality of position, whereby the class structure can be regarded, in large part, as comprising social locations (for example occupations) characterized by different and unequal levels of advantage. On the other hand, there is what conventionally has been termed inequality of opportunity, this being a measure, not of the differential privileges or rewards enjoyed by members of the various classes, but of the inequality of access to the different class positions themselves. This distinction, though fundamental, can be difficult to grasp. Perhaps the following example will serve to explain what we have in mind.

Imagine two societies—A and B. Both have a very simple class structure; in fact they have only two classes, T (Topdogs) and U (Underdogs). In Society A, the two classes, though unequal in terms of the advantage enjoyed by their members, are only marginally unequal. Members of T earn a bit more than members of U, own houses that are a little larger, and enjoy slightly better working conditions, but the differences between the two classes considered as positions are not great. However, it is almost impossible for children whose parents are Underdogs to climb into the Topdogs, and very easy for children whose parents are Topdogs to stay there. In terms of our distinction, Society A is one in which there is little inequality of position, but marked inequality of access. Compare this with Society B, in which there are huge inequalities of position between the two classes—here Topdogs earn vastly more than Underdogs, live in mansions, and work in comfortable offices, whereas Underdogs live in hovels and labour under appalling conditions—but those born into Underdog homes have almost as good a chance of ending up in Topdog positions as do the children of Topdog parents. In other words, there is gross inequality of condition, but hardly any inequality of access to the different positions.

It may clarify the issue further if we respond to two possible objections to this example and the distinction it illustrates. The first is that these scenarios are unlikely: it is simply not realistic to postulate a society, like Society B, in which classes differ widely in the money and other components of advantage that they enjoy but where this inequality of position is not accompanied by a significant degree of inequality of access. Conversely, if inequality of position between the two classes is not great, as in Society A, why should it be so difficult for people to move up from U to T? This first objection disputes the empirical likelihood of Society A and Society B actually existing.

The second wonders whether it makes sense to separate the advantage that characterizes different class positions from the likelihood that the occupants of those positions will be able to transmit that advantage to their children. Is not one component of the advantages enjoyed by someone in class T precisely the ability to ensure that his or her children themselves have a good chance (better than the children of someone in class U) of attaining a position among the Topdogs? The example postulates that the classes in Society B have very unequal rewards and privileges but denies that they have unequal abilities to transmit their advantages intergenerationally. Since, however, part of a person's advantage is his or her ability to convey that advantage to his or her children, does it really make sense to say that they have such unequal levels of advantage?

Both objections contain a grain of truth. With regard to the first, we entirely agree that the scenarios are empirically unlikely. For present purposes, however, their sociological plausibility is beside the point. What matters is whether there is a conceptual distinction between these two kinds of inequality. If there is, then the question of how they interrelate can be investigated empirically. The suspicion that they tend to be associated can be put to the test, and if it is proved correct, the sociologist can proceed to offer, and further explore, some explanations for the association.

As for the second objection, we do not deny that one of the respects in which members of a class may be advantaged over members of another is their ability to transmit privilege intergenerationally. But this would only constitute an objection to our distinction if *all* advantage were of this kind—which it surely is not. Of course, it is true that one reason why it might be thought better to be a top business executive than an unskilled manual worker is that the former is more likely to be able to help his or her children get on in the world, but this is not the only reason. Unskilled workers would be worse off than executives even if the chances of their children getting good jobs were the same (however empirically unlikely our first objection might hold this to be).

What we take these examples to indicate, then, is that when one investigates the issue of social class, it is useful to distinguish two kinds of inequality: the degree to which a society's class structure manifests inequality of position, and the extent to which mobility between the classes that constitute that structure exhibits inequality of access to those unequal positions. These are features of the society that can and should be examined quite separately—and they bear different relations to normative questions of social justice.[12]

The analysis we will present in the following chapters addresses questions about inequality of access rather than those related to inequalities of position. For example, although we make the general claim that the class positions between which social mobility occurs are characterized by unequal degrees of advantage, we have not asked whether inequality between class positions in Britain is greater or less now than in the past; nor, indeed, whether it is more pronounced here than it is in other industrialized societies. Such inequalities of condition are in fact already well documented, even in cross-national perspective, and we have little to add to the extensive commentaries presently available. There is a sizeable research industry—comprising academics, government agencies, independent consultants, and political pressure groups—surrounding the collection of data pertaining to the ownership and distribution of property, wealth, earnings, housing, health, durable consumer items, and the many other dimensions of class advantage and disadvantage in modern societies. Variations between regions, races, age groups, and men and women are a growing feature of these accounts, but social class differences in the distribution of such goods remain at the forefront of discussion. Of course, there is still a substantial measure of outspoken disagreement about the precise shape of the disposition and about the direction of any trends, but—as we stated at the outset—there is consensus about the fact that the allocation of rewards in modern Britain is obviously unequal. Quite how unequal need not detain us here.[13]

In the context of the discussion of the previous section, it should be clear that our focus on data relating to (in)equality of access therefore manifests a concern with only a particular subset of issues that might be thought relevant to social justice. Put bluntly, it can be argued that there is more to social justice than fair access to unequal positions.[14] Even if a society did offer all of its members genuine equality of access to different class destinations, this might not be sufficient to establish that the society was just, for there would remain the question of whether the inequalities of position between the class destinations were themselves justified. Consider again, for example, Society B—in which there is almost complete equality of access. We can still ask whether it is really just that those who end up in T enjoy so much more advantage than do those who end up in U. However fair the processes by which people arrive at places in the structure of unequal positions, it remains a further question whether the extent of the inequality of that structure can itself be justified. Even if it were the case that everyone in Britain today had the same chance of becoming Chief Executive of British Gas, we might still think it unfair that the incumbent of that advantaged position earned quite so many times more than the average wage.[15]

Just as we have not in this book sought to present data on the extent of inequality of position in Britain (or anywhere else), so we are not here concerned to assess whether that inequality can be justified. It would take research of a quite different kind fully to investigate whether the differential advantages enjoyed by members of the different classes were just. Precisely what research would depend on one's view of what exactly one thought justice requires that people should be rewarded for. On one account, perhaps, people should be rewarded for how hard they work, in which case we would want to compare the efforts of those in different kinds of occupation.[16] On another, justice might demand that people get the value of their product (or something at least proportional to it), in which case there would need to be a way of determining that value. On yet another, inequalities might only be justified if they served the long-term advantage of the worst-off group in society, in which case one would need an economic theory able to discern the kinds of inequality that met this condition.

These examples, and the obvious difficulties they immediately present, perhaps indicate one reason why we have not attempted this alternative task. More importantly, however, we would argue that, in much of the relevant social and political debate, the question of what might justify inequalities of outcome is often reduced simply to that of fair access. On this account, the justice of distributive outcomes is taken to be no more than a function of whether everybody had an equal chance of achieving the various shares. In so far as this is the legitimation of inequality that is most commonly offered, then it clearly makes sense for us to confront the issue of access directly. In other words, this book does not consider the possible justice or injustice of the differential advantage of class positions, except in so far as this is taken to be an issue concerning access to these different locations. This is by no means to say that we regard fair access as all that there is to justice. It merely reflects our decision to focus, in this book, on the kind of inequality that has been most prominent in current debates about the relation between social class and social justice.

IV

Our concern in this chapter has been to identify alternative ways in which class inequality might be just, and to clarify a number of quite different issues that tend to be run together.

On the one hand, we have seen that inequality of position is sometimes defended on the grounds that it results from the free choices of individuals or (rather differently) promotes productivity and serves to advantage everybody over time; on the other, it has also been endorsed because it gives people what they are entitled to or (something else again) reflects the fact that people deserve differently. These justifications may coincide—as, for instance, when people freely give resources (to which they are entitled) to others who have particular talents (that form the basis of desert claims) and in doing so promote the long-run well-being of the least advantaged—but they need not necessarily do so. We have also explained that our focus on social mobility reflects an interest specifically in issues of fair access to unequal class positions, and does not seek to address other aspects of the justice (or injustice) of class inequality. Together, these elementary clarifications provide the basic framework for our analysis and the foundations of our approach to the issue of social justice. We will build upon them in subsequent chapters.

NOTES

1. Campbell (1988) offers a helpful overview of the extensive political and philosophical literature on social justice.

2. For a good account of the conceptions of justice developed within specific political ideologies, see Goodwin (1987: ch. 13).

3. Much of the opposition to class society, most obviously within the Marxist tradition, has derived from some such understanding. However, as we shall see in due course, in practice even communist regimes abandoned equality of outcome as an objective of practical social policy.

4. We regret that some of our earlier publications (e.g. Marshall and Swift 1993; 1996) reproduced the common misrepresentation of Rawls according to which he holds the strong view that ability to make an effort is itself something beyond the individual's control. For the source of the misrepresentation, see Nozick (1974: 213–14); for its correction, and a valuable discussion, see Cohen (1989: 906–14).

5. One of our own critics, Peter Saunders (1994: 87), is therefore quite wrong to insist that the entitlement theory associated with Nozick is 'central to the ethical case for a meritocracy'.

6. This is obvious from the exposition of new right ideas to be found in e.g. King (1987) or Gamble (1988).

7. See also Joseph and Sumption (1979: 34): 'The recent obsession with formal qualifications has obscured the fact, which the lives of . . . self-made millionaires bring out very clearly, that the enrichment of individuals has very much more to do with luck and with the strength of their motivation than the quality of their upbringing.' It is important, from the point of view of the argument we ourselves will make in later chapters, also to note here that these authors further observe: 'There is no reason to suppose that intensity of motivation goes naturally with the material advantages of a prosperous background. All the evidence suggests that the opposite is true.'

8. It should also be noted, however, that Hayek's defence of the market mechanism and price system rests upon its importance in generating information and bearing knowledge—not upon its motivational aspects. As he puts it, 'the term "incentives" is used in this connection with somewhat misleading connotations, as if the main problem were to induce people to exert themselves sufficiently. However, the chief guidance which prices offer is not so much how to act, but *what to do*' (Hayek 1978b: 187). For Hayek the price signal is functional, but primarily because it tells people where they may most productively deploy their abilities, not because it gives them the rewards necessary to induce them to do so. By contrast, functionalist explanations of stratification tend to emphasize the necessity both of instilling motivation in the proper individuals to fill certain social roles and, once they have assumed these roles, of instilling the desire to perform the appropriate duties accordingly (see e.g. Davis and Moore 1945).

9. See also Daniels (1978), and Haslett (1994: 240), who argues for equality of opportunity on the grounds that 'the closer we come to equal opportunity for all, the more people there will be who, as a result of increased opportunity, will come to realize their productive potential. And, of course, the

more people there are who come to realize their productive potential, the greater overall productivity will be.'

10. For a full exploration of this issue, see Cohen (1995).

11. In *Social Class and Stratification*, for example, Peter Saunders appeals to a conception of justice rooted simultaneously in the writings of Nozick, Hayek, and the theory of meritocracy, apparently unaware that these point in quite different and mutually inconsistent directions (see esp. chs. 3 and 4). See also Green (1990), esp. ch. 4.

12. Given this distinction between kinds of (in)equality, it is important that class analysts do not build what some call the 'mobility propensities' of the different classes into the very definition of class itself, in the tradition established by one reading of Max Weber's (1968: 302) theory of stratification—that which places undue emphasis on his definition of a 'social class' as 'the totality of those class situations within which individual and generational mobility is easy and typical'. To do this would be to confuse issues of position and access. Things get complicated further when one considers that one component of a person's current advantage is his or her chance of intragenerational (or career) mobility. In principle, this is amenable to the same kind of analysis as that offered in the text, but it cannot be denied that, since people might prefer jobs with poor current rewards but good chances of promotion over jobs with better current rewards but little chance of promotion, in practice the distinction is hard to maintain.

13. For a review of the evidence, see e.g. Hudson and Williams (1989) or Westergaard (1995).

14. Compare Herbert Gintis's (1980: 13) claim that 'capitalism gives us a whole lot more mobility than it does other ingredients of social justice'.

15. One strand of the aforementioned literature on inequalities of condition deals with precisely this issue. The evidence seems to suggest that Britons think that the chief executive of a large national company should earn between five and seven times as much as an unskilled worker. (The exact ratio varies according to the particular statistical measure employed.) This perception of the proper differential between the pay of those in top jobs and those in manual labour makes us among the most inegalitarian of nations in our beliefs: Americans are the only respondents in surveys who consistently endorse a (marginally) higher ratio. By comparison, Australians, Poles, Hungarians, and Swedes are more egalitarian, and believe that the legitimate ratio between the two sorts of occupation is somewhere between two and three. See e.g. Kelley and Evans (1993) and Svallfors (1995). The real degree of income inequality in all of these societies is substantially higher, not only than most people think fair, but also than they perceive it to be—although the conceptual and methodological difficulties involved in answering these sorts of questions are truly formidable (see Atkinson 1980; Rubinstein 1986; Phelps Brown 1988; Coulter 1989; and, for a cross-national perspective, either Mahler 1989 or Atkinson and Micklewright 1992).

16. Notice that, even if we could measure effort directly, it seems plausible to think that the best scale we could devise would be ordinal, ranking each individual, or the typical person in each occupation, according to the amount of effort exerted. Quantifying the amount of effort contributed by each individual so as to permit the construction of a ratio scale—thereby allowing us to conclude that (for example) one job required twice as much effort as another—seems an impossible task. It is this kind of scale that would be needed to justify particular inequalities of reward along the lines suggested in the text.

3

Social Class

I

If the concept of social justice is complex, and subject to diverse interpretations, to what extent is this true also of the other topic that is
central to our study? What—precisely—do we mean when we speak of
social class?

There are many ways of thinking about class. Within the sociological
literature alone, classes have been conceptualized quite differently in
terms of ownership or non-ownership of the means of production, control of various assets within bureaucratic organizations, and possession
of marketable workplace skills. Sometimes, classes are defined by occupational prestige scores, arranged in hierarchical fashion; or, more
loosely, in terms of generalized social standing in the community at
large. American sociologists have tended to differentiate classes according to what many European observers think of as life-styles—or what
Max Weber termed 'social status'. Classes have also been described as
competing cultures, subcultures, or value-systems. Indeed, some Marxists have gone further, seeing class as a phenomenon defined by the
shape of various so-called class struggles—usually as these have been
expressed through collective action in pursuit of industrial and political
power.

There is a large and diverse literature within which these and other
positions are forcefully represented. Fortunately, those new to the topic
are well served by a generous selection of substantial textbooks, offering an overview of the different approaches and an introduction to
current debates. Indeed, one of us has previously published a lengthy
assessment of the leading contenders in the class analysis field, in terms
of both theoretical grounding and empirical applications.[1]

Rather than repeat these arguments here, it would seem to be
more appropriate in this chapter simply to describe the specific

approach that we will adopt, and then examine its implications for the study of social justice. We may start, therefore, from the observation that, throughout this volume, the term 'social class' is intended to refer to the class categories devised by John Goldthorpe and his colleagues for the Oxford Social Mobility Study of England and Wales during the 1970s.

There are several reasons why we have chosen to think about class in this particular way. The most important of these is that (as we shall see) the author of this schema has, over the years, provided a comprehensive account both of its conceptual foundations and of the procedures to be used when allocating individuals or families to classes in actual research practice. Goldthorpe's approach is therefore more developed theoretically, and better documented from the point of view of operationalization, than are most of the alternatives. Moreover, his schema has been refined specifically for use in cross-national comparative analyses of social mobility, and is widely deployed in this way. For these reasons, the Goldthorpe classification has become increasingly prominent in discussions of inequality of opportunity, among both proponents and critics of the thesis that social class is compatible with social justice.

Finally, there are pragmatic reasons for adopting the Goldthorpe classes for our own investigation, not the least of which is that most of the relevant data-sets available to us already contain information about respondents that has been codified in this way. There is also some virtue in maintaining this convention, since comparability with earlier studies of social mobility means that we can examine class processes over time, an important consideration if one wishes (as we do) to say something about trends in merit-selection during recent decades.

II

What then are the Goldthorpe classes? For the Oxford Social Mobility Study, Goldthorpe developed a sevenfold classification, the categories of which were said to aggregate occupational groupings whose members shared similar 'market situations' and 'work situations'. The scheme attempted, in Goldthorpe's own words,

to combine occupational categories whose members would appear, in the light of the available evidence, to be typically comparable, on the one hand, in terms of their sources and levels of income, their degree of economic security and chances of economic advancement [market situation]; and, on the other hand, in their location within the systems of authority and control governing the

processes of production in which they are engaged, and hence in their degree
of autonomy in performing their work-tasks and roles [work situation].
(Goldthorpe et al. 1980: 39)

The requirements of conducting comparative research involving nations having occupational structures quite different from that found in
England and Wales led Goldthorpe and his colleagues in the later
CASMIN (Comparative Analysis of Social Mobility in Industrial Nations) Project to subdivide some of the original class categories. In a
series of revisions to the initial framework, routine non-manual employees were subdivided into clerical (higher) and personal service (lower)
categories; *the petite bourgeoisie* of own-account workers was separated into its constituent elements of small proprietors with employees,
small proprietors without employees, and farmers and smallholders;
and agricultural workers were distinguished from other rank-and-file
semi-skilled and unskilled manual labourers. These amendments yield
the now standard elevenfold Goldthorpe class scheme shown in Table
3.1.[2]

As the categories of the schema have been refined over the years,
so too have its theoretical foundations. For example, in the second
edition of his monograph reporting the results of the Oxford study,

TABLE 3.1. *The Goldthorpe Class Categories*

I	Higher-grade professionals, administrators, and officials; managers in large industrial establishments; large proprietors
II	Lower-grade professionals, administrators, and officials; higher-grade technicians; managers in small industrial establishments; supervisors of non-manual employees
IIIa	Routine non-manual employees, higher grade (administration and commerce)
IIIb	Routine non-manual employees, lower grade (sales and services)
IVa	Small proprietors, artisans, etc., with employees
IVb	Small proprietors, artisans, etc., without employees
IVc	Farmers and smallholders; other self-employed workers in primary production
V	Lower-grade technicians; supervisors of manual workers
VI	Skilled manual workers
VIIa	Semi-skilled and unskilled manual workers (not in agriculture, etc.)
VIIb	Agricultural and other workers in primary production

Note. The convention of labelling the classes by a combination of roman numerals and letters
is understandably confusing. The former define the original 7-category typology of the Oxford
Mobility Study. The latter reflect refinements made during subsequent comparative mobility
analyses.

Goldthorpe's (1988: 40) definition of market situation emphasizes the typical 'conditions of employment' of class members. Similarly, in their report of the findings from the CASMIN Project, Erikson and Goldthorpe (1992*a*: 37) state that the rationale of the schema is 'to differentiate positions within *labour markets* and *production units* or, more specifically . . . to differentiate such positions in terms of the *employment relations* they entail'. For this reason it is important to distinguish between the self-employed and employees. However, within the fairly heterogeneous category of employee, it is also possible to make 'meaningful distinctions' according to differences in (what has now become) 'the labour contract and the conditions of employment':

Employment relationships regulated by a labour contract entail a relatively short-term and specific exchange of money for effort. Employees supply more or less discrete amounts of labour, under the supervision of the employer or of the employer's agents, in return for wages which are calculated on a 'piece' or time basis. In contrast, employment relationships within a bureaucratic context involve a longer-term and generally more diffuse exchange. Employees render service to their employing organisation in return for 'compensation' which takes the form not only of reward for work done, through a salary and various perquisites, but also comprises important *prospective* elements—for example, salary increments on an established scale, assurances of security both in employment and, through pension rights, after retirement, and, above all, well-defined career opportunities. (Erikson and Goldthorpe 1992*a*: 41–2)

It is clear that, despite these minor changes in terminology, the nature of the employment relationship is and always has been central to the differentiation of classes. As Erikson and Goldthorpe (1992*a*: 42) themselves insist, it is 'the distinction between employees involved in a service relationship with their employer and those whose employment relationships are essentially regulated by a labour contract that underlies the way in which, within our class schema, different classes have been delineated'. So-called service-class (or salariat) occupations offer incremental advancement, employment security, and the possibility of exchanging commitment to the job against a high level of trust on the part of employers. Working-class occupations, on the other hand, tend to have closely regulated payment arrangements and to be subject to routine and greater supervision. If the circumstances of those who buy labour, and of those who neither buy the labour of others nor sell their own (that is, employers and the self-employed respectively), are also taken into account, then the origins and basic structure of the class scheme can readily be grasped.[3]

III

These, then, are the social class categories that will inform the empirical analysis which follows. It may help to clarify that analysis further if we pause at this point to consider two possible objections to our use of Goldthorpe's schema. Both have been voiced by critics in other contexts, and both bear directly upon the issue of class and justice. The first is that the concept of the salariat or service class is too broad, since it fails to distinguish between the employment situations of the capitalist élite on the one hand and the mass of professional and managerial employees on the other. The second is that the scheme has not been validated and may not measure those characteristics—relations or conditions of employment—that are central to Goldthorpe's concept of class. Let us consider these points in turn.

We begin with the long-standing contention that the Goldthorpe classification is of limited value because its service-class category—if not in the original conception then certainly as this has been applied in research—embraces individuals having quite distinct class locations: those associated with relatively privileged managerial and professional employment on the one hand, but also the capitalist élite of large proprietors, speculators, and others who have no specific occupation, but whose income is derived instead from inherited wealth or investments. In other words, although the scheme reserves a particular class location for the self-employed *petite bourgeoisie*, it fails to distinguish members of the bourgeoisie proper from the mass of salaried employees. This is, of course, anathema to many class theorists—and not only Marxists (see e.g. Penn 1981).

Erikson and Goldthorpe (1992*a*: 40–1) have explained their reasoning on this issue at some length. They argue that a randomly selected national sample of respondents—of the type that forms the basis for most empirical studies of class inequality and social mobility—is not an appropriate strategy for investigating top industrialists. Very few such individuals will be selected for analysis in even the largest of surveys. In fact, the CASMIN team estimate that across the Western industrial societies in their study, large employers account for only some 5–10 per cent of all men in Class I (which itself comprises only about the same proportion of the total workforce). Even so, these large proprietors are typically the owners of garages, hotels, transportation firms, and such like, rather than the captains of industry and finance. They are therefore included in the service class, not because of their entrepreneurial activities, but because proprietors of such businesses tend also to be extensively involved in management. In this respect they are rather similar to the salaried managers in Class I, many of whom also have shares in the ownership of the enterprises in which they are employed. Moreover, the distinction between employee, self-employed, and employer is at this relatively privileged level often rather ambiguous and sometimes merely formal, being artificially induced for reasons of legal or fiscal convenience. In short, even if it were possible to identify genuinely large employers accurately, their numbers would in any case be too small to allow separate study in a class analysis of this type. Of course, in Eastern European societies the category of large employer was until recently mainly irrelevant, except perhaps in relation to class origins.

It must be conceded at the outset, therefore, that the following analysis of social class and social justice does not deal—other than exceptionally—with the circumstances of the very privileged. That specific topic would require an altogether different research design. However, more specialized investigations have in any case already confirmed that the élites in question share a small and relatively closed membership, tending to pass on their considerable wealth intergenerationally in the form of land and capital assets.[4] By contrast, ours is a study of social mobility and educational attainment among whole populations, and Goldthorpe's failure to reserve a discrete class for the capitalist bourgeoisie seems to us to raise no particular problems from this point of view.

Our second objection accepts the underlying logic of the classification—including the theory of the service class—but then questions its implementation in research practice. In particular, a number of critics have pointed out that, despite his intensive use of the scheme as a research instrument, Goldthorpe offers no systematic evidence of its internal (or criterion) validity as a measure of the class characteristics of occupations (see e.g. Savage et al. 1991: ch. 1; Baxter et al. 1991: ch. 4).

Specialists will know that, in translating their theory about the importance of the labour contract and conditions of employment into concrete research practice, Goldthorpe and his colleagues generally refer to an individual's occupational title (for example electrician or lawyer) and employment status (self-employed with employees, manager in large establishment, and so forth) as indicators of the market situation and work situation characteristics that are central to the classification. They claim, at the outset, to have allocated an appropriate class standing to each combination of occupational title and employment status in the light of the available information from official statistics, monographic sources etc., regarding the typical market and work situations of the individuals comprised: e.g. on levels of income, other monetary and non-monetary benefits, degree of economic security, chances of economic advancement, and location in systems of authority and control.[5]

The fact that we are not shown the information in question is, as Geoffrey Evans (1992: 212) has put it, a 'methodological lacuna' that is potentially, at least, highly problematic.

Fortunately, Evans has been prompted to conduct an exhaustive validity test which shows that the scheme is indeed highly predictive of the characteristics that are central to Goldthorpe's concept of class: employment and payment conditions, authority relations, levels of pay, and control over work activities. Using data from the Essex Class Survey (a large national sample of those eligible for employment in Britain), Evans examines the association between Goldthorpe class and some eighteen separate items describing the nature of work relationships, including security of employment, supervisory responsibilities, routes to increased pay, rules governing attendance at the workplace, control over work tasks, and salary guarantees. The results show unambiguously that class membership is strongly predictive of these characteristics; or, as Evans concludes, that 'the substantial association between class and indicators of a service relationship versus a labour contract confirms empirically the main distinction embodied in the schema'. Analysis also verifies that 'the various aggregation procedures adopted for British and crossnational research do not greatly reduce the validity of the shorter versions of the schema'.[6]

Evans's final observation perhaps requires additional explanation. It points to another feature of the Goldthorpe scheme, and one that is directly relevant to the present project: the various class categories can meaningfully be collapsed in ways that are appropriate for crossnational comparative work with relatively small sample sizes. In studies such as ours, it is often difficult to maintain standards of comparability at the full eleven-category level of differentiation, either because of imprecise occupational information for one or more nations or because the resulting numbers are simply too small to be reliable. The CASMIN Project researchers themselves, despite their concern for matters of detailed occupational coding and their access to relatively large datasets, were forced in the main to work with a version of the Goldthorpe scheme which combined classes I and II, IVa and IVb, and V and VI, into a unified service class, *petite bourgeoisie*, and skilled working class respectively. Only in this way could comparative mobility analysis reliably be conducted (see especially Erikson and Goldthorpe 1992*a*: 52–3 and table 2.1).

Our own study, which draws in large part on much smaller data-sets, has encountered similar problems. It proved impossible to distinguish the higher and lower elements of the service class in the same way across all countries—so we work (in the main) with an undifferentiated salariat. Although we can distinguish small proprietors according to the size of their workforce in several data-sets, the cases involved are so few that differentiation within this class is counter-productive, since it serves merely to create large numbers of empty cells in some of our tables (especially in the former communist states). For this reason we follow CASMIN practice and merge classes IVa and IVb. Finally, since there are good reasons for maintaining comparability with the CASMIN study itself (in order to examine changes over time within particular countries), we have in most (but not all) instances collapsed classes V and VI. Later in our analysis, as additional variables such as educational attainment enter into the picture, our relatively small samples compel further merging of classes—for example into the broad salariat (I and II), intermediate (III, IV, V), and working (VI and VII) categories, although it is also important in most countries to maintain a distinct agricultural sector (classes IVc and VIIb).

The aggregated versions of the scheme will be explained as they are introduced in the text. The most appropriate collapse for our purposes is to the seven-category version used by the CASMIN team. For those countries (such as Britain) in which the agricultural sector is relatively small, this can be further reduced to a five-category scheme embracing the salariat, routine clerical employees, *petite bourgeoisie* (including farmers and smallholders), skilled manual employees, and unskilled working class (including agricultural labourers). All of these shorter versions of the schema have been successfully used at different times and in a variety of projects.[7] The important point to grasp here is that, even where the distinction is apparently as crude as that between salariat, intermediate, and working classes, the Goldthorpe categories ensure more than merely nominal comparability by allocating occupations involving the same sorts of employment relations to the same classes across countries. Hitherto, national conventions as to what constituted (for example) the working class have tended to vary, as indeed has the class placement of borderline groups such as supervisors. Even the collapsed Goldthorpe classes offer greater assurance of comparability of data across different studies and countries.

IV

Goldthorpe's approach to class analysis seems to us, therefore, to be well suited to the cross-national study of inequalities of access to unequally rewarded positions. This is not to say that we regard his typology as ideal for our particular purposes. Two sorts of complication need to be mentioned here.

The first of these arises out of the fact that the Goldthorpe schema does not order social classes in a simple hierarchical fashion. An important feature of the classification, at least from the point of view of the present study, is its distinction between more and less privileged market and work situations—a reference to advantage and disadvantage which is clearly pertinent where issues of social justice are concerned. But the employment status and sectoral components in the scheme do mean that the classes cannot be arranged along a single such dimension. Distinctions are made, not only between classes having relatively advantaged and disadvantaged conditions of employment, but also between individuals located in different sectors (agricultural and non-agricultural) and individuals having different employment statuses (notably the self-employed and employees). Seen in this light, therefore, it is difficult to conceive of the transition between (say) agricultural labourer (class VIIb) and unskilled manual worker (class VIIa) as being a move upward or downward in mobility terms. The same could be said of mobility between classes IV (the self-employed) and III (routine non-manual employees). This would seem to be a matter of some importance for the issue in hand, since sceptics might reasonably ask why an interest in social justice should lead us to care about movements between classes that are no better or worse than one another, and how mobility patterns so described can be thought of as in any way indicative of inequalities of access or opportunity.

In fact, there seem to us to be good reasons for thinking that non-vertical mobility might also be relevant to questions of social justice, although these raise complex issues relating to theories of justice (so we have restricted our observations on this matter to the confines of Appendix E). Nevertheless, it might still be thought that, given this problem, we should at the outset have explored the relationship between social class and social justice in terms of an alternative system of classification—specifically one which was explicitly hierarchical.

This is certainly possible in principle. Indeed, it is precisely what is attempted by those working in the so-called status attainment tradition, who analyse mobility between occupations ranked along a unidimensional scale of socio-economic status or prestige: and who, by incorporating strong assumptions about the precise positions of different occupations on that scale, are able to employ powerful regression techniques to investigate the possible determinants of individual success or failure.[8] However, we believe that there are a number of more straightforwardly sociological reasons for eschewing the status attainment approach, and persisting with an analysis couched specifically in terms of social class.

One reason for favouring a class approach over models that seek to analyse social stratification and mobility in terms of a single dimension of advantage is simply that we believe the former provides a better means of understanding the sociological processes that underlie the phenomena in question. To group together occupations solely on the basis of their 'general desirability', however understood, would be to regard as equivalent occupations holding quite different places in the social structure. While not a problem if one were interested solely in those occupations as indicators of the advantage accruing to their holders, this approach would make it difficult to analyse the sociological processes underpinning mobility patterns. One could not, for example, seek to explain such patterns in terms of macro-societal influences on the occupational structure, such as shifts in demand, technological innovation, or government economic policies.[9] Here, perhaps, the relevant political theory and sociology pull in slightly different directions—the latter insisting on the explanatory significance of factors that go beyond the individual attributes to which the former directs our attention. Understood in this way, our decision to adopt a class analysis rather than an individualistic approach may be thought to give priority to our view about best sociological practice, over that which would seem to be implied by the normative literature alone.[10]

In any case—and this is probably a more important reason for persisting with an approach rooted in class analysis rather than status attainment—it should be remembered here that the Goldthorpe class scheme does in fact have a strong hierarchical element that is clearly relevant to social justice. As was explained above (and as is confirmed by the work of Evans and others), the scheme is constructed so that there are significant inequalities of position between the working, intermediate, and service classes. Whatever qualifications might be appropriate at greater levels of detail, these three groupings can certainly be considered to form a hierarchy, so we can be confident that, at this three-class level of analysis, we are investigating mobility between not just different but also unequal positions.[11] We have been careful to pay particular attention to this problem throughout the empirical analyses in this volume.

Indeed, in one sense at least, the absence of any more comprehen-
sively hierarchical claims for our approach may be seen as positively
beneficial. If we were to seek to construct a unidimensional scale, in
terms of which all occupations could then be ranked, it would be necessary for us to make strong and controversial claims about the nature of
the 'advantage' the fairness of access to which we were concerned to
investigate. By deliberately opting for a system of classification that
contains only general and relatively unproblematic claims about what
makes one position better than another, we intend to avoid getting
bogged down in the difficult issue of how one should understand 'advantage' (and the no less difficult problem of how to operationalize it for
empirical investigation).[12]

A second general complication that follows from our decision to
explore the relationship between class and justice by means of the
Goldthorpe categories is that, although this schema is commonly used in
comparative stratification research, it is by no means uncontroversial
among class analysts themselves. On the contrary, Goldthorpe's whole
approach to the study of social mobility has been the subject of several
rather acrimonious debates, more than one of which has involved the
authors of this volume. For example, it is sometimes claimed that his
scheme lacks a robust theoretical foundation, that it deals inadequately
with the class positions of women, and that it may be undermined in
practice because of cross-national variation in the conventions by which
occupations are classified.

We are not insensitive to these sorts of issue. Neither do we think that
they are all equally salient to the matter here under consideration.
Though not without interest, much of this discussion simply falls outside
the scope of an investigation into the relationship between class and
justice, and deals instead with (for example) the precise way in which
Goldthorpe's class categories have been operationalized in the practical
settings of specific research projects. For this reason, we have consigned
our discussion of some of the disputed but more abstruse theoretical
and methodological aspects of the scheme to the decent obscurity of
Appendix C, to which specialists in class analysis are now referred. The
appendix also gives full details of the particular coding conventions that
were followed in the various surveys from which our data have been
derived.[13]

Our next task, in pursuing the implications of social class for social
justice, is to examine patterns of intergenerational social mobility in
Britain and elsewhere. Do children from different social backgrounds
have the same opportunities to enjoy distributive advantage? Of course,
the issue of mobility chances takes us on to terrain already well trodden

by earlier class analysts, most obviously by the CASMIN team them-selves. However, the apparently simple problem of determining the degree of openness in class societies is surrounded by no little (ongoing) controversy, not the least of which—as we shall now see—concerns the interpretation of particular patterns and trends as evidence for and against the claim that industrialism induces equality of opportunity— and therefore greater social justice.

NOTES

1. See Marshall (1988), Marshall et al. (1988), and Marshall and Rose (1990). Recent textbooks include Scase (1992), Edgell (1993), Crompton (1993), and Breen and Rottman (1995*a*).
2. Because of its complex genealogy, the class scheme has variously been described in the literature as the Goldthorpe, Erikson–Goldthorpe, EGP (Erikson–Goldthorpe–Portocarero), and CASMIN typology. In Britain, the conventional terminology is 'Goldthorpe classes', and at the risk of offending Goldthorpe's collaborators we have followed this usage throughout.
3. For a diagrammatic representation of this account of the derivation of the class schema, see Erikson and Goldthorpe (1992*a*: fig. 2.1). See also Goldthorpe (1995*a*: 314–15), in which the following summary is offered: 'In earlier work, I referred (following Lockwood) to *market* and *work situation* as being the two major components of class position, and sought to implement this view in the development of the class schema. However, I now believe it is better simply to say that class positions are differentiated in terms of *employment relations*. The primary division here is then according to employment status, that is, between employer, self-employed and employee positions; while the secondary division is according to different types of employee relationship (or different forms of the regula-tion of employment), with the "service relationship" being counterposed to the "labour contract". This reformulation appears to me desirable chiefly in order to bring out that the view of class that I take ... is *not* a "work-centred" one: that is to say, it *is* employment relations that determine class positions, not the nature of work-tasks and work-roles *per se*, nor yet the degree of autonomy, authority etc. that is conferred on the individuals performing them ... There are, to be sure, good reasons for expecting that those positions that are defined by a service relationship will tend to be ones that do involve incumbents in the exercise of some degree of professional autonomy and/or managerial or administrative authority. But where any discrepancy in this respect occurs, it is the nature of the employment relationship, and not of the work-tasks and work-roles, that is relevant. Thus, for instance, in the case of

positions supposedly carrying managerial titles for purely "cosmetic" reasons, what matters is whether or not a service relationship exists. If it does, then such positions are service-class positions—even if those fortunate enough to hold them are required to do no more than sort paper clips.'

4. See, for details of the British case, Scott (1982; 1991). Moreover, as will be seen in due course, we focus our attention on the meritocratic defence of class inequalities, and issues of merit scarcely arise in this context: theories of social justice which emphasized entitlement would more easily be accommodated.

5. Goldthorpe and Payne (1986: 21). Note here that the reference to 'chances of economic advancement' refers to prospective elements of the service relationship itself—salary increments, pension rights, and the like—rather than mobility propensities as such. (Compare Ch. 2, n. 12, above.) Ideally, therefore, class position would be determined on the basis of direct information about the employment relations of each respondent. Goldthorpe and his colleagues accept that occupational title and employment status serve only as proxies in this respect. This logic does mean, however, as Goldthorpe (1995a: 315) notes, that 'the class schema is "occupationally based" only in so far as it is supposed that groupings of occupations, with the same employment status, will be characterised by similar employment relationships.'

6. Evans (1992: 226–7). For an earlier (and cruder) test of the criterion validity of the Goldthorpe schema, see Marshall et al. (1988: ch. 4). See also Evans (1996).

7. See e.g., the 5-category and 3-category versions used in Heath et al. (1985), and the two-category collapse in Erikson and Goldthorpe (1992b).

8. Classic studies include Blau and Duncan (1967) and Featherman and Hauser (1978). The status attainment programme sees the principal interest of mobility studies as lying in the attempt to specify those attributes which are characteristic of individuals who end up in the more desirable rather than the less desirable jobs. Typically, these studies investigate the extent to which the present occupational status of individuals is associated with the status of their family of origin, rather than individual achievements such as educational attainment or other indicators of skill and ability. This approach depends upon the assumption that individuals are allocated to positions ordered in a continuous unidimensional hierarchy. In some studies this social hierarchy was conceptualized narrowly as being one of occupational prestige—most commonly, how people rate the relative 'general standing' of different occupations. In others, it was generalized to include additional aspects of socio-economic status, such as income and years of schooling. This approach is controversial, partly because many of its advocates have seemed to argue that social order rests mainly on shared values, and that the prestige hierarchy is a function of widespread convergence in moral evaluations. It has thus been criticized as an extension of the

functional theory of stratification. For an overview by one of its leading exponents, see Featherman (1981).

9. See also Erikson and Goldthorpe (1992a: 30–1, 34, 45), who observe that 'occupations that are found in close proximity to each other on scales of prestige or status need not, and often do not, have much in common with each other, and may indeed hold quite disparate locations within the social division of labour. Thus, within the same narrow band of scale values one may find, say, groupings of skilled industrial workers brought together with certain types of small proprietor and minor official; or, again, farmers and smallholders placed alongside artisans, industrial labourers, and personal service workers. In consequence, where mobility is analysed in a hierarchical context as represented by occupational prestige or status scales, it becomes difficult for the structural influences that bear on mobility rates and patterns to be adequately isolated and displayed. Occupational groupings that are treated as equivalent will in fact often be ones that are . . . following, within the overall course of economic development, quite divergent trajectories of expansion or decline.'

10. Moreover, the empirical evidence shows that distinctions indicating sectoral differences and employment status are of great significance for the explanation of socio-political class formation. For example, research consistently confirms that the self-employed are among the politically most conservative of social classes, and in this respect are ideologically quite distinct from their occupational peers who are employed by others—see e.g. Heath et al. (1985: 17–20). It is also firmly established (see Newby, 1977) that the conditions of agricultural as against industrial labour encourage manual employees in factories and the countryside to develop significantly different life-styles, values, and beliefs. The distinctive value added by retaining the class analysis perspective is, then, that socio-political class formation may itself have implications for understanding both popular conceptions of, and attempts to realize, social justice. On this last point, see Swift et al. (1995).

11. In one sense it might be argued that the scheme is blind to differences introduced by gender, since within each class the employment relations and conditions of females are usually inferior to those of males (although Evans demonstrates convincingly that the differences are very small); but the data confirm that women are no less class-divided in these terms than are men. Rewards are, in other words, differentially distributed by class within the sexes.

12. There is an extensive literature on this issue in political theory. See e.g. Sen (1995) and Cohen (1989). In contrast to the philosophical precision of such discussions, note that the sociological concept of socio-economic status, which is regularly used as the dependent variable (that which people attain) in status attainment research, has a bizarre history and referent. In the most widely used index of socio-economic status (that devised by O. D. Duncan), an occupation's socio-economic status is determined by a weighted combi-

nation of the average income and years of schooling characteristic of those in the occupation (though we are never told why), but the weights are derived as those that best fit perceptions of the occupational prestige attaching to people in certain specific occupations (for the details, see Duncan 1961). Is this then a measure of the occupation's prestige or its socio-economic resources? For a trenchant critique of this and similar indices, see Goldthorpe (1990: 414–16).

13. A good overview of much of the controversy surrounding Goldthorpe's work on social class and social mobility can be gleaned from the exchanges reported in Clark et al. (1990). For an extended defence of this particular approach to class analysis, see Goldthorpe and Marshall (1992).

4

Class Mobility

I

In this chapter, we examine the social mobility patterns that are to be found in eleven contemporary industrialized societies, including, of course, those for modern Britain. Our analysis will more easily be understood if two distinctions are borne in mind. One of these was introduced in an earlier chapter, but is worth repeating here, since it has generated a certain amount of controversy in previous discussions of class mobility. The other is (so far as we are aware) entirely uncontroversial, and is mentioned mainly for the benefit of readers new to mobility studies.

The latter can be dealt with briefly, since it points only to an established contrast between two types of class mobility research. On the one hand, the present class location of an individual may be compared with that of his or her parents, that is to say in relation to social origins or social class background. People will, in other words, have been mobile or immobile *inter*generationally. Alternatively, it is possible to think in terms of *intra*generational mobility, and to visualize a person's class mobility as a work-history—from, say, first to present employment. Most studies of social mobility have been concerned with origins-to-destinations trajectories of the former type. This particular volume is no exception: our subject is intergenerational rather than career mobility.[1]

The distinction between outcome and access—between the advantage enjoyed by occupants of particular social positions and the chances of mobility between those positions—is perhaps more problematic. Indeed, critics of mobility research have often conflated the two, and claimed—wrongly in our view—that because some mobility studies suggest that inequalities of opportunity may not have diminished much over the past half-century or so, their authors are somehow blind to the fact that (almost) everybody has gained from the general betterment of people's positions that has been achieved during this time.[2] It is important to understand, therefore, that nothing in social mobility studies (our own included) tackles the issue of whether or not people are generally more affluent now than they were at some point in the past. That would raise questions about the (average) improvement in the material circumstances of the various positions within the class structure. In fact, however, no mobility researcher known to us has ever denied that Britons are (on average) now better off in absolute terms than they were hitherto: as a nation, and considered in the long run, we have tended to earn more, live longer, and so on. Mobility researchers are interested instead in the quite separate issue of equality of opportunity—of access to the different (unequally advantaged) positions within that class structure—and it is this problem that we have identified as being central to the arguments of this book.

With these clarifications in mind, we may now proceed to the comparative analysis of class mobility patterns, as these have been recorded by the various sample surveys. Sociologists will be aware that this is in fact one of the most intensively researched topics in contemporary social science. A plethora of complex and increasingly technical issues have been raised over the years. These have been effectively summarized elsewhere (for example, see Kurz and Müller 1987; and Ganzeboom et al. 1991). In any case, for present purposes it is sufficient to consider only a few of the principal arguments, since our interest is here circumscribed by our particular focus on the relationship between social class and social justice. More specifically, we will pursue the issue of social mobility in cross-national comparative perspective, only in so far as—and only because—some prominent earlier commentators have related these sorts of data directly to arguments about equality of opportunity and meritocratic selection.

II

The closely related themes of equal opportunities and meritocracy are most obvious in the writings on social stratification of American social scientists such as Talcott Parsons, Clark Kerr, and Daniel Bell. The theory of industrial society developed by these and like-minded authors has been described as 'liberal' because it is premised on the assumption that industrial economies are most compatible with—and in the long term actually promote—a liberal or pluralist form of society. Indeed, in strong versions of the theory, industrialism is said to impose an irresistible logic on its social and political structures, reinforcing features which are functionally consistent with the technical and economic rationality of industrial production, and so generating convergence in the developmental paths of all industrial societies.

Reviewing this literature for the CASMIN Project of the 1980s, Erikson and Goldthorpe summarized in three succinct propositions the implications of the liberal theory of industrialism for social stratification, emphasizing in particular the contrast between pre-industrial and advanced industrial societies. In the latter, as compared to the former, rates of social mobility are high (with upward mobility prevailing over downward mobility); opportunities for mobility are more equal; and both mobility rates and the degree of equality of opportunity tend to increase.[3]

As Erikson and Goldthorpe also point out, different writers offered different explanations as to why these particular tendencies were inherent in the industrialization process, although every account was implicitly functionalist in tenor. Some argued that the sectoral shifts occasioned by industrialization itself yielded high rates of intergenerational mobility, as the economically active population was progressively redistributed from agriculture to manufacturing and then to services, a tendency reinforced by the associated expansion of bureaucratic organizations and of occupations requiring specialized technical and professional skills. The conjoint effect of industrialization, bureaucratization, and automation is therefore to reduce the relative size of the labouring classes, especially the numbers involved in merely routine activities, and greatly to increase the proportion of skilled workers, technical experts, managers, and administrators. In this way, industrial societies become increasingly middle-class, and—since upward mobility is more likely than downward mobility—the chances of success are improved for all.

A second explanation for the contrast between mobility in pre-industrial and industrial societies moved beyond consideration merely of changes in the structure of opportunities itself, and pointed instead to a transformation in the processes by which individuals were allocated to particular positions in the social division of labour, emphasizing in particular the functional necessity of a shift away from ascription and towards achievement as the principal criterion for social selection. It is at this point that the theme of meritocracy comes to the fore. Liberal theory envisages the emergence of dynamic societies in which rational technologies call forth an increasingly differentiated and specialized division of labour. As the demand for highly qualified personnel grows, so too does the requirement to expand education and training and to

make this increasingly accessible to all individuals, regardless of their
social background. Gradually, therefore, the efficient use of human
resources promotes an increase in educational provision and in
meritocratic selection to occupations. The 'traditional' association between social origins and class destinations is in this way weakened, as
opportunities for mobility (or so-called mobility chances) become more
equal between classes, and societies become more open or fluid. In
some accounts, other aspects of industrialism (such as increasing geo-
graphical mobility, the growth of mass communications, and greater
equality in living conditions or incomes) are said to undermine further
the historical link between origins and destinations, by loosening ties of
kinship and locality, raising aspirations, and redistributing the resources
necessary for the realization of ambitions.

Finally, Erikson and Goldthorpe point to a number of accounts in
which the effects of economic growth and of the shift to achievement as
the basis for social selection are seen to interact, such that meritocratic
procedures operate most strongly within the expanding technologically
advanced sectors of the economy and the growing numbers of large-
scale bureaucratic organizations. Conversely, ascriptive tendencies are
confined to declining sectors and outmoded organizational forms, for
example agriculture or the small family-based firm. In this way, an
increasing proportion of the population is exposed to the new
meritocratic mobility regime, both because of the spread of that regime
itself and because the forms of economic activity most resistant to it are
in decline.

The implications of this theory for the present study are obvious.
Industrialism, it is claimed, promotes both greater opportunities for
social mobility and meritocratic selection to occupations. It follows,
therefore, that nations which have attained different levels of industrialism should display different mobility regimes. The more advanced the
society, the higher the rates of mobility (especially upward mobility),
and the greater the fluidity or openness. Furthermore, as a particular
society approaches industrial maturity it should show signs of convergence with other advanced societies, notably in a tendency towards
increased equality of opportunity over time. From the point of view of
our interest in the relationship between social class and social justice, we
should therefore see evidence both that mobility rates are higher and
opportunities more equal in Britain than are those to be found in (say)
the less advanced post-communist states of Central and Eastern
Europe, and also that mobility rates and social fluidity have increased
over time within these societies as they have advanced along the route
charted by liberal theory.

Do the data provided by recent surveys support either of these propositions? We do not believe so. To explain why, we will first consider the total mobility rates within each of the eleven countries for which we have information, our analysis culminating in the observation that sectoral shifts occasioned by industrialism tend to increase the possibilities for social mobility generally within societies by changing the structure of opportunities. We then address the issue of equality of opportunity by examining the distribution of those mobility prospects across the various social classes. In other words, we calculate relative mobility chances. Issues relating to social change will also be explored by examining cross-sectional data for particular societies at two different points in time. We conclude by noting the implications of our findings about social mobility for arguments about social justice—arguments which are then pursued in subsequent chapters that deal explicitly with the role of education as a mediator between social origins and class destinations.

The distinction—just drawn—between absolute (or total observed) mobility and relative mobility chances (also called social fluidity) will be central to our analysis. Both concepts are well established and fully elaborated in the earlier mobility literature. The absolute mobility rates in any society can be observed from a cross-tabulation of each individual's class origins against his or her class destinations. The main weakness of absolute rates—at least from our point of view—is that they confound mobility due to changes in the shape of the class structure with that which reflects relative mobility chances. That is to say, the simple cross-tabulation of origins against destinations fails to distinguish mobility induced by structural changes in the economy which cause the expansion and contraction of classes (these are reflected in the changing percentages to be found in the marginal totals of the mobility table), from mobility net of (after allowing for) these external influences. Only changes in the latter would indicate a redistribution of mobility chances in favour of greater equality—or inequality—of opportunity.

The two sorts of effect can be separated out by calculating so-called odds ratios. These describe (in this particular context) comparative mobility chances, regardless of how class structures may have changed over time (or, indeed, how they may vary across societies), merely because of the various structural processes which alter the relative sizes of the classes. Odds ratios are, precisely, a measure of the relative chances of mobility and immobility of those born into different social classes—and are, therefore, the best available indicator of the degree of equality and inequality of opportunity in any society. They are also the basis for more sophisticated log-linear modelling of social mobility data.

These models provide formal statistical tests of whether or not the mobility patterns observed in any society or societies are consistent with certain hypotheses relating to the associations found in contingency tables—in this case, those between social origins, class destinations, and the absence or presence of changes in this association across different nations and time periods.

Class analysts will be familiar with these concepts and the accompanying statistical techniques. Other readers, who may well be encountering for the first time either the distinction between absolute and relative mobility or the techniques themselves, may find it helpful to read Appendix B before proceeding further with this chapter. Certainly, an appreciation of the logic of odds ratios will make it easier to understand our tables, especially the log-linear analyses reported later in the exposition.

III

We begin, however, by reviewing the simple distribution of origin and destination classes among respondents to the eleven surveys taken from the recent International Social Justice Project (ISJP). In Table 4.1, the destination class distributions of males and females are given separately in terms of their own employment, and their class origins in relation to that of their fathers when respondents were aged 15.[4]

It is possible, in these data, to observe some of the sectoral changes— the move from agriculture to manufacturing and services—that are central to liberal theories of industrialism. The expansion and contraction of particular classes is also obvious, as is differentiation in the class destinations of the sexes, and marked differences between countries in terms of their distributions of both the origin and destination classes. The different national patterns could in each case be situated within their local historical contexts; for example, they might be related to reforms in landholding and the organization of agriculture, to developments in government industrial strategy, or even to something as specific as changes in fiscal and tax policy with respect to self-employment. However, our interest in social justice hardly warrants such an exhaustive treatment, especially since this is readily available elsewhere.[5] In any case, given the relatively small sample sizes of these surveys, it would be unwise to read too much into the precise numbers obtained for any particular country.[6] Instead, we wish only to point to three general conclusions that can be drawn from these aggregate mobility data, and which bear directly on the arguments of liberal theory.

TABLE 4.1. *Distribution of Respondents in Eleven Nations, by Class of Origin and Destination, and by Sex (Percentage by Column); and Delta (Dissimilarity Index) Values for Origin and Destination Distributions*

Males

	BUL	CZA	GDR	EST	GBR	JAP	POL	RUS	SLO	USA	FRG
Class of origin (% by column)											
I, II	15	17	22	18	21	12	13	24	10	30	26
IIIa	3	6	6	2	4	9	3	2	6	5	8
IVa + b	2	2	7	1	8	17	5	0	5	8	11
IVc	15	6	12	9	4	36	33	0	27	5	9
V, VI	25	36	36	3	33	20	26	29	26	25	31
VIIa, IIIb	18	24	16	44	27	5	17	32	24	24	14
VIIb	22	9	2	23	4	0	3	13	2	3	2
Class of destination (% by column)											
I, II	27	28	29	30	41	26	17	36	24	36	40
IIIa	6	4	7	2	5	8	6	3	7	8	12
IVa + b	4	3	6	2	11	22	10	1	7	9	8
IVc	0	0	2	1	1	18	14	0	5	1	2
V, VI	31	34	40	41	20	19	30	29	32	20	27
VIIa, IIIb	21	20	14	24	21	11	21	27	24	26	12
VIIb	11	10	2	0	1	0	2	3	1	1	0

Females

	BUL	CZA	GDR	EST	GBR	JAP	POL	RUS	SLO	USA	FRG
Class of origin (% by column)											
I, II	21	18	28	23	24	19	16	31	16	25	28
IIIa	5	5	9	3	4	9	4	1	4	4	11
IVa + b	1	1	6	1	8	21	3	0	6	8	13
IVc	10	6	10	11	5	33	26	1	19	9	6
V, VI	21	34	33	5	36	16	22	25	30	31	25
VIIa, IIIb	19	24	11	42	20	2	23	27	21	21	16
VIIb	24	12	4	15	2	0	7	15	5	2	1
Class of destination (% by column)											
I, II	31	31	37	39	29	15	26	48	25	42	32
IIIa	22	20	21	18	30	22	19	14	24	19	31
IVa + b	1	1	5	0	8	21	5	0	4	5	8
IVc	0	0	3	0	1	9	12	0	4	1	0
V, VI	14	13	10	8	10	13	8	10	16	7	6
VIIa, IIIb	27	25	22	31	25	20	29	24	26	26	22
VIIb	5	9	3	3	2	0	1	4	1	0	0

TABLE 4.1. Continued

All

	BUL	CZA	GDR	EST	GBR	JAP	POL	RUS	SLO	USA	FRG
	Class of origin (% by column)										
I, II	18	17	25	21	23	12	14	28	13	27	27
IIIa	4	6	8	3	4	9	4	2	5	5	9
IVa + b	2	2	7	1	8	17	4	0	6	8	12
IVc	12	6	11	10	4	36	30	1	23	7	8
V, VI	23	35	34	4	35	20	24	27	28	28	29
VIIa, IIIb	18	24	13	43	24	5	20	29	23	23	15
VIIb	23	10	3	19	3	0	5	14	3	2	2
	Class of destination (% by column)										
I, II	29	29	33	34	33	26	21	43	24	39	37
IIIa	14	12	14	10	18	8	12	9	16	13	19
IVa + b	3	2	5	1	9	22	8	1	6	7	8
IVc	0	0	3	0	1	15	13	0	5	1	1
V, VI	22	24	25	26	15	19	20	18	23	14	19
VIIa, IIIb	24	23	18	27	23	11	25	25	25	26	16
VIIb	8	10	2	2	1	0	1	4	1	0	0
Deltas for origin and destination distributions											
Males	26	14	12	51	25	23	20	15	23	12	18
Females	36	30	32	35	33	31	34	31	35	37	31

Notes
1. Percentages may not sum exactly because of rounding.
2. Nations are Bulgaria (BUL), Czechoslovakia (CZA), East Germany (GDR), Estonia (EST), Great Britain (GBR), Japan (JAP), Poland (POL), Russia (RUS), Slovenia (SLO), the United States (USA), and West Germany (FRG).

The first is simply that the distributions of origin and destination classes show considerable variation across the eleven countries under investigation. Clearly, these are societies having reached different stages in the long march to industrial maturity, at least as this is envisaged in liberal theory. Some, such as Poland and Japan, retain a sizeable (though declining) agricultural workforce. Others, including Britain and the United States, already have relatively small agricultural populations in even the origin class distributions. During the period covered by the surveys, the manual working class was expanding in Bulgaria, Estonia, Japan, and Poland—although elsewhere (as in Britain, the United States, Russia, and the former West Germany and Czechoslovakia) it formed a declining proportion of the economically active population. The numbers involved in non-manual work have everywhere grown— although the relative rate of expansion has been greater in some societies than in others. In Slovenia and Japan, for example, the percentage of employees in the salariat virtually doubles between the origin and the destination distributions shown in Table 4.1. In Bulgaria and Poland the growth rate is only one-half of this. In what was East Germany it is more modest still, at approximately one-third. In other words, it is clear that these nations have attained different levels of industrialism, and this is reflected in their widely varying distributions of destination classes.

Second, we may note that, although these societies therefore occupy a range of positions along the trajectory of industrialism described in liberal theory, there is no evidence that absolute social mobility rates are higher in the more industrialized societies of the capitalist West. This can readily be seen from the calculation of overall mobility rates shown in Table 4.2. Here, for each of the countries under consideration, we report male and female total mobility rates (TMR), which (following the example set by the CASMIN researchers) we have in turn decomposed into total vertical (TV) and total non-vertical (TNV) mobility. Vertical mobility is then partitioned further into total upward (TU) and total downward (TD) mobility.[7]

One striking feature of this table is that the societies with the highest total mobility rates, at least among males, are those of the industrially less developed post-communist world—Estonia, Bulgaria, Slovenia, and East Germany. Another obvious finding is that there is no systematic tendency (in the case of either sex) for the more mature industrial societies to have higher ratios of vertical to non-vertical mobility, or of upward to downward mobility, than do the former state socialist societies of Central and Eastern Europe. For example, the balance of vertical and non-vertical mobility among men is the same in Russia as it is in the United States, in Japan as it is in Bulgaria, and virtually the same in Slovenia as in the former West Germany. Similarly, as regards male upward and downward mobility, identical or nearly identical ratios can be observed in Poland as compared to West Germany, and the United States in comparison with East Germany.

In other words, the balance of vertical as against non-vertical and of upward as against downward mobility was at least as favourable among the male workforces in many of the less developed formerly communist states as it was among economically active males in more mature industrial nations, such as West Germany and the United States. Similar sorts of observations could be made about total mobility rates among females. Clearly, findings such as this cannot easily be reconciled with the assumption made by liberal theorists that continuing industrial development leads to ever-higher rates of social mobility (especially of an ascending nature) because of the progressive upgrading of employment that is involved.

TABLE 4.2. *Decomposition of Total Mobility Rates (TMR) in Eleven Nations, into Total Vertical (TV) and Total Non-vertical (TNV) Mobility, and of Total Vertical Mobility into Total Upward (TU) and Total Downward (TD) Mobility, by Sex*

Males

	TMR	TV	TNV	TV/TNV	TU	TD	TU/TD
Estonia	79	65	14	4.6	56	10	5.6
Bulgaria	73	56	17	3.3	41	15	2.7
Slovenia	71	57	14	4.1	42	15	2.8
East Germany	69	55	14	5.9	34	21	1.6
Great Britain	66	56	10	5.6	39	17	2.3
United States	65	56	9	6.2	33	23	1.4
Russia	65	56	9	6.2	37	20	1.9
Czechoslovakia	64	53	11	4.8	34	19	1.8
Poland	63	47	16	2.9	32	15	2.1
West Germany	62	50	12	4.2	34	16	2.1
Japan	60	46	14	3.3	35	11	3.2

Females

	TMR	TV	TNV	TV/TNV	TU	TD	TU/TD
West Germany	76	57	19	3.0	31	26	1.2
Czechoslovakia	74	56	18	3.1	35	21	1.7
United States	74	61	13	4.7	39	23	1.7
Great Britain	74	55	19	2.9	28	28	1.0
East Germany	74	57	17	3.4	31	26	1.2
Estonia	73	58	15	3.9	44	14	3.1
Slovenia	73	53	20	2.7	36	17	2.1
Bulgaria	71	53	18	2.9	38	15	2.5
Poland	71	49	22	2.2	34	15	2.3
Japan	67	43	24	1.8	22	22	1.0
Russia	66	56	10	5.6	39	17	2.3

Finally, on the basis of these results at least, it seems that there is no obvious tendency towards a convergence that derives merely from the logic of the industrialization process itself. No ordering or grouping of nations which is consistent with the convergence thesis can readily be derived from the figures shown in Table 4.2. Early-industrial and late-industrializing countries do not form tidy categories having their own characteristic patterns or rates of social mobility. The distinction between democratic capitalist and state socialist or post-communist societies is equally unhelpful. As we have already observed, for example, the balance of vertical and non-vertical mobility is the same among Russian men as it is among their counterparts in the United States, while that of upward and downward mobility is not much different.

Indeed, if we calculate dissimilarity values (deltas) for pairwise comparisons of the different national distributions (as in Table 4.3), then the difficulties of reconciling our results with liberal propositions about social mobility become even more apparent.[8] For example, looking at the origin distributions for males, the dissimilarity index values for Slovenia as compared to most of the other state socialist societies on the one hand, and Britain, Japan, the United States, or West Germany on the other, are all rather similar (falling in the range 23–9)—this despite their widely differing levels of industrialization. In terms of male class

TABLE 4.3. *Deltas for Pairwise Comparisons of Eleven Nations*

Males

	BUL	CZA	GDR	EST	GBR	JAP	POL	RUS	SLO	USA	FRG
BUL	—	22	21	31	30	43	22	30	25	29	31
CZA	5	—	16	37	13	49	30	19	23	19	23
GDR	16	16	—	50	14	38	24	29	24	19	10
EST	17	14	12	—	42	68	52	34	49	44	51
GBR	22	24	24	24	—	47	30	17	26	12	17
JAP	36	39	31	41	29	—	22	61	27	45	35
POL	22	30	23	27	25	25	—	40	10	29	29
RUS	17	17	23	15	16	42	28	—	37	21	27
SLO	13	16	14	15	21	29	13	19	—	24	29
USA	22	24	23	22	8	29	26	14	17	—	16
FRG	25	26	18	23	15	29	29	20	22	16	—

Females

	BUL	CZA	GDR	EST	GBR	JAP	POL	RUS	SLO	USA	FRG
BUL	—	19	28	27	27	48	23	23	25	24	30
CZA	5	—	21	31	16	52	22	19	18	17	28
GDR	13	13	—	42	15	38	31	30	20	13	15
EST	13	14	12	—	41	58	35	28	39	36	45
GBR	14	15	13	20	—	46	28	26	17	6	17
JAP	29	31	27	39	27	—	34	61	38	42	35
POL	18	20	18	18	22	24	—	31	11	24	33
RUS	23	22	17	16	32	41	31	—	32	25	28
SLO	11	15	14	22	13	22	13	19	—	13	27
USA	16	17	12	10	17	33	16	17	18	—	15
FRG	18	19	14	20	7	29	22	27	19	15	—

Notes
1. Nations are as in Table 4.1, n. 2.
2. Figures in upper right-hand triangle refer to origin distributions; figures in lower left-hand triangles refer to destination distributions.

destinations, the most marked contrasts are between Japan and almost every other nation in our study, post-communist or capitalist and mature industrial or late-industrializing alike. Similarly, the Czech destination distribution for men is most akin to that found in some of the other post-communist states (such as Bulgaria), contrasts rather more with the distributions in the three Western capitalist societies (Britain, West Germany, the United States), but is yet further removed from the pattern of destination classes found in state socialist Poland. Again, the results for females are no less discouraging, when considered from the liberal point of view.

In sum, the findings reported in these three tables all tend to point to the same conclusion: that there is no obvious propensity towards convergence around the rates displayed by the most advanced nations. True, one can detect a tendency for distributions of class destinations to be more similar cross-nationally than are those of class origins, so that (for example) a discrepancy of 30 per cent or greater will be found in more than two-fifths of all male class-of-origin comparisons but in only one-tenth of those involving male class destinations. However, the discrepancy is still 20 per cent or above in almost two-thirds of the latter comparisons, and (more importantly) the overall pattern of dissimilarities does not support liberal claims that the industrialization process generates convergence on some modal class structure. In order to salvage such claims, and to explain why the mobility profiles for all mature industrial (or all late-industrializing or newly industrialized) societies are not basically the same, it would be necessary to invoke an implausible profusion of theories of exceptionalism.

IV

It would seem, from the above analysis, that the general arguments advanced by liberal theorists of industrialization are of doubtful validity if judged against the absolute mobility rates observed in these eleven countries. However, since our interest here is in determining the possible implications of social class specifically for social justice, it is predictions about the distribution of mobility opportunities rather than total rates that are of particular interest. This brings us naturally to questions of relative mobility, in other words the comparative mobility chances of those born into different classes, and thus the degree of equality of opportunity in the societies under review.

It is important to remember, in addressing this issue, that the concept of equality of opportunity—which is central to liberal accounts of social mobility in industrial societies—is inherently comparative. It necessarily invites us to examine the opportunities of different groups or different individuals and to assess these opportunities relative to one another. That is simply in the nature of the concept of equality—whether it be of opportunity or, for that matter, of outcome. Equality of opportunity therefore means precisely that—*equality* of opportunity. Some observers (e.g. Saunders 1995: 25) have quite wrongly assumed that questions about equal opportunities may be answered merely by pointing to the increased 'room at the top' created by the expansion of the salariat over time in Britain and elsewhere. However, this is tantamount to saying that we should not be interested in the distribution of opportunities, but simply in the fact that (as can be seen from a study of absolute rates alone) the structure of opportunities now is rather different from that found in the past. In short, we should not be concerned with equality of opportunity at all, but rather with the fact that industrialism tends to provide more opportunities all round for upward social mobility.

That conclusion could certainly be drawn from the mobility rates reported above. The proportion of the workforce employed in non-manual work has everywhere grown. The resulting changes in the class structure have, over time, led to a general increase in chances for upward mobility within industrialized societies. This is evident, for example, in the ratio of total upward to total downward mobility rates—which in all countries is (for men at least) greater than 1 (and nowhere less than 1 for women). However, the issue at the heart of liberal theory is one of *relative* access to the different positions within the class structure, since industrialism is supposed to generate an increase, not only in total mobility rates, but also in equality of access to positions of advantage and disadvantage. The theory states unambiguously that, as nations progress along the route to industrial maturity, ascribed status (as determined by such criteria as social origins or sex) must give way to achieved status (determined by what Talcott Parsons refers to as 'the valued results of the actions of individuals'). Parsons goes on to argue that, in advanced industrial societies such as contemporary America, 'we determine status very largely on the basis of achievement within an occupational system which is in turn organized primarily in terms of universalistic criteria of performance and status within functionally specialized fields'. The resulting class structure therefore 'requires at least a relatively high degree of "equality of opportunity" which in turn means that status cannot be determined primarily by birth or membership in kinship units'.[9]

Parsons's later work situates this assessment within the evolutionary perspective that came to dominate his and other liberal theories of industrial society:

The United States' new type of societal community, more than any other factor, justifies our assigning it the lead in the latest phase of modernization. We have suggested that it synthesizes to a high degree the equality of opportunity stressed in socialism. It presupposes a market system, a strong legal order relatively independent of government, and a 'nation-state' emancipated from specific religious and ethnic control. The educational revolution has been considered as a crucial innovation, especially with regard to the emphasis on the associational pattern, as well as on openness of opportunity. Above all, American society has gone farther than any comparable large-scale society in its dissociation from the older ascriptive inequalities and the institutionalization of a basically egalitarian pattern. (Parsons 1971: 114)

Similar assessments will be found in the work of Kerr, Bell, and other liberal theorists. For example, Donald J. Treiman (one of the leading exponents of liberal theory in the field of stratification studies) maintains that mobility chances not only increase but equalize with economic development, so that equality of opportunity is inherent in the logic of industrialism (see Treiman 1970: 221; Ganzeboom et al. 1989: 3–4). Presumably, therefore, relative mobility chances should be more equal in mature industrial societies (such as Britain and the United States) than in late-industrializing countries (such as Russia and her former satellite states in Eastern Europe). Is this in fact the case?

One way of resolving the issue is to fit a model of so-called common social fluidity (CmSF) to the eleven male and eleven female mobility tables taken from the ISJP. Such a model proposes that, across the tables in question, we will find an association between the distribution of class origins and the countries; or, in other words, that the proportions of the population found within each of the origin classes is different in different societies. There will also be a further association between the distribution of class destinations and countries. Finally, the model suggests that although there is an association between class origins and destinations within each table, this does not itself vary across societies—hence the fitted model is one which hypothesizes 'common social fluidity' across countries. If liberal propositions about equality of opportunity are sound, then this model should not fit at all well; and, moreover, the discrepancies ought to indicate greater social fluidity in the most advanced societies.

In fact, although the results show that it is indeed the case that the model does not fit the data for either sex (see Table 4.4), they also

TABLE 4.4. *Results of Testing the Model of Common Social Fluidity in Eleven Nations, by Sex (Respondent's Class Determined by Reference to Own Employment)*

Males

Model	G^2	df	p	rG^2	delta
Independence	672.82	99	0.000	—	13.97
Common Social Fluidity	127.85	90	0.005	80.9	5.17

Females

Model	G^2	df	p	rG^2	delta
Independence	562.96	99	0.000	—	13.48
Common Social Fluidity	150.35	90	0.001	73.3	6.52

Notes
1. Class origins (O) and destination (D) class each have 4 levels: salariat (I, II); intermediate (IIIa, IVa + b, V); working (VI, VIIa, IIIb); and agricultural (IVc, VIIb).
2. Nations (N) are as in Table 4.1, n. 2.
3. Independence model = ON + DN.
4. Common social fluidity model = ON + DN + OD.
5. G^2 = log-likelihood ratio; rG^2 = % reduction in G^2 achieved by the CmSF model (treating the conditional independence model as a baseline); delta = proportion of misclassified cases.

demonstrate clearly that there is a substantial measure of cross-national similarity in the degree of social fluidity. Formally, we must reject the hypothesis that relative mobility chances are exactly the same for men or for women, across the eleven industrialized countries in question. (Readers who are new to log-linear techniques, and perhaps uncertain as to how to interpret the table, may find the relevant section of Appendix B helpful at this point.) In the case of males, for example, the CmSF model returns a G^2 of 127.85, on 90 degrees of freedom, and misclassifies just over 5 per cent of cases. The fit is slightly worse in the case of females—where more than 6 per cent of individuals are wrongly classified. On the other hand, these figures represent improvements of over 80 per cent (for males) and 73 per cent (among females) on the simpler independence model, which allows only for different origin and destination distributions within each country but posits no common association between origins and destinations across countries.[10]

In other words, while it cannot be argued (at least on the basis of these data) that mobility chances are identical across all industrialized nations (whatever their level of industrialization), one might nevertheless conclude that, to the extent that class origins are in fact associated with class destinations within particular countries, by far the largest part of that association is common to all of the societies here examined.[11]

Moreover, and crucially, there is nothing in our results to suggest that relative mobility chances vary cross-nationally in a way that is consistent with the propositions of liberal theory. For example, if we look at the largest residuals under the CmSF model—that is, the cells of the mobility table for which there are the greatest discrepancies from what would be expected under the model of common social fluidity—we find that, in the case of males, the model underestimates the numbers who are upwardly mobile into the salariat from origins in other classes, but does so in East Germany and Estonia as well as the United States. Alternatively, we might note that it underestimates mobility between the salariat and working class in both directions in the case of Estonia, but overestimates the numbers involved in these same trajectories in the case of Poland. In other words, Estonia would seem to be relatively more open to this particular form of long-range intergenerational mobility than would the other countries in our sample, while Poland is relatively more closed. Rather importantly, there is no evidence that the model of common social fluidity systematically underestimates the degree of fluidity in the more advanced societies such as Britain, West Germany, or the United States, as compared to those of the former Soviet empire.

Similarly, in the case of women, inspection of the residuals reveals that the CmSF model underestimates the amount of mobility into the salariat in a number of advanced industrial and late-industrialized countries alike—including the United States on the one hand and Czechoslovakia and Estonia on the other, as well as Japan and both parts of the formerly divided Germany. Downward mobility from the salariat to the working class is likewise underestimated in both Russia and the United States. Again, as in the case of males, there is no evidence that the common social fluidity model underestimates the openness of the industrially more mature societies in comparison with those which are industrially less developed.

Alternatively, we might note that at least one of the possible hallmarks of advanced industrialism and social fluidity—long-range mobility in both directions between the salariat and working classes—is (if anything) more obvious in some of the former state socialist societies than in those of the democratic and capitalist West.

Consider, for example, the results reported in Table 4.5. The salariat versus working-class odds ratios shown in the table explain some of the variance that is not captured by the common social fluidity model. These have been calculated from the same four-class mobility table as was the

TABLE 4.5. *Salariat versus Working-Class Odds Ratios, by Sex, for Eleven Nations*

Males		Females	
East Germany	2.11	East Germany	2.27
Estonia	2.21	Estonia	2.27
Bulgaria	2.51	Russia	2.79
Russia	3.09	United States	2.98
Czechoslovakia	3.17	Czechoslovakia	4.37
United States	3.72	West Germany	4.46
West Germany	5.39	Bulgaria	5.28
Great Britain	5.48	Great Britain	6.25
Slovenia	6.67	Poland	6.67
Japan	7.68	Japan	12.78
Poland	7.90	Slovenia	12.88

model itself. They point to a form of long-range social mobility that is unambiguously hierarchical and, one assumes, particularly desirable from the point of view of equal opportunities. The results make it clear that the chances of being intergenerationally mobile between these two broad classes vary substantially across nations, and do so in a way that cannot easily be explained by reference to liberal theory. They also show that, in this respect at least, the degree of inequality of opportunity in Britain is probably greater than that to be found in many other industrialized societies. In this country, boys and girls having service-class parents are five or six times more likely to be found in the service class (and not in the working class) than are their peers who hail from working-class backgrounds, a finding which puts Britain closer to the bottom than the top of this particular mobility league.

Finally (and perhaps most convincingly of all), if we then subject to formal test the liberal proposition that the logic of industrialism tends to equalize the opportunities for class mobility, the results confirm that, to the contrary, there is no apparent secular trend towards greater equality of opportunity implicit within the industrialization process. This conclusion is evident from the findings reported in Table 4.6. Here, our eleven nations have been ranked in terms of overall fluidity (separately for each sex), as this has been estimated under Goldthorpe and Erikson's model of uniform difference. In other words, the nations have been arranged in order of increasing openness, with (among males) Japan at one extreme (as the least fluid society) and Estonia at the other (as the most open).[12]

Note that the beta parameters shown in the table are a measure of only general or overall fluidity. They do not imply that adjacent nations

TABLE 4.6. *Ranking of Eleven Nations, by Overall Fluidity, by Sex*

Males		Females	
Nation	Fluidity (beta value)	Nation	Fluidity (beta value)
Estonia	− 0.49	United States	− 0.46
East Germany	− 0.35	East Germany	− 0.42
Czechoslovakia	− 0.30	Russia	− 0.26
Russia	− 0.21	Estonia	− 0.23
Bulgaria	− 0.19	Czechoslovakia	− 0.15
United States	0.05	Great Britain	− 0.09
Poland	0.11	West Germany	0.18
Slovenia	0.15	Poland	0.19
Great Britain	0.25	Bulgaria	0.21
West Germany	0.48	Japan	0.49
Japan	0.50	Slovenia	0.53

in the table will also have patterns of fluidity that are similar. In other words, to the extent that countries deviate from the model of common social fluidity, they may do so in ways not at all obvious from their relative standings in the table. Nevertheless, the ranking does reflect the degree to which nations show greater or less openness overall, and this would seem to be the aspect of fluidity that is of central interest to liberal theory.[13]

That ranking hardly confirms the liberal prediction that industrialism tends to increase the overall fluidity of societies. In the case of males, for example, the most open nations—those having greater than average fluidity—seem to be the less advanced states of formerly communist Europe. The democratic capitalist countries—Japan, the United States, West Germany, and Britain itself—all appear to have class structures that are less open than the average for these eleven societies considered as a whole. In the case of females, the ranking is no less unhelpful to liberal theory, since certain advanced capitalist states appear to display much the same degree of general social fluidity as other less advanced communist states, more or less throughout the range shown in the table. Thus, not only the United States but also the German Democratic Republic appear among the most fluid nations, while both Slovenia and Japan seem to be most closed.[14]

These findings encourage us to draw two general conclusions. The first is that, to the degree to which the common social fluidity model fails to fit the data for those countries in our sample, this is not because the more mature industrial societies are somehow more open than their late-industrializing counterparts. Equality of opportunity is not inherent in some underlying logic of industrialism. Second, and as a corollary of this, it is hard to see how the more advanced countries can be seen as moving towards a convergence on some sort of 'open society'. Not only are the mobility regimes in these countries not that different from those of their much less industrialized post-communist neighbours but, furthermore, to the extent that they are indeed distinct then this is not because they are uniformly more open.

V

If the foregoing results are sound, they cast serious doubts on the arguments advanced by liberal theorists of industrialism, especially in respect of the social mobility regimes that are said to characterize nations at different stages of development. Relative mobility chances are not more equal in mature industrial as compared to less advanced societies. Nor do differences in total mobility rates correspond to the predicted pattern—although the latter finding is of less obvious relevance to the concerns of this particular volume. The only outstanding issue, as regards liberal theory and its bearing on our specific interest in social class and social justice, is, then, the question of social change within societies rather than in cross-national perspective. The theory predicts that the degree of equality of opportunity tends to increase over time. To what extent does the available evidence substantiate this final strand in the liberal argument?

One way of addressing this issue would be to examine chances of mobility and immobility across different cohorts within a particular country. The Oxford researchers did precisely this, and found that relative mobility chances for British men had altered little throughout the course of the twentieth century, up until the time of their study.[15] There was a 'trendless fluctuation' in such chances rather than any clear indication of a move towards either greater openness or closure in the class structure. The comparative chances of mobility among men born before the First World War were rather similar to those that prevailed among men born during and after the Second World War. Has this pattern been maintained throughout the decades up to the time of our own investigation?

Table 4.7 suggests that the short answer to this question is yes. Our analysis here draws on the male mobility tables from the Oxford Social Mobility Study (1972), Essex Class Project (1984), and the British sur-

TABLE 4.7. *Social Fluidity among Males in Britain, 1972–1991*

Surveys included	Model	G^2	df	p	rG^2	delta
A + B + C	OD + DT + OT	40.43	32	0.146	97.6	1.11
A + B + C	UNIDIFF	36.71	30	0.185	97.8	0.97
A + C	OD + DT + OT	21.70	16	0.153	98.7	0.60
A + B	OD + DT	27.39	20	0.125	98.3	0.73
B + C	OD + DT	18.61	20	0.548	90.1	5.05
C + A (standardized sample size)	OD + DT	16.73	20	0.670	90.1	4.60

UNIDIFF parameter estimates (Oxford survey set to zero): A + B = − 0.1272 (ns): B + C = − 0.1945 (ns).

Notes
1. A = Oxford Mobility Study, 1972, B = Essex Class Project, 1984, C = British Social Justice Project, 1991.
2. O = class of origin, D = class destination, T = (time of) survey. O and D have 5 levels: salariat (I, II); routine clerical (IIIa +b); *petite bourgeoisie* (IVa + b + c); skilled manual workers (V, VI); unskilled manual workers (VIIa + b).
3. G^2 = log-likelihood ratio; rG^2 = % reduction in G^2 achieved by each model (treating the main effects as a baseline); delta = proportion of misclassified cases.
4. Main effects = O + D + T.
5. ns = not significant.

vey within the ISJP (1991). In order to examine possible variations in the strength of the association between class origins and destinations over time, we have compared successively the three sets of results, and then each of the three possible pairs. (This perhaps cumbersome strategy is intended to guard against the possibility that a three-way comparison alone may be misleading if the results are unduly influenced by the much larger Oxford sample.) As a final check, the results from the 1972 survey were compared with those from 1991, but standardized down to the base provided by the latter sample.

The model shown in Table 4.7 for the three-survey (A + B + C) comparison provides a good fit to the data and reports associations between the distribution of class origins (O) and time (T)—or, in other words, confirms that the distribution of class origins has changed over the years; between the distribution of class destinations and time (DT); and, finally, between origins and destinations (OD). Since this last association does not itself vary across the surveys—the interaction term ODT is not significant—we may describe the fitted model as one which proposes 'constant social fluidity' (CnSF) over time. In fact, the CnSF model provides a satisfactory fit to the data however the surveys are compared—pairing any survey with any other, and on a standardized as well as unstandardized sample size. This would seem to suggest that the association between origins and destinations has not changed significantly across the surveys. In other words, the pattern of relative class mobility chances has remained basically the same over time.[16]

Again, Erikson and Goldthorpe's UNIDIFF test allows for more sophisticated analysis than does the global test provided by the constant social fluidity model, in this case by investigating whether or not the odds ratios display a monotonic directional trend across the three surveys in question. In fact, however, as will be seen from the results shown in the table, the UNIDIFF test does not improve significantly upon the fit obtained by the CnSF model (reducing the deviance by only 3.72 for the sacrifice of two degrees of freedom). It is true that the uniform-change parameter estimate points perhaps to a marginal increase in fluidity over the years: if the parameter for the Oxford survey is set at zero, the estimate is negative for both the later studies, indicating a slight and progressive decrease in the odds ratios (and therefore marginally greater social fluidity) among the more recent samples. But the modest size of this effect, and failure of the uniform difference model to return a significant improvement in fit, suggests that any difference in underlying relative rates is very slight indeed—if in fact it exists at all. Application of this more stringent test does not therefore lead us to qualify the earlier conclusion of trendless fluctuation.

Nor can we find any evidence of a definite change in social fluidity among females over the past decade or so (see Table 4.8).[17] The model that hypothesizes changing class origin and destination distributions

TABLE 4.8. *Social Fluidity among Females in Britain, 1984–1991 (Women's Class Determined by Reference to own Employment)*

Surveys included	Model	G^2	df	p	rG^2	delta
B + C	OD + DT + OT	21.11	16	0.174	82.8	4.96
B + C	UNIDIFF	20.49	15	0.153	83.3	4.90

UNIDIFF parameter estimate (Essex survey set to zero) = − 0.1627 (ns).

Notes
1. B = Essex Class Project, 1984, C = British Social Justice Project, 1991.
2. O = class of origin, D = class destination, T = (time of) survey. O and D have 5 levels: salariat (I, II); routine clerical (IIIa + b); *petite bourgeoisie* (IVa + b + c); skilled manual workers (V, VI); unskilled manual workers (VIIa + b).
3. G^2 = log-likelihood ratio; rG^2 = % reduction in G^2 achieved by each model (treating the main effects as a baseline); delta = proportion of misclassified cases.
4. Main effects = O + D + T.
5. ns = not significant.

over time, but no change in the association between origins and destinations between the surveys (the constant social fluidity model
OT + DT + OD), once more provides an adequate fit to the data. As in
the case of British males, the UNIDIFF test confirms that there is no
significant monotonic move towards greater openness in the British
class structure in so far as female employment is concerned, although
the parameter estimate is again negative (perhaps suggesting a marginal
reduction in female class inequalities considered in this way). Here too,
however, such a reduction—if it exists—will be found to be very slight
indeed.

It would seem that, in the case of Britain at least, the pattern of
relative class mobility chances—or, as some might claim, the degree
of equality of opportunity—has remained basically the same throughout the years covered by the Oxford Mobility Study, Essex Class
Project, and British Social Justice Survey. Is this same constancy to be
found in other societies of the industrialized world?

One way of addressing this question is to compare the results of the
International Social Justice and CASMIN Projects for those countries
which are common to both. Apart from Britain itself, there are five
other nations for which we have comparable surveys from the two
studies, although only for males: West Germany, the United States,
Poland, Czechoslovakia, and Japan. If we revert to the seven-category
Goldthorpe class collapse favoured by the CASMIN researchers, then
the Japanese mobility table from the ISJP suffers from problems of
sparseness, although (fortuitously) the results for the other countries
are not at all problematic in this regard. In most cases the CASMIN
survey and corresponding ISJP survey are separated by some fifteen to
twenty years. Have mobility opportunities in these societies become
more equal during this period?

The findings reported in Table 4.9 suggest that the answer to this
question is in all four cases negative. The CASMIN tables are based on
much larger samples than are those taken from the corresponding ISJP
surveys. The former have therefore been standardized down. The results show that the model proposing constant social fluidity over time
provides a good fit to the data in all instances. There is no significant
interaction effect between class origins, class destinations, and time (as
represented by the interval between each pair of surveys). Nor does the
uniform difference test offer any advance over the fitted model: in no
case does the improvement achieved reach levels approaching statistical
significance. Furthermore, we can also see that each UNIDIFF parameter estimate is in any case positive, again suggesting that there is no
uniform tendency for the odds ratios to move towards unity in the later

TABLE 4.9. *Social Fluidity among Males in the Federal Republic of Germany (1976–1991), Poland (1972–1991), Czechoslovakia (1984–1991), and the United States (1973–1991)*

	Model	G^2	df	p	delta	beta
FRG	Independence	322.24	72	0.000	19.54	
	CnSF	28.05	36	0.826	4.66	
	UNIDIFF	28.05	35	0.792	4.66	0.0035 (ns)
POL	Independence	349.60	72	0.000	23.74	
	CnSF	32.74	36	0.625	5.07	
	UNIDIFF	32.35	35	0.597	5.16	0.0874 (ns)
CZA	Independence	124.94	72	0.000	15.65	
	CnSF	17.30	36	0.996	4.99	
	UNIDIFF	16.96	35	0.996	4.91	0.1224 (ns)
USA	Independence	182.09	72	0.000	15.81	
	CnSF	22.18	36	0.966	4.42	
	UNIDIFF	21.74	35	0.961	4.28	0.1137 (ns)

Notes
1. Class origins (O) and destination class (D) each have 7 levels, as in Table 4.1. Time (T) represents the interval in years between the surveys within countries.
2. Nations are FRG (Federal Republic of Germany), POL (Poland), CZA (Czechoslovakia), and USA (United States).
3. Independence model = OT + DT.
4. Constant social fluidity model = OT + DT + OD.
5. G^2 = log-likelihood ratio; delta = proportion of misclassified cases.
6. beta = UNIDIFF parameter estimate; CASMIN surveys set at zero; ns = not significant.

as compared to the earlier survey for each nation (since the CASMIN surveys are set to zero as reference points).

Of course, these results must be treated with due caution, since we may have lost information by standardizing down to the sizes of the smaller samples. But it is worth noting, in this regard, that our findings are entirely consistent with those obtained by the CASMIN researchers themselves. Erikson and Goldthorpe, for example, examined inter-generational class mobility data for four birth-cohorts within each of nine countries (including Poland and the United Kingdom) but were unable to find any general tendency towards greater social fluidity. Indeed, not only was there considerable stability in relative rates across successive birth-cohorts, but the very slight movement that was some-times detected by more nuanced models was not (as predicted by liberal theory) regularly in the direction of more equal rates.[18]

In short, and when seen against this background of findings all tend-ing to point in the same direction, we are led to conclude that there is no obvious evidence of any generalized loosening in the class structures of industrial societies over time. Certainly, on the basis of our own and earlier results taken together, we can reasonably maintain that the study of trends in social mobility does not provide evidence sufficient to salvage liberal claims. Increased equality of opportunity—as defined in terms of convergence in relative class mobility chances—is not somehow inherent in the process of industrialism.

VI

This is as far as we need—or indeed are able—to pursue our investigation of intergenerational class mobility. As was noted at the outset, this particular topic has already attracted a great deal of specialized sociological attention, and in this context some of our samples may look small and our models simple. Nevertheless, we have no reason to doubt the reliability of these data, and are convinced that our analysis—though uncomplicated—is adequate to the specific focus of this particular volume.

What then do our findings suggest about class mobility in contemporary Britain? Twenty years on we would appear to have arrived at conclusions broadly similar to those reached by the researchers who conducted the Oxford mobility inquiry. Using new data available from the British survey for the International Social Justice Project, we have found that substantial absolute rates of upward and downward mobility coexist alongside relative class mobility chances which have remained largely unchanged throughout the years covered by the two studies—in effect most of this century up to the present day. Class boundaries seem to be neither more nor less permeable now than they have been in preceding decades. Rather, sectoral shifts towards non-manual work have created additional 'room at the top', but this has not been accompanied by greater equality in opportunities to get there from social origins embodying different degrees of class advantage.

Of course we cannot deny that these results paint a fairly crude picture of social mobility in this country. A refined account would require a larger sample and an extended version of the Goldthorpe class scheme. However, it is also worth noting that a more nuanced analysis would provide scope for detailing further inequalities, having possible implications for the issue of social justice. There is little doubt, for example, that our collapsed (class I and II) salariat conceals additional class mobility differentials. The data from the Essex Class Project show that, among males, the skilled working class versus upper salariat odds ratio was substantially higher than that for the transition between the skilled working class and class II (at 7.7 and 5.7 respectively). Were we able to distinguish classes I and II in all our data-sets, we might well find greater rather than smaller inequalities of access across the different classes.[19]

Similarly, it might be argued that, in a book about social justice in modern Britain, there are good grounds for considering the plight of those who are involuntarily excluded from the labour market alto-gether—and thus, in turn, from the class schema and mobility tables (at least as we have construed these).[20] Of course, by restricting our analysis to those actually holding formal employment at the time of the survey (or during the preceding twelve months), we are merely following estab-lished practice in class analysis. But here too this further refinement might well serve to increase the inequalities of opportunity observed above. We know from previous research that unemployment is charac-teristically a working-class experience.[21] Against the background of Britain's declining manufacturing base and the reduced availability of manual employment in recent decades, many working-class individuals who would otherwise be so engaged are in effect forced out of the labour market, and hence the class mobility table. We also know (from studies of class composition) that the great majority of skilled and unskilled manual employees are (at least) second-generation working-class. Were the currently unemployed to be included in our analysis, on the basis of their last recorded employment, most would there-fore appear as intergenerationally stable in classes VI or VII. Their omission probably serves therefore to underestimate working-class intergenerational immobility, and so diminishes (artificially, as it were) the degree of inequality in mobility chances that we have documented for modern Britain.

In sum, our data and analyses are adequate for the purposes of this volume, in that they provide for a reasonably accurate assessment of the overall degree of openness in contemporary British society. They confirm that inequalities of opportunity—at least in so far as these are measured by relative mobility chances—have not diminished to any appreciable extent throughout the largest part of the twentieth century.

Moreover, the substantial measure of temporal and cross-national stability in the association between class origins and destinations that is then demonstrated by our comparative data seems to falsify the claims of liberal theorists, notably the suggestion that relative mobility chances—and therefore equality in opportunities—increase concomi-tantly with economic development. Our analysis suggests clearly that this claim is false, whether one considers it in relation to nations at different levels of industrial development or in terms of social change within particular societies.

What, then, are the implications of these findings for arguments about social justice? The evidence is that mobility chances are unequal, with (for example) children of British service-class parents being five or six times more likely to obtain service-class jobs than are those whose origins lie in working-class homes. Where differences of this magnitude are found, and indeed appear to persist across several decades and many nations, can we reasonably conclude that they testify to inequalities of opportunity between those born into different social classes and thereby to social injustice?

Not yet. It is entirely plausible to argue that different rates of mobility across classes reflect an unequal distribution of justice-relevant talents and abilities among individuals. As Peter Saunders (1990: 82) has suggested, by comparing actual patterns of mobility with a norm of 'openness' according to which social origins have no effect on destinations, mobility research effectively 'assumes that genetic or natural advantages (including factors like differential parental support and encouragement) either do not exist or are randomly distributed between different social strata'.

In other words, and as we noted in Chapter 1, class mobility studies stand accused of ignoring the possibility that talents are unequally distributed, with the most able people tending to rise to the highest social positions, and then passing on some of their advantages to their children. On this account, critics could argue that the mobility patterns we have identified thus far are not in fact evidence of inequalities of opportunity, but rather reflect the differential take-up of equal opportunities. Lack of perfect fluidity does not necessarily testify to lack of openness in anything but a technical sense.[22] Whether grounded in the idea that people deserve to be rewarded for the exercise of those talents and abilities, or via a functional appeal to the social value of having people do what they do best, it could be argued that our data are perfectly consistent with an ideal of justice as meritocracy. In the remainder of this book, therefore, we focus on the claim that differential mobility chances result from the differential distribution of justice-relevant talents and abilities.

NOTES

1. The best introduction to the general field of social mobility studies is still Heath (1981). Note that studies of class mobility rates and mobility chances

are, strictly speaking, as much investigations into class immobility and of the chances of being socially immobile. For example, success for children from privileged social backgrounds consists in staying where they are, or in class continuity rather than change. However, in order to avoid repetition of this clumsy terminology in the text, it should be understood that our use of such terms as class mobility and mobility chances is intended to refer to the likelihood of individuals ending up in one class destination rather than another—and this may or may not involve social *mobility* as such.

2. See e.g. the arguments of Saunders (1989; 1995: 25–6). Note that the point about general betterment is distinct not only from the issue of inequalities of access (with which we are concerned) but also from that of inequalities of outcome (with which we are not). Since there could be general betterment, but without any reduction in the inequalities of positions that were generally getting better, it should be clear that Saunders's insistence on the importance of rising standards implies a relative lack of interest in both these kinds of inequality.

3. Erikson and Goldthorpe (1992a: 3–6). For a more extended commentary, see Goldthorpe (1991). Note that the themes of equal opportunity and meritocracy were also a prominent feature of state socialist ideology during the same period. The Soviet literature on meritocratic socialism therefore has close parallels with that reviewed by Goldthorpe and Erikson (see Appendix F).

4. Some might argue that, in countries where women have had high employment rates for a considerable time (such as the former state socialist societies of Europe), the use of fathers' occupations to indicate origin classes should be seen as problematic. However, since occupational information on mothers is unavailable in these data, it is not possible to pursue alternatives to the strategy here adopted. More broadly, our practice of identifying males and females separately throughout the analysis raises the general issue of how class and gender might in this context interrelate, a question which has been the subject of extensive previous debate. Aspects of the discussion are relevant to the topic of class and justice, and these will be pursued in Chapters 5 and 6 below, but much of the controversy is not really germane to our particular problem. For a summary of the main points of contention, and of our own position in relation to these, see Appendix G. Note also that a response rate of only 52% (yielding but 777 cases) raises obvious questions about the reliability of the ISJP Japanese sample (see Appendix A).

5. For example, Erikson and Goldthorpe (1992a: 399–422) list the principal sources for each of the countries included in the CASMIN Project, in their comprehensive bibliography. (The relevant discussion of absolute mobility rates in Britain, West Germany, Japan, Poland, and the United States occurs in chs. 6, 9, and 10.) For a detailed discussion of the Russian experience, see Marshall, Sydorenko, and Roberts (1995). On Czechoslovakia, see Boguszak (1990). The East German case is discussed in Marshall (1996).

6. On the matter of sample size, it is worth making the point here that we have restricted our analysis to those respondents who are currently in employment, or have been employed within the preceding 12 months. This rather exclusive approach contrasts with some earlier studies, which have allocated class positions to the long-term unemployed and retired, usually on the basis of their last employment. Such a strategy would increase the numbers in our mobility tables by about one-quarter. However, we confine ourselves to those currently (or very recently) in employment in order to maintain broad comparability with the earlier Oxford Mobility and Essex Class Projects, since this allows us (as we shall see shortly) to pursue the issue of trends in class mobility over time. In any case, we have repeated all of the mobility analyses reported in this chapter on a sample which includes the long-term unemployed and retired respondents in our study, and can find no differences of substance to report. This operational issue is discussed more fully, and its implications for wider issues in class analysis examined in detail, in Marshall et al. (1996).

7. The extent to which Goldthorpe class categories can be regarded as ordered hierarchically, and social mobility between classes therefore considered as upward or downward, was explained in the previous chapter. This issue is clearly of some significance as regards questions of social justice.

It will be recalled that an important feature of the Goldthorpe class schema, and one which distinguishes it from (for example) the various scales widely used within the status attainment tradition of mobility studies, is that the former does not embody a central hierarchical principle from which a simple or uniform ordering of the classes can be obtained. Nevertheless, there are hierarchical elements to the scheme, and these reflect broad differences in the relative advantages of the different origin classes and relative accessibility and desirability of classes of destination. The salariat comprises occupations which offer the most advantaged and desirable employment situations in modern societies. They also present the strongest barriers to entry. The working-class locations cover the least desirable occupations, offer fewest advantages as classes of origin, and present the weakest barriers to access. Intermediate classes are indeed intermediate as regards the advantages, accessibility, and desirability of the positions they embody. The tests for criterion validity referred to in Chapter 3 confirm many of these characteristics of the classes.

It is possible, therefore, to specify a hierarchy matrix for the Goldthorpe scheme, and one which distinguishes between upward and downward mobility, taking each movement between levels as a separate shift. Erikson and Goldthorpe (1992a: 124, 195) themselves provide such a matrix. For the sake of convenience this is reproduced here. Base level 1 cells imply no hierarchical mobility, in the sense that the origin and destination to which they refer fall within the same hierarchical division, while level 2 cells do imply mobility. Furthermore, except for those cells on the main diagonal,

Hierarchical Effects Matrix for Goldthorpe Classes

	I + II	III	IVa + b	IVc	V + VI	VIIa	VIIb
I + II	1	2	2	2	2	2	2
III	2	1	1	1	1	2	2
IVa + b	2	1	1	1	1	2	2
IVc	2	2	2	2	2	1	1
V + VI	2	1	1	1	1	2	2
VIIa	2	2	2	2	2	1	1
VIIb	2	2	2	2	2	1	1

level 1 cells imply non-vertical mobility while those on level 2 imply vertical mobility. Among the latter, those on the first row and the last two columns of the matrix imply downward mobility, the remainder upward mobility. Note that farmers and smallholders fall into the lowest division when taken as a class of origin, but the intermediate division when considered as a destination class, on the grounds that the commercialization of family farming over the years has tended to increase the size and value (therefore the desirability and advantages) of this as a class destination. The results shown in Table 4.2 are based on this hierarchical effects matrix, and are therefore comparable with those reported for the countries included in the CASMIN project.

8. The dissimilarity index for any 2 marginal distributions (e.g. the origin and destination distributions for a particular country, or—as here—the origin or destination marginals for pairs of countries) is calculated by summing the differences between the numbers in each pair of class marginals and dividing by 2. The result indicates the proportion of cases that would need to be reallocated in order to make any two sets of marginal distributions the same.

9. Parsons (1940: 78–9). In a later essay, reprinted in the same volume, he reiterates this assessment and makes explicit the connection with the educational system: 'As has several times been noted, we treat American society as having a value-system very close to the universalistic-achievement or performance ideal type . . . The context of application of universalism concerns the allocation of performance-capacities and opportunities for productive achievement. The focus of it is the universalistic definition of "equality of opportunity" as applied both to individuals and to collectivities. The differences of hereditary capacity must of course be accepted as "facts of nature". But within this framework there is a strong predilection to universalize opportunity. This seems to be the source of our high valuation of . . . education. Without . . . as much training as a person has capacity to utilize, he cannot realize his potentialities for productive achievement' (Parsons 1953: 415, 417). See also Blau and Duncan (1967:

435), who conclude: 'The high level of popular education in the United States, perhaps reinforced by the lesser emphasis on formal distinctions of social status, has provided the disadvantaged lower strata with outstanding opportunities for long-distance upward mobility.' The role of education in social mobility is examined in Chs. 5 and 6 below.

10. Note that these results are derived from a collapsed version of our Goldthorpe class mobility tables. Unfortunately, if we attempt to fit the CmSF model to all 11 mobility tables for either sex using the standard 7-category collapsed version of the Goldthorpe scheme that we have tended (following the practice of the CASMIN researchers) thus far to employ, the result is highly unreliable because of the large number of cells with zero or very low counts. It is not so much that the overall array of the data is unduly sparse, more the fact that the distribution is extremely uneven, across both classes and countries. For this particular modelling purpose, too many of the mobility tables for the post-communist states contain too many empty or nearly empty rows and columns, in most cases because particular political regimes have legislated in ways which have effectively abolished particular classes. For example, many of the former state socialist countries simply forbade the sorts of property holding and economic activities that elsewhere support a *petite bourgeoisie*, and many also subjected independent farmers and smallholders to forced collectivization. It is this unevenness, combined with our relatively small (and themselves uneven) sample sizes, that creates the problem.

In order that our models might be robust, we have therefore had to collapse our classes to the familiar salariat, intermediate, and working categories, although (because of the importance of agriculture in so many countries) we have retained agricultural workers (including farmers and smallholders) as a distinct class. Although this means that, in some Western societies, the few landowning farmers in the samples are placed in the same class location as their labouring workforce, the numbers involved here are very small indeed, so that this particular strategy does not in fact threaten the substance of the analysis. Furthermore, the notion of a single agricultural class has a certain logic in many (though not all) state socialist societies, since the distinction between 'agricultural labourer' and 'farmer or smallholder' has historically been something of a moot point under communism. Many individuals have, almost literally overnight, been transferred from one status to the other at the behest of a governing élite in pursuit of agricultural collectivization or privatization.

11. This conclusion also bears upon a quite separate debate about the so-called Featherman–Jones–Hauser (or FJH) hypothesis. These authors proposed that the pattern of relative mobility chances was 'basically the same' in all industrial societies. Throughout the 1980s, cross-national comparative analysis of intergenerational social mobility rates was dominated by discussion of this thesis, although the issues were construed in ways largely tangential to our own interest in social class and social justice. The—rather

limited—implications of our findings for this earlier debate are spelled out in Appendix H below.

12. The uniform difference (UNIDIFF) test is a relatively recent development in contingency table analysis. The idea behind the model is fairly straightforward.

It will be recalled that, in Table 4.4, we showed the results obtained from fitting a model of common social fluidity to 11 mobility tables for each sex. That model suggests that the proportions to be found in the various origin and destination classes will vary across nations, but proposes that once these differences in the marginal distributions have been allowed for, relative mobility chances—as expressed in the pattern of odds ratios calculated for competing pairs of origin and destination classes within each table—will be the same across countries. In fact, as we have seen, the CmSF model does not quite fit our data—although much the largest part of the association between origins and destinations that is reported in the tables is indeed held in common.

However, the common social fluidity model itself offers only a global or generalized test of underlying relative rates, so that small but nevertheless sociologically interesting specific differences in mobility chances can easily be overlooked. The uniform difference model, developed by Erikson and Goldthorpe during the CASMIN study, offers a more powerful means of assessing whether or not the class structure is more open in one society as against others. This has an added advantage over the standard CmSF model in that the UNIDIFF test addresses the further issue of whether or not two sets of odds ratios display a monotonic trend in one particular direction. More specifically, it tests for the possibility that the different sets of odds ratios relating to competing pairs of class origins and destinations move uniformly (though not by a constant amount) either towards or away from unity, in one mobility table as compared to another.

The columns of Table 4.6 show, for each of our 11 nations, the uniform difference (or beta) parameters estimated under the model. The average parameter across all nations has been set at zero. Where nations have positive beta values, this means that the odds ratios defining the origin–destination association tend to be further from independence than under the general pattern of association, whereas in nations with negative beta values these odds ratios tend to be closer to independence.

For a precise specification and more detailed explanation of the model, see Erikson and Goldthorpe (1992a: 90–2). The same test appears also to have been developed independently by Yu Xie (1992), who refers to it as the 'log-multiplicative layer effect model'.

13. Much of the recent specialized literature in the field of cross-national comparative mobility analysis has been concerned precisely with modelling similarities and differences in the *patterns* of intergenerational mobility. For example, Erikson and Goldthorpe (1992a) have proposed that the key features of cross-national common social fluidity patterns can be repre-

sented in a 'core model', which postulates specific hierarchical, inheritance, affinity, and sectoral effects. Richard Breen and Christopher Whelan (1994) have proposed an alternative AHP (Agriculture, Hierarchy, Property) model for the Republic of Ireland—principally by amending the importance of the hierarchy dimension of Erikson and Goldthorpe's core model. Similarly, Raymond Sin-Kwok Wong (1992) has modelled a number of vertical and non-vertical effects on the structure of mobility chances between and within countries, concluding that both are almost equally important to the explanation of cross-national variation in mobility regimes. This (still vigorous) debate about the relative importance of hierarchical, sectoral, and other effects in modelling mobility chances within different nations lies well beyond our own concern with the implications of social class for social justice. That concern focuses attention specifically upon the issue of whether or not industrialism necessarily generates increasing equality of opportunity overall (in the form of diminishing class differentials in relative mobility chances). Cross-national nuances in fluidity patterns are, from this point of view, of lesser significance—although clearly central to the debate about the FJH hypothesis (summarized in Appendix H below).

14. It is worth noting here that our findings in this regard are consistent with those observed from the earlier CASMIN data-sets studied by Erikson and Goldthorpe. With one exception only, the rank ordering of countries in terms of male overall fluidity rates that they report is mirrored exactly in Table 4.6, for those nations which the two analyses have in common (Czechoslovakia, the United States, Poland, Great Britain, West Germany, and Japan). The last of these provides the exception, since Japan appears as one of the most fluid nations in the CASMIN study, and one of the most closed in our own. However, this discrepancy is probably an artefact of the ISJP data-set, specifically its relatively small size and (possibly) unreliable sample.

Note also that, in a rather more controversial extension of their argument, the CASMIN team pursue the analysis of overall fluidity further by considering their ranked nations in relation to four independent indices of industrialism (measuring industrial development, educational inequality, economic inequality, and the political complexion of government respectively within each nation). When these variables are incorporated as factors into the analysis (independently and conjointly), the beta parameter estimates still do not follow the pattern predicted by liberal theorists, in that fluidity does not increase steadily with improvements in industrial development, educational equality, and so forth. These results seem to contradict the original findings reported by Treiman and Yip. However, it is difficult to compare these studies directly, not only because the latter use Treiman's Standard International Occupational Prestige Scale scores (rather than Goldthorpe classes) as the basis for the dependent variable, but also because (and this is probably the most controversial aspect of the debate) each pair of authors constructs the (complex and composite) independent variables in somewhat different ways (cf. Erikson and Goldthorpe 1992a: 379–89, and Treiman and Yip 1989).

15. See Goldthorpe et al. (1980: 77–84). There is some evidence of a trend towards greater social fluidity in Victorian and Edwardian Britain. However, as the author of this claim concedes, the problems of obtaining reliable data for the period are formidable, mainly because of the imprecision with which occupational identities were recorded (see Miles 1993).

16. Note that, in order to maintain comparability between the 3 surveys, it is necessary to standardize on the Oxford study by reallocating sales and service workers (class IIIb) to the routine clerical class.

17. The findings from 2 studies only are included in this table because the Oxford national mobility inquiry was one of the male population (aged 20–64) in England and Wales. Again, the coding of occupations to classes has been standardized across the studies, mainly by combining classes IIIa and IIIb.

18. Erikson and Goldthorpe (1992a: 86–96). See also Goldthorpe (1995b). Cf. Erikson and Jonsson (1996: 3), who note: 'Unlike most other comparable nations, relative social mobility—or "social fluidity"—has increased in Sweden, and the degree of "social inheritance" is relatively low.' Note also, however, that these authors immediately concede: 'In another perspective . . . it is perhaps more striking how *similar* nations are with respect to social fluidity. The *pattern* of inequality is very much the same in Sweden as in other nations, and even if the degree is somewhat lower, the differences are not great. Our impression is that Sweden deviates less from other nations when it comes to inequality of social opportunity than in terms of inequality of living conditions. This suggests that the mechanisms behind inequality of opportunity are highly resistant to change.'

19. See Marshall et al. (1988: table 4.8). Disaggregating classes I and II would also reveal a well-documented sex differential in class destinations. Females who gain employment in the salariat most commonly do so in junior management or administration, teaching, nursing, and other occupations to be found in the lower echelons of this class. The higher-level executive and professional positions of the upper salariat tend to be filled by men. In the Essex Class Project, for example, it was found that only 4% of employed females were successful in securing employment in the upper salariat (class I), as compared to 13% of employed men, whereas females were more commonly employed in the (class II) lower salariat (19% of employed females as against 17% of employed men). Women therefore constituted 18% of class I as against 44% of class II. This pattern is confirmed by the more recent British General Election Study of 1992, which suggests that 21% of males arrive at upper salariat destinations (with a further 16% in class II), whereas the corresponding figures for females are 6% and 22%. The upper salariat is still 80% male, while the lower salariat is 54% female.

20. This would be particularly important for those who consider that social justice has something to say, not only about the distribution of rewards that accrue to those in different jobs, but also (and perhaps especially) about the distribution of the reward of having a job at all. On this second issue, which we do not address, see Elster (1988) and Arneson (1990).

21. See e.g. Goldthorpe and Payne (1986). Again the data from the more recent British General Election Study of 1992 confirm this pattern, and show that 70% of those unemployed at the time of the survey were previously in working-class employment, with 73% of the unemployed having working-class social origins.

22. It should therefore be clear that when referring to 'inequality of opportunity' or 'unequal mobility chances' in this and earlier chapters, we were using these terms in their specifically technical and descriptive sense, without any accompanying claim about the reasons why those born into different classes might have different chances of achieving the various class destinations.

5

Education: Patterns

I

Is it possible, as critics of social mobility research have sometimes claimed, to construct a meritocratic defence of class inequalities in mobility chances by explaining the association between origins and destinations in terms of the unequal distribution of ability?

Proponents of meritocracy have conventionally taken this to be an argument about the role of education in class reproduction. In the previous chapter, for example, we saw that Talcott Parsons placed access to education at the heart of his conception of equality of opportunity. In Parsons's view, educational expansion played a crucial role in effecting the historical shift from ascription to achievement, as the principal determinant of status in advanced societies (see also Parsons 1961).

Other liberal theorists have been similarly forthright, linking education to equality of opportunity in general, and often to the notion of meritocracy in particular. For example, constructing his agenda for the emerging social structures of the twenty-first century, Daniel Bell insists that the coming 'post-industrial society . . . is a meritocracy'—by which he means that 'differential status and differential income are based on technical skills and higher education'. Or again, that 'the post-industrial society, in this dimension of status and power, is the logical extension of the meritocracy; it is the codification of a new social order based . . . on the priority of educated talent'. For this reason, according to Bell, 'the university, which once reflected the status system of society . . . has now become the arbiter of class position. As the gatekeeper, it has gained a quasi-monopoly in determining the future stratification of society.'[1]

Against this background, meritocrats have argued that if people in an advanced society were distributed to occupations strictly according to merit, we might well *expect* a person's class background to influence his or her class destiny—but only in so far as it determined educational accomplishments. For example, if children from privileged class backgrounds are more likely to achieve educational qualifications, then it could (and should) be this properly meritocratic criterion which explains their relative advantage in the labour market. In practice, therefore, empirical testing of the meritocracy thesis has come to be construed as an argument about the relationship between social origins, class destinations, and educational attainment.

II

These arguments about the role of merit in class mobility are perhaps best understood in relation to the diagram shown in Fig. 5.1. The meritocracy thesis—or what has sometimes also been called the hypothesis of increasing merit-selection (IMS)—suggests that, in modern industrial societies, merit becomes the principal determinant both of an individual's access to education beyond the legal minimum requirement, and of his or her subsequent position within the social division of labour. Ascriptive characteristics, such as class background, are increasingly irrelevant to both processes.[2]

More specifically, the argument goes, because of educational change we should expect the association between class origins and educational attainment to decline over the years, as talented children from working-class backgrounds avail themselves of the expanding opportunities to gain credentials. Furthermore, the concomitant replacement of ascription (according to class background) by achievement (indicated by formal qualifications) as the principal criterion of social selection and reward will enhance equality in occupational opportunities, so strengthening the association between educational attainment and eventual

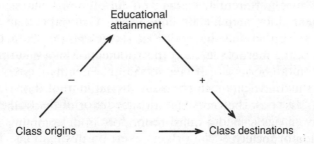

FIGURE 5.1. The Hypothesis of Increasing Merit-Selection. (*Note*: negative sign denotes weakening effect; positive sign denotes strengthening effect.)

class destinations. Inevitably, as a corollary of both processes, the direct transmission of class privileges—that is, the association between origins and destinations, net of educational achievement—will also steadily decline.

Research into these propositions has generated conflicting reports. For example, in their American data for 1962, Peter Blau and Dudley Duncan (1967) found some evidence (although they admitted that it was by no means conclusive) of an increasing effect of education on socioeconomic status among males. They also detected a weakening influence of class origins on occupational destinations—although they were unable to discern whether class origins were of generally decreasing importance for educational achievement. A decade later, David Featherman and Robert Hauser (1978) found the strength of the association between education and destination to be unchanged; reported a diminished relationship between origins and destinations; and detected some (they admit inconclusive) evidence of a weakening influence of social origins on educational attainment.

These are somewhat mixed findings from the point of view of providing support for the hypothesis of increasing merit-selection—especially since the United States might be expected to constitute the most favourable of test cases for the argument. Indeed, the implications for arguments about equality of opportunity and meritocracy of the (largely) American status-attainment literature as a whole are still unclear, and a matter of some controversy. (For a brief overview of this material, see Appendix I.)

Similar research in other countries has proved no less equivocal in its implications. From his analysis of the data gathered for the Oxford Mobility Study of 1972, A. H. Halsey concluded that among men in England and Wales there was a decreasing influence of origins on destinations and a tightening bond between educational attainment and occupational outcomes. However, Halsey also reported that an individual's class origins were increasingly associated with his or her level of educational achievement, a finding which he interprets as being inconsistent with the idea that industrial societies are characterized by a secular trend towards greater meritocracy. Halsey surmised that increasing merit-selection in the labour market had been offset by decreasing merit-selection in the educational market. For this reason, although 'education is increasingly the mediator of the transmission of status between generations', still there has been no reduction in the overall influence which social origins exert on destinations. To use his metaphor, the dice of social opportunity continues to be weighted by class, and ' "the game" is increasingly being played through strategies of child rearing refereed by schools through their certifying arrangements'. In this way, as Halsey puts it, 'ascriptive forces find ways of expressing themselves as "achievement"'.[3]

By contrast, Anthony Heath and his colleagues (Heath et al. 1992) have more recently argued that evidence from the 1973 and 1985 General Household Surveys shows that, among both males and females in England and Wales, educational qualifications (most notably those at middling levels of attainment) are a declining asset in the labour market. These same data point to an unchanging association between class origins and educational attainment, on the one hand, and on the other an uncertain (partial and statistically insignificant) decrease in the relationship between origins and class destinations. Analogous research by Jan Jonsson (1993a; 1993b) focuses on Sweden. He argues that, among both men and women in that particular country, there is evidence of all three associations weakening over time (although this is not compelling in the case of the relationship between credentials and destinations). In the Republic of Ireland, on the other hand, data analysed by Richard Breen and Christopher Whelan (1993) seem to show that, although the average level of educational attainment has increased during successive decades, there has been a simultaneous decline in the returns to higher credentials. The effect has been to leave both the gross and the partial relationships between origins and destinations (i.e. the overall relationship, and the association net of educational attainment) largely unchanged throughout the largest part of this century.

Other relevant evidence bears upon only part of the argument about increasing merit-selection—but it is no less contradictory than these more extensive studies. Alan Kerckhoff and Jerry Trott (1993) re-examined the Oxford Mobility data, specifically to test for the impact of the 1944 Education Act on the link between class origins and educational attainment, and found that, despite the reforms, origins were indeed exerting an increasing influence on educational achievement (as Halsey had earlier suggested). By contrast, Jan Jonsson and Colin Mills (1993) have claimed that the evidence provided by a different data-set shows class-based inequalities in educational outcomes to be declining, in England as well as Sweden. Michael Hout and his colleagues (Hout et al. 1993) have reported the same trend in the United States. Some studies of other industrial societies point, however, to an apparent lack of change. Citing data from the 1974 Israeli Mobility Survey, Yossi Shavit and Vered Kraus (1990) argue that the effect of father's occupation on the various educational transitions remained substantial and constant across cohorts who attended school in the 1940s, 1950s, and 1960s. Similarly, Jaap Dronkers (1993) has examined the evidence on educational attainment among successive cohorts of Dutch male students, and found that the effects of parental occupation have not changed significantly throughout the postwar years.[4]

It is not easy to account for the discrepancies in these findings. The usual suspects should probably be rounded up: unmatched data-sets, of varying quality and representativeness, analysed in terms of different techniques based on contrasting assumptions, and tending therefore to yield disparate results. Social class and educational achievement have also been defined and operationalized in diverse ways. Another obvious possibility is, of course, that there are indeed genuine cross-national differences in some or all of the key associations.

Our own reservations with respect to this literature are, however, more fundamental. If we look again at Fig. 5.1 we see that the thesis of increasing merit-selection involves claims about changes in three distinct associations between the three variables that make up what is sometimes referred to as 'the meritocratic triad'. In our view, it has often not been sufficiently appreciated that the interpretation of these associations—and hence of any changes over time that might be discovered in them—is rather complex, at least in so far as they are regarded as the basis of claims about meritocracy. The same evidence can be interpreted in a variety of different ways—primarily depending upon different understandings of the extent to which it is legitimate to equate education with 'merit'.

To see this, suppose that a society were discovered to have a very tight linkage between education and destination; that is, what people achieved educationally very strongly determined their occupational and (hence) class position. In such a society, one might say, there is a high degree of merit-selection by education, where this is understood to be a claim specifically and solely about the role played by education in selecting people for places in the class structure

Now suppose that we discover also a very strong association between social origins and education—or, in other words, that what people achieve educationally depends to a very great extent upon their class background. It is clear that this could not touch the claim about merit-selection by education, because this is an assertion about the link between education and destination alone; but would it tell against the argument that the society is genuinely meritocratic—where this means that people are selected for destinations in accordance with their merits?

Clearly, one's answer will depend upon whether or not it is accepted that people's merits can satisfactorily be operationalized by measuring their educational achievements. If one does accept this, and holds therefore that the strong association between origin and education simply reflects the fact that merit is differently distributed across those born into different classes, then this will indeed be evidence of a meritocratic society. The fact that class of origin strongly influences class of destination is no evidence of a lack of meritocracy, simply because it exerts that influence in the appropriate way—that is, through processes whereby people's class-related unequal abilities and motivations are reflected in their educational achievements, and in turn convert into unequal outcomes.

Most sociologists who have examined the issue of meritocracy or equality of opportunity have not, however, accepted this equation of merit with educational attainment. Rather, they have assumed that the distribution of real merits between classes is less unequal than the distribution of actual educational qualifications, with class differences in the achievement of those qualifications being better understood as the result of various class-related distortions in the educational process than as evidence of class differences in ability or motivation. One way to see this is to notice that the thesis of increasing merit-selection, as presented in Fig. 5.1, posits a decreasing association between origins and education. It takes any loosening of this association as evidence of an increase in genuinely meritocratic selection processes.

It is clear that data on origins and education alone cannot decide what is actually the question of whether, and to what extent, it is appropriate to equate merit with educational qualifications. If one takes seriously the possibilities that ability and motivation may differ across classes, then it becomes in principle possible to reconcile *any* association between origins and education with the claim that a society is meritocratic, and any change in that association over time with the claim it is becoming more so. By the same reasoning, of course, it is possible to argue that any such associations do *not* necessarily indicate meritocratic processes, nor any tendency in their direction. In order fully to decide such questions, one needs to unpack the mechanisms that link people's class origins and their educational attainments.

So much for the issues relating to the links between education and the other two components of the meritocratic triad. How are we to interpret the direct association between origin and destination—the relationship that is not mediated by education? This is to consider the bottom arrow in Fig. 5.1, which has a minus sign attached to it, indicating that increased merit-selection is usually taken to involve a reduction in this direct effect. Now, if we assume that education is an exhaustive indicator of merit then this makes good sense: any intergenerational transmission of advantage that does not go via educational qualifications would have to be regarded as indicative of a lack of meritocracy, for advantaged parents would be handing down that advantage to their children in ways that did not involve the passing on of meritorious attributes. But if we reject the equation of merit with education, then the interpretation becomes rather more difficult. One might argue, for example, that class differentials in occupational outcomes net of education indicate, not an absence of meritocracy, but rather the allocation of individuals to destinations in accordance with aspects of merit that are distributed unequally across classes of origin but that are not captured by a model which looks at education alone. Perhaps middle-class parents pass on to their children, whether genetically or through socialization, not only abilities relevant to educational attainment (such as intelligence or the motivation to achieve in school) but also abilities directly relevant to occupational success (such as willingness to take risks or to be innovative at work). In that case, a person of middle-class origins who failed in educational terms might still be more likely to merit an advantaged destination than someone of working-class origins, and any unexplained class effects need not tell against meritocratic claims broadly understood. Again, then, one needs further research, and of a different kind, to draw any firm conclusions about such matters.

Given complexities such as these, and the many more that we do not mention here, it is important that we should make clear our strategy in the remainder of this book. In this and the next chapter, we look at the evidence on the role played by education in mediating the association between origins and destinations, and we assess the extent of, and changes over time in, merit-selection by education. For those who are happy to equate education with merit—or whose definition of the term 'meritocracy' simply identifies it with a society in which people find occupational roles on the basis of educational attainments—this analysis may be thought of as assessing the extent to which Britain is, or is becoming, a meritocratic society. Since in our view, however, such an equation is fraught with difficulties, we ourselves would rather regard these chapters as addressing the more limited and empirical issue of the role played by education in the intergenerational transmission of class advantage and disadvantage. We make no attempt, at this stage, to consider what conclusions about *meritocracy* might be inferred from our evidence about either the association between origins and educational achievements or the unmediated association between origins and destinations. What might or might not be suggested by that evidence is discussed at some length in Chapter 7.

Then, in Chapter 8, we will return to the normative issue, touched on in Chapter 2, of whether it can be just that people should enjoy unequal rewards for possessing attributes the distribution of which is a matter of chance. Even if one accepted that people's educational achievements are a good indicator of their actual abilities and motivations—and hence reflect their 'merits' in the commonsensical understanding of that term—one might still doubt that it is just or fair that these should be rewarded with relatively advantaged places in the class structure, on the straightforward grounds that it is implausible to regard people as responsible for the fact that they happen to have more of them than others. This view might challenge any identification of merit with 'natural ability and effort' because it took the idea of merit to have something to do with desert, and held that people's abilities, including perhaps their ability to make an effort, are beyond their control in such a way as to make them unable to support claims to relatively advantaged social positions.

As these hints of what is to come may suggest, Chapters 7 and 8 will cover a great deal of ground, both sociological and political-theoretical. The point of mentioning them now is to justify our strategy in the next two chapters of inspecting the evidence about class mobility and educational achievement on the basis of our own data. We do so, not because we are unaware that it is problematic to equate education with merit, but simply because we can only do one thing at a time. With this extended caveat in mind, therefore, let us consider whether the different rates of intergenerational mobility across classes that we have identified in the previous chapter do indeed reflect the unequal distribution of educational attainment. We begin by looking at the current situation, and move on, in the next chapter, to review the picture over time.

III

Consider, first of all, the case of Britain. In order to allow for reasonably detailed examination of the relationships in question, we have pooled the relevant data from three large-scale social surveys: the 1991 British Social Justice Project and British General Election Surveys of 1987 and 1992. This generates a sample of more than 4,000 individuals for whom reliable and comparable information about social mobility and educational attainment is readily available.[5]

The key variables in these data-sets have been defined and operationalized in (already familiar) ways that have been validated by earlier research. We have standardized the coding of the education variables on a fourfold classification which distinguishes between low, ordinary, advanced, and degree-level qualifications. These categories are explained and defined precisely in Appendix D.

Two refinements were also made to the Goldthorpe class categories themselves. As in previous chapters, we have retained as far as possible the sevenfold classification used by the CASMIN researchers, in order to maintain comparability between the two sets of findings. However, in an investigation of the relationship between social mobility and educational attainment, it may be particularly useful to distinguish the higher-grade professionals and managers of the upper salariat (Goldthorpe class I) from their lower-grade counterparts in Goldthorpe class II, since the argument is sometimes made (in relation to both class background and sex) that while credentials facilitate access to salariat-type jobs, class origins (and being male) are especially important for entry to the most senior positions within many service-class occupations. This distinction cannot reliably be made across the various national surveys included in the ISJP, but it is possible to sustain for class destinations (though not class origins) in the British study alone, because (for reasons explained in Appendix C) this particular occupational point was in fact coded twice—and one such coding was to the full eleven-category version of the class schema. The information contained in the British General Election Studies also allows researchers to make this distinction.

Our second modification is to exclude almost entirely from the analysis those individuals who currently occupy the various *petit bourgeois* positions that comprise Goldthorpe class IV. For the sake of conveying complete information to readers, this category is included in the first of the cross-tabulations that follows, but is then excluded from the subsequent models. It can reasonably be argued that these particular class destinations are arrived at principally on the basis of access to (and sometimes inheritance of) capital or property. For the most part they are not dependent primarily upon the attainment of appropriate educational qualifications.[6] The inclusion of self-employed farmers and small-business owners in a study of meritocratic class processes *might* therefore distort the findings—although, of course, one could argue not only that those who successfully create small businesses are entitled to their wealth but also that this is no less than they deserve as a reward for hard work and initiative. Nevertheless, since educational credentials are at the nub of most contemporary arguments about merit, it is probably wise at this juncture to omit the *petite bourgeoisie* and to concentrate instead upon employees.

Having made these preliminary clarifications, we may now turn to the analysis of our pooled data-set. Table 5.1 shows the outflow percentages

TABLE 5.1. *Class Distribution in Britain, by Class of Origin and Educational Attainment (Percentage by Row)*

Class origins	Class destination						N
	I	II	III	IV	V/VI	VII	
Education level 1							
I, II	8	11	14	14	13	39	105
III	7	17	12	10	14	38	42
IV	7	6	8	28	15	36	177
V, VI	2	7	10	8	23	50	517
VII	2	8	9	8	16	57	507
Education level 2							
I, II	12	19	27	10	11	19	315
III	15	14	29	16	10	17	93
IV	9	13	28	17	12	19	190
V, VI	6	13	25	9	25	21	564
VII	8	13	20	9	26	25	396
Education level 3							
I, II	29	33	22	4	7	5	256
III	29	38	23	0	8	2	52
IV	28	32	11	15	8	7	117
V, VI	21	35	14	4	13	13	224
VII	18	29	21	3	14	16	117
Education level 4							
I, II	48	41	5	4	2	0	227
III	52	40	10	0	0	0	42
IV	42	37	4	12	0	7	57
V, VI	38	43	12	3	0	5	112
VII	37	50	6	2	4	4	52

N = 4,162.

Note: Classes are I: higher salariat; II: lower salariat; III: routine non-manual; IV: *petite bourgeoisie* (including farmers and smallholders); V: lower-grade technicians and supervisors of manual workers; VI: skilled manual employees; VII: unskilled manual employees (including agricultural labourers and rank-and-file service workers).

from class origins to class destinations for each of the four levels of educational attainment. Clearly, and not surprisingly, an individual's educational credentials have substantial implications for his or her employment. Those least qualified (educational level 1) are rarely found in the salariat and usually gain manual employment: only 11 per cent obtain service-class occupations (at higher or lower grades), while half take on unskilled manual labour. Greater educational attainment increases the chances of gaining employment in the salariat. However, at each level of education there is differentiation in the destinations reached by individuals, according to the social backgrounds from which they originate. Persons having service-class (or even routine non-manual) origins are more likely to arrive at relatively privileged positions within the class structure.

This form of differentiation by class is most prominent among those with low and, in particular, ordinary and advanced qualifications (levels 1–3). For example, among individuals at the lowest level of educational attainment, those having service-class origins are four times more likely to achieve service-class employment than are their working-class peers. In other words, an advantaged class background would seem to offer some protection against the labour-market consequences of educational failure, whilst enhancing the prospects of those who obtain modest (or even advanced) credentials. Class of origin appears to be of less consequence for class destination among people holding the highest (level 4) qualifications. Over 80 per cent of individuals from each class of origin, and who also possess a university degree or equivalent, gain salariat employment. Even here, however, there is differentiation, according to class origins, within the salariat itself. Individuals having white-collar social backgrounds are more likely to secure the more desirable higher-salariat positions. Forty-eight per cent and 52 per cent respectively of those from service-class and routine non-manual backgrounds gain employment in class I. This compares with only 37 per cent and 38 per cent of those from unskilled and skilled working-class origins.

It is possible to test the thesis of merit-selection through education formally by applying log-linear techniques to the analysis of these data. The educational merit-selection (or conditional independence) model in Table 5.2 proposes that an individual's mobility chances are mediated entirely through education; that is, that there are associations between class origins and educational attainment, educational attainment and class destinations, but that there is no direct influence of class background on class destination. This model is clearly inadequate. It fails to capture significant associations in the data and misclassifies almost 8 per cent of all cases. The parameter estimates obtained when Erikson and Goldthorpe's UNIDIFF model is then fitted confirm that there is no significant tendency for the association between class origins and class destinations to become progressively weaker with greater educational attainment.

Examination of the residuals under the meritocracy model reveals that the misclassified cases deviate systematically in a way which tends

TABLE 5.2. *Results of Testing the Educational Merit-Selection Model for Britain*

Model	G^2	df	p	rG^2	delta
Merit-selection	184.0	64	0.000	—	7.8
OE + ED + OD	60.6	48	0.104	67.1	4.1
UNIDIFF	59.9	45	0.068	67.4	4.1

UNIDIFF parameter estimates (low educational attainment set to zero) = -0.1247 (ns); -0.2375 (ns); and -0.1687 (ns).

N = 3,787.

Notes
1. Class origin (O) has 5 levels: salariat (I, II); routine non-manual (IIIa); *petite bourgeoisie* and farmers (IVa + b + c); skilled manual (V, VI); and unskilled manual (VIIa + b, IIIb).
2. Class destination (D) has 5 levels: higher salariat (I); lower salariat (II); routine non-manual (IIIa); skilled manual (V, VI); and unskilled manual (VIIa + b, IIIb).
3. Educational attainment (E) has 4 levels, as in Table D.1.
4. Merit-selection model = OE + ED.
5. G^2 = log-likelihood ratio; rG^2 = % reduction in G^2 (treating the merit-selection model as baseline); delta = proportion of misclassified cases.

to suggest that class inequalities in modern Britain cannot easily be justified as a consequence of merit-selection by education. Thus, most notably amongst those with middling levels of educational attainment, there is an over-representation in the salariat of individuals from the more privileged backgrounds. For example, among those with what we have termed ordinary (or level 2) qualifications, 39 individuals from salariat origins gain higher-salariat employment. The merit-selection model suggests this figure should be only 26. Conversely, those from manual backgrounds are under-represented in the salariat: according to the merit-selection model 84 such individuals should be in higher-salariat employment, when only 63 are in fact to be found in these positions. The picture is similar among persons holding advanced (level 3) qualifications. Here, among those to be found in higher-salariat jobs, there is a 14 per cent over-representation and a 20 per cent under-representation of individuals from salariat and manual backgrounds respectively.

These direct class effects are also evident, although to a lesser extent, among people with both the lowest and highest qualifications (levels 1 and 4). This suggests that it may be harder to circumvent meritocratic principles, at least in so far as these are represented by occupational rewards for educational attainment, where educational credentials are either negligible or (at the other extreme) very good. The greatest scope for deviating from meritocratic principles, thus interpreted, would seem to be where there is evidence of some educational attainment—

evidence which is, presumably, open to varying interpretations, and seems to be of differing worth to different individuals according to their class background.

This association between class origins and class destinations must be taken into account in order to provide a model that fits our data satisfactorily. When the OD term is included, a reduction of more than two-thirds in the G^2 for the baseline independence model is achieved, and the proportion of misclassified cases is almost halved. This confirms our earlier observation that social origin, further to an individual's educational achievements, determines his or her class destination. In other words, the existence of a significant and substantial association between class origins and destinations (the OD term in the model) tells against the thesis of educational merit-selection, in so far as the latter assumes perfect mobility conditional upon education (and therefore no such association between class background and current employment).[7]

IV

The meritocracy thesis, as conventionally formulated, addresses the specific issue of social class. There is nothing in the relevant literature that refers to other ascriptive characteristics such as gender and ethnicity. However, it is an interesting issue as to whether the association between class mobility and educational attainment differs among men and women, or varies across ethnic groups. Unfortunately, this additional question can be pursued only so far by means of our pooled data-set, which does indeed contain both males and females—although the preponderance of white respondents means that the ethnic dimension cannot seriously be explored. To consider ethnicity properly would require a quite different sort of (targeted) sample.[8]

How are the sexes distributed in the labour market? Table 5.3 shows the allocation of males and females to the various class destinations at each level of educational attainment. (For the purposes of this particular argument, and as in earlier chapters, every respondent's class is here determined by reference to his or her own employment.) This table tells the now familiar story (compare, for example, Table 4.1 and the discussion in Appendix G below) of a pronounced sex-segregation of the class structure in modern Britain. Irrespective of credentials, females are more often found in routine clerical and unskilled manual employment, while males more frequently arrive at skilled manual and salariat destinations. It is also true that, for males and females alike, educational attainment greatly improves the chances of gaining salariat and avoiding manual employment. However, within the salariat and regardless of the level of qualification obtained, it is always males who are the more likely to be found in the most privileged positions. Females tend to occupy lower-grade, rather than higher-grade, service-class occupations. This is true among both those with few if any qualifications (educational levels 1 and 2) and those holding advanced and degree-level certificates (educational levels 3 and 4).

Log-linear analysis of these data (see Table 5.4) reveals that, after allowing for the associations between educational attainment and class destinations, and between educational attainment and sex, sex-segregation in the class structure is still very important (compare models 3 and 4). Furthermore, the three-way association between education, sex, and class destination is also significant, and must be included to achieve a model having a satisfactory fit to the data. In other words, sex affects the likelihood of arriving at particular class destinations, but differently across the various levels of educational attainment. For example, unqualified or poorly qualified women are less likely than are their male peers to arrive at lower-salariat positions, but more likely to do so when they have obtained advanced or degree-level qualifications. Similarly, women are more likely than men to be found in working-class destinations, except when they hold the highest-level qualifications—in

TABLE 5.3. *Class Distribution in Britain, by Educational Attainment and Sex (Respondent's Class Determined by Reference to Own Employment): Percentage by Row*

Educational level	Sex	Class destination					N
		I	II	III	VI/VI	VII	
1	Male	6	10	4	28	52	664
	Female	2	6	18	11	63	687
2	Male	14	19	9	39	19	788
	Female	5	12	48	5	30	738
3	Male	35	26	11	18	9	427
	Female	13	45	30	3	10	357
4	Male	57	36	3	1	2	319
	Female	24	57	14	1	3	184

N = 4,164.

Notes
1. Class destination has 5 levels, as in Table 5.2.
2. Education has 4 levels, as in Table D.1.

TABLE 5.4. *Class Distribution in Britain, by Educational Attainment and Sex (Respondent's Class Determined by Reference to Own Employment): Models*

Model	G^2	df	p	rG^2	delta
1. E + D + S	2,613.3	31	0.000	—	35.3
2. ED + S	941.6	19	0.000	64.0	19.5
3. ED + ES	864.4	16	0.000	66.9	18.4
4. ED + ES + SD	211.6	12	0.000	91.9	7.8

N = 4,164.

Notes
1. Class destinations (D) has 5 levels, as in Table 5.2.
2. Education (E) has 4 levels, as in Table D.1.
3. S = sex.
4. G^2 = log-likelihood ratio; rG^2 = % reduction in G^2 (treating the main effects model as baseline); delta = proportion of misclassified cases.

which case the differences between the sexes largely disappear. In short, and glossing over much of the detail which could be extracted from the tables, we can conclude that the educational attainment to class-destination profiles of males and females are markedly distinct, and with considerable advantage to the former, especially where the chances of obtaining a higher-grade (rather than lower-grade) salariat position, and skilled rather than unskilled manual employment, are concerned.

How, if at all, does this additional finding bear upon the argument about meritocracy? It might reasonably be argued (indeed, it often has been) that the persistence of ascriptive processes associated with gender is in itself sufficient to undermine explanations of labour-market outcomes which are couched in terms of merit-selection via education.[9] However, using our pooled data for Britain, we can also test explicitly whether or not the inclusion of sex as a variable would lead us to modify our conclusions about the *class* processes relating origins to destinations. The results shown in Table 5.5 indicate that disaggregating the data in this way does nothing to salvage the meritocratic case. As can be seen from the table, the best-fitting model (model 2) fits the associations SED plus SOE plus OD, showing that it is still not possible to achieve a satisfactory explanation of our data without including an association between class origins and destinations (compare models 1 and 2). The three-way interaction terms in this model confirm what we know from previous research: compared to men, women historically have tended to attain lower credentials across all classes of origin (SOE). They also arrive at different occupational destinations, even where educational

TABLE 5.5. *Results of Testing the Educational Merit-Selection Model for the Sexes in Britain*

Model	G^2	df	p	rG^2	delta
1. SED + SOE	254.4	128	0.000	—	8.7
2. SED + SOE + OD	131.4	112	0.102	48.3	5.6
3. SED + OE + ODS	136.2	108	0.035	46.4	6.1
4. ED + SOE + ODS	190.3	108	0.000	25.2	7.0
5. SED + SOE + ODS	118.7	96	0.058	53.3	5.1

N = 3,787.

Notes
1. Class origins (O) and Destination (D) each have 5 levels, as in Table 5.2.
2. Education (E) has 4 levels, as in Table D.1.
3. S = sex.
4. G^2 = log-likelihood ratio; rG^2 = % reduction in G^2 (treating model 1 as baseline); delta = proportion of misclassified cases.

attainment is held constant, because of sex segregation and discrimination in the labour market (SED). Net of both of these effects, however, there is still an unmediated association between origins and destinations—which (as a comparison of models 2 and 5 shows) does not itself vary significantly by sex. (Inclusion of the three-way ODS interaction term reduces the G^2 by only 12.7 for the loss of 16 degrees of freedom.) In short, it is simply not possible to fit satisfactorily the model of merit-selection through education to these data, whether or not the sexes are considered separately.[10]

V

We have argued that the conventional defence of class inequalities as meritocratic posits an association between class origins and destinations that is mediated by educational attainment; that the reality of modern Britain is that people from different class origins have unequal chances, not only of educational but also of occupational success, despite taking actual credentials into consideration; and that these class processes are evident among men and women alike.

By way of conclusion, we will briefly pursue two additional issues that follow from this analysis. Each has been the subject of some speculation. The first raises the question of whether or not merit-selection by education is a feature particularly of specific sectors within modern economies. The second places Britain in cross-national comparative perspective in order to determine whether or not this country looks less meritocratic than do its near industrial neighbours. In the remainder of this chapter we consider these problems in turn.

The sectoral issue is relatively straightforward. Some analysts have argued that recruitment practices are oriented more towards credentials (and likely therefore to be more educationally meritocratic) in public enterprises than in those located in the private sector. In Britain, for example, the National Health Service, schools and colleges, local government, and so on might be expected to rely more on formal qualifications for recruitment and promotions than do private businesses. Indeed, the argument that advanced societies generally progress towards merit-selection by education (a thesis that is tested formally in the following section) is sometimes based explicitly on the assumption of an expanding public sector, which cannot afford to utilize its human capital otherwise. For example, Donald Treiman (1970) has suggested that there is evidence of increased merit-selection in the United States, and has attributed this mainly to the growth of public bureaucracies within which education constitutes the most widely recognized criterion for recruitment. By way of contrast, Jan Jonsson (1991) has more recently argued that it is at least as plausible to assume that increasingly competitive markets will encourage those involved in the private sector to place greater emphasis on skills reflected in educational qualifications, where questions of recruitment and promotion arise.[11] Against this background, it is interesting to pose the question of whether or not our own findings for Britain might be attributable mainly to allocation practices in the private rather than the public sector.

To test this proposition, we fit further log-linear models to our data on social mobility and educational attainment, but distinguishing between respondents employed in the public and private sectors, as shown in Table 5.6. Only the models of interest are reproduced here. Our baseline model of merit-selection by education (model 1) now hypothesizes that the association between educational qualifications and class destinations will also vary across the different sectors of the economy. (We would not expect the association between class origins and credentials to vary by sector—and the comparison with model 2 confirms this to be case.) Of course, since this model does not allow for the direct influence of class background on class destinations that we know to be present in our data, it fits rather poorly (misclassifying more than 9 per cent of cases in the table). When the further association between origins and destinations is then added (model 3), a satisfactory fit to the data is achieved, and the deviance in the baseline model is reduced substantially.

TABLE 5.6. *Results of Testing the Educational Merit-Selection Model for the Public and Private Sectors in Britain*

Model	G^2	df	p	rG^2	delta
1. SED + OE	260.3	144	0.000	—	9.1
2. SED + SOE	243.8	128	0.000	6.3	8.4
3. SED + OE + OD	142.2	128	0.184	45.4	6.3
4. SED + OE + ODS	127.6	108	0.095	51.0	5.9

N = 3,764.

Notes
1. Class origins (O) and Destination (D) each have 5 levels, as in Table 5.2.
2. Education (E) has 4 levels as in Table D.1; S = Sector (public, private).
3. G^2 = log-likelihood ratio; rG^2 = % reduction in G^2 (treating model 1 as baseline); delta = proportion of misclassified cases.
4. The private sector includes some self-employed professionals and proprietors in salariat destinations (see n. 12 to this chapter).

Note, however, that the association between origins and destinations does not itself vary significantly across different sectors of the economy (compare models 3 and 4). In other words, although the pattern of recruitment by educational attainment is somewhat different in the public and private sectors, the former is no more (in this sense) meritocratic overall than is the latter. For example, it is clear that people employed in the public sector tend to have higher educational qualifications than do those involved in private enterprises, at least according to our data. Thus, 24 per cent of those employed in the public sector have no formal qualifications, as compared with 35 per cent of those privately employed. Similarly, among those presently to be found in higher-salariat (Goldthorpe class I) positions in the public sector, 44 per cent hold degree-level (or equivalent) educational certificates. The corresponding figure for private-sector employees is only 35 per cent. Four per cent of higher-salariat employees in the public sector have no formal qualifications. In the private sector this figure is 10 per cent. Nevertheless, and taking these sorts of difference into account, the evidence suggests that the thesis of merit-selection by education cannot be salvaged by focusing attention upon public-sector employees alone. Indeed, if the model of merit-selection (OE + ED) is fitted separately to our data for public-sector and private-sector employees, 8.7 per cent and 8.2 per cent of cases respectively are misclassified, these proportions being reduced to 6.3 per cent and 5.2 per cent when the further association between origins and destinations is then added (in both cases providing a model that fits satisfactorily). In sum, the two sectors do not differ greatly, at least in the degree to which they seem educationally unmeritocratic.

Examination of the residuals under the baseline model reveals patterns that are at odds with the principle of educational merit-selection in the public as well as the private sector. Individuals from less privileged social origins—particularly those with middling levels of educational attainment—are under-represented in the salariat. In private enterprises, for example, among those with ordinary (level 2) and advanced (level 3) qualifications, 258 individuals from working-class backgrounds should be in salariat positions under the conditions of merit-selection. In reality this figure is only 218—a shortfall of some 16 per cent. This coincides with an 18 per cent over-representation of those from salariat backgrounds in these same service-class positions. Correspondingly, in the public sector, under conditions of merit-selection 162 individuals from manual backgrounds should be in salariat employment. In fact only 145 are so located—an under-representation of some 10 per cent. At the same time there is an 11 per cent over-representation of people from salariat backgrounds in these positions. It would appear that, in the case of these particular mobility channels, class background exerts a similar influence in the private and public sectors alike.

Recruitment practices are somewhat more sector-specific for those with low (level 1) qualifications. Relatively few such people gain salariat employment in the public sector—only three from a total of 277 (1 per cent) in our sample. With one or two exceptions, such as an over-representation of individuals from unskilled manual backgrounds in unskilled manual jobs, differentiation according to class of origin is not marked among the least educated in the public sector. However, as we have already noted, proportionately more individuals with limited education do gain salariat employment in the private sector— where, in addition, such employment forms a greater proportion of the total positions available. Furthermore, in the private sector, people from relatively privileged salariat backgrounds are more likely than are those from the working class to overcome educational limitations, and to arrive at salariat destinations: they are in fact over-represented by no less than 89 per cent. Conversely, and by comparison, those from working-class backgrounds are under-represented in these class positions by more than 20 per cent. In other words, a privileged class background is more likely to enhance employment prospects among low educational achievers in the private than in the public sector. In this respect, at least, recruitment and promotion practices within specifically private enterprises are clearly less rooted in educational merit-selection.

Finally, amongst those with degree-level qualifications, most individuals in both sectors gain service-class employment. Although this level of education almost guarantees access to the salariat, those from relatively privileged backgrounds are slightly more successful in obtaining salariat positions, across both the public and private sectors alike. For example, in the private sector, highly qualified people from service-class backgrounds are over-represented in the salariat (under the conditions of merit-selection) by 14 per cent. In the public sector the corresponding figure is 8 per cent.

In summary, the direct effects of class—rather than those mediated by education—appear to be somewhat more prominent in the private sector, particularly among those with limited education. However, on the above evidence, claims that the public sector is characterized by far-reaching educational merit-selection in recruitment and promotion would appear to be greatly exaggerated. An individual's class origins do have a stronger impact on employment prospects in the private sector, net of the qualifications gained, but the evidence for the public sector does not justify optimistic assumptions about the inherently meritocratic nature of public bureaucracies.[12]

VI

How then does the situation in Britain compare with that to be found in other advanced industrial societies? This question is surprisingly difficult to answer by reference to earlier studies of the role of educational attainment in class reproduction. Relatively few systematically comparative cross-national analyses have in fact been conducted. Only a handful of these have addressed explicitly the issues raised by the theory of meritocracy.

For example, although the CASMIN researchers considered in some detail the issue of cross-national variation in the relationship between educational and mobility regimes, this was done mainly in relation to class differentials in educational outcomes, on the one hand, and educational differentials in class outcomes on the other. In other words, attention was focused on the ways in which access to education is dependent upon family background, and on the importance of educational credentials as assets in the labour market. The role of education as a mediator of the association between class origins and destinations, at least in relation to the effects of direct class inheritance, was therefore imparted only by implication (see e.g. Müller and Karle 1993).

One such study, by Walter Müller and three of his colleagues (Müller et al. 1990), suggests that, in every nation examined as part of the CASMIN project, the link between class of origin and educational qualifications is weaker than that between educational qualifications and class destination. Furthermore, there is a large degree of cross-national commonality with respect to both relationships, nations differing more in terms of each of the constituent elements than they differ in terms of the end result. In other words, although the relative strength of the associations between class origins and educational attainment (on the one hand) and educational attainment and class destination (on the other) might differ from country to country, their conjoint effect was such that the overall pattern of association between class of origin and class destination is similar across nations. Finally, and somewhat contrary to the expectations of the researchers themselves, the variation in the relative importance of the two associations involving educational credentials did not correspond to any simple distinction between East European (or communist) and West European (or capitalist) regimes. For example, the differences between Hungary and Poland were at least as large as those observed between West Germany and Sweden, while Poland was similar to the countries constituting the United Kingdom (which tended to have lower than the cross-national average degree of association between both class origins and qualifications and qualifications and class destinations).[13]

Our own data are taken from the more recent International Social Justice Project. These studies have relatively modest sample sizes, so we are constrained to the limitations of a summary measure (as shown in Table 5.7), which does not distinguish between the different social processes affecting each separate class mobility trajectory. As in our earlier discussion of the British case, we are here testing the general thesis of educational merit-selection, which proposes that—across the class structure considered as a whole within each of the eight nations for which data are available—differential intergenerational class mobility chances are mediated entirely through education. Nevertheless, despite the relative crudeness of this analysis in comparison to some earlier studies of educational merit-selection, our results do shed additional light upon Britain's relative standing in relation to other advanced societies.[14]

Perhaps the first thing to note about the upper panel of Table 5.7 is that it reveals a reassuring convergence between our basic findings and those reported from the much larger samples utilized by the CASMIN Project.[15]

TABLE 5.7. *Results of Testing the Educational Merit-Selection Model in Eight Countries*

Model		G^2	df	p	rG^2	delta
(a) Country by country						
USA	Main effects	532.9	54	0.000	–	25.2
	OE + D	438.8	45	0.000	17.7	23.8
	Merit-selection	69.0	36	0.001	87.1	7.3
	OE + ED + OD	34.0	27	0.165	93.6	4.0
FRG	Main effects	1,089.3	54	0.000	–	34.1
	OE + D	792.0	45	0.000	27.3	30.1
	Merit-selection	150.6	36	0.000	86.2	7.6
	OE + ED + OD	24.2	27	0.617	97.8	3.3
GDR	Main effects	399.9	54	0.000	–	23.9
	OE + D	342.7	45	0.000	14.2	22.4
	Merit-selection	73.1	36	0.001	81.7	9.6
	OE + ED + OD	30.3	27	0.299	92.4	5.4
BUL	Main effects	1,113.7	54	0.000	–	32.9
	OE + D	817.8	45	0.000	26.6	28.7
	Merit-selection	65.9	36	0.002	94.1	6.9
	OE + ED + OD	24.3	27	0.617	97.8	3.2
CZA	Main effects	701.2	54	0.000	–	34.0
	OE + D	591.1	45	0.000	15.7	33.0
	Merit-selection	95.1	36	0.000	86.4	9.5
	OE + ED + OD	45.2	27	0.015	93.6	5.5
POL	Main effects	1,122.5	54	0.000	–	36.3
	OE + D	926.6	45	0.000	17.5	33.5
	Merit-selection	167.1	36	0.000	85.1	12.8
	OE + ED + OD	33.7	27	0.174	97.0	3.8
RUS	Main effects	717.8	54	0.000	–	28.4
	OE + D	546.2	45	0.000	23.9	25.8
	Merit-selection	59.0	36	0.009	91.8	7.0
	OE + ED + OD	26.8	27	0.477	96.3	3.2
SLO	Main effects	805.5	54	0.000	–	36.7
	OE + D	635.4	45	0.000	21.1	34.7
	Merit-selection	86.6	36	0.000	89.3	9.5
	OE + ED + OD	27.4	27	0.443	96.7	3.5
(b) Across all countries						
1. NED + NOE		766.4	288	0.000	–	8.7
2. NED + NOE + OD		351.9	279	0.002	54.1	5.1
3. NED + OE + ODN		380.8	279	0.000	50.3	6.0

TABLE 5.7. Continued

Model	G^2	df	p	rG^2	delta
4. ED + NOE + ODN	703.7	279	0.000	8.2	8.3
5. NED + NOE + ODN	245.9	216	0.079	67.9	3.9

N = 8,821.

Notes
1. Class origin (O) has 4 levels: salariat (I, II); intermediate (IIIa, IVa + b, V); working (VI, VIIa, IIIb); and agricultural (IVc VIIb).
2. Class destination (D) has 4 levels: salariat (I, II); intermediate (IIIa, V); working (VI, VIIa, IIIb); and agricultural (IVc VIIb).
3. Educational attainment (E) has 4 levels, as in Table D.1.
4. Nations (N) are as in Table 4.1, n. 2.
5. Main effects model (upper panel) = O + E + D.
6. Merit-selection model = OE + ED.
7. G^2 = log-likelihood ratio; rG^2 = % reduction in G^2 (treating the main effects model as baseline in upper panel and model 1 as baseline in lower panel); delta = proportion of misclassified cases.

One such similarity involves the relative importance of the two associations involving educational attainment. As will be evident from the table, the relationship between class origins and educational attainment is in all cases weaker than the further association of educational attainment with class destinations, although (as in the earlier studies) the relative strengths of these relationships is not identical across countries. The association between origins and qualifications seems to be stronger in (say) Bulgaria and West Germany than in Czechoslovakia and the United States. (Note that we are looking here at the pattern followed by the delta statistics for each analysis, rather than the percentage reductions in the G^2, since the latter will be partly an artefact of such things as the variable size of the national samples.)

Furthermore, we find (as did the CASMIN researchers) that the net effect of educational attainment in the overall pattern of class reproduction by intergenerational social mobility is broadly similar across countries, in each case reducing the proportion of misclassified cases substantially (by between 60 per cent and 80 per cent if the main effects model is taken as a baseline). Of course, the merit-selection model does not fit equally badly across countries, and the proportion of misclassified cases is lower in Bulgaria and Russia, at one extreme, than in East Germany and Poland at the other.

However—and this would be our second major observation—in all cases that model fails to provide a satisfactory fit to the data, since in each country (as we saw earlier for Britain) a further direct association between class origins and destinations is significant, and must be included to obtain a well-fitting model. The basic model of merit-selection by education does not square with the facts for any of the industrialized nations here under consideration. It appears that, in all such countries, an individual's social origins influence his or her class destination, over and above their effects on his or her educational achievements.

The results reported in the lower panel of the table then lead us to our third conclusion, which is that the association between social origins and class destinations is itself cross-nationally variable, as can be seen from a comparison of models 2 and 5. Model 2 allows for cross-national variation in the relationships between both educational attainment and class origins, on the one hand, and educational attainment and class destinations on the other. It also posits that the association between origins and destinations is identical across nations—net of these other relationships. This model provides a poor fit to the data. An acceptable degree of fit is achieved only when—as in model 5—the relationship between origins and destinations is allowed to vary across nations. The other models shown in the table confirm that the degree of cross-national variation in how educational credentials are related via labour markets to occupational outcomes (the ED term in the models) is substantially greater than the degree of cross-national variation in the association between class origins and educational outcomes (OE).

It is something of a novelty, in the context both of the earlier literature on class mobility and of this particular volume, to uncover an association between origins and destinations that does indeed seem to vary substantially across industrial nations. However, the differences in question provide cold comfort for anyone seeking to use them as a lifeline for liberal theory, since we must also report that the economically most advanced nations (such as the United States and West Germany) are—in these terms—not necessarily the most 'meritocratic', as will be seen from the evidence of Table 5.8. Here, we are subjecting to formal test an extended version of the liberal claim that the logic of industrialism tends to promote equality of opportunity, understood in terms of merit-selection through education. Using these same data from the ISJP, we have ranked nations in terms of their overall propensity to educational merit-selection, as this has been estimated under Goldthorpe and Erikson's model of uniform difference. The analysis is therefore analogous to that reported earlier in Table 4.6. In other words, the most open societies among these nine nations considered as a whole—that is, those in which the odds ratios are closer to 1 than is the average for all nine—have the largest negative beta parameters. Those

TABLE 5.8. *Ranking of Nine Nations, by Overall Fluidity, within Four Levels of Educational Attainment*

Nation	Fluidity (beta value)	Nation	Fluidity (beta value)
Level 1		*Level 2*	
Russia	− 0.50	Bulgaria	− 0.68
Czechoslovakia	− 0.29	United States	− 0.57
Bulgaria	− 0.28	East Germany	− 0.39
United States	− 0.18	Russia	− 0.09
Poland	− 0.08	Great Britain	− 0.06
Slovenia	0.03	Poland	0.01
East Germany	0.13	Slovenia	0.03
Great Britain	0.35	Czechoslovakia	0.06
West Germany	0.83	West Germany	0.85
Level 3		*Level 4*	
East Germany	− 0.80	Bulgaria	− 1.20
Slovenia	− 0.77	Slovenia	− 0.55
Czechoslovakia	− 0.19	Poland	− 0.40
West Germany	− 0.02	Russia	− 0.39
Russia	0.12	Czechoslovakia	− 0.17
Bulgaria	0.29	East Germany	− 0.02
United States	0.47	West Germany	− 0.01
Poland	0.92	United States	0.52
Great Britain	0.98	Great Britain	2.22

in which the odds ratios are higher than the average have positive estimates. In this case, however, there are four such rankings—pertaining to each of the four levels of educational attainment with which we have been concerned.

These rankings suggest no obvious ordering of nations in terms of socio-political regimes or degree of economic development. At each level of educational achievement, advanced capitalist and former communist countries will be found adjacent to each other, and at both ends of the tables. For example, at the lowest level of formal qualifications, the United States appears as slightly more open a society than is average among these nine countries. However, it is less open than Russia, Czechoslovakia, or Bulgaria. Moreover, since the parameter estimates express differences between countries in a standardized form, we can say that—in relation to overall fluidity at least—the United States (at this educational level) looks more like Poland than it does West Germany. Note also that the rank order of countries changes across the different levels of educational attainment. Thus, for example, Slovenia is found to be more fluid than most other societies here considered—but only among those individuals holding advanced or degree-level qualifications (categories 3 and 4 of our educational-attainment schema). In short, therefore, these findings lend further support to the argument of Müller and his colleagues, since both our data and theirs suggest that the relationship between social mobility regimes and educational attainment does not correspond to distinct societal types, when seen in cross-national perspective.

Finally, and to return to the question posed at the outset, it should be noted that, when viewed in these particular terms, Britain looks considerably less educationally meritocratic a society than do most of her industrialized counterparts. Only in the case of respondents holding educational level 2 ('ordinary') qualifications does this country appear to be (slightly) more open than the average. It is at the bottom (or nearly so) of the league of nations here studied with regard to each of the other three levels of educational achievement. In other words, the direct effect of class origins on class destinations is greater among individuals holding advanced and degree-level qualifications in Britain than it is in any of the other eight advanced societies with which it has here been compared. Among those with little or no credentials, only the former West Germany appears less meritocratic.

This last point is perhaps more easily made in terms of simple odds ratios. For example, if we look (using the ISJP data-sets) at the odds ratios for the salariat versus working class at each of the four levels of educational attainment with which we are here working, then for the United States the relevant figures are 1.0 (low educational attainment), 1.1 (ordinary-level attainment), 2.4 (advanced), and 1.4 (degree-level credentials). The corresponding figures for West Germany are 1.7, 2.8, 1.4, and 1.1. Among the former state socialist societies, these same odds ratios are 1.0, 1.4, 1.5, and 1.4 (Czechoslovakia); 1.0, 1.6, 2.1, and 0.7 (Russia); and 1.0, 1.3, 1.8, and 2.6 (Poland). In Britain they are 5.1, 2.4, 3.4, and 2.9. Even allowing for sampling error, the general tendency is obvious, and suggests that, at all four levels of educational attainment, the degree of class inequality in social mobility (in this case of a long-range, unambiguously hierarchical nature) tends to be greater in Britain than in other advanced industrial nations—which is, of course, precisely the conclusion earlier reached (via a slightly different route) by Müller and his colleagues.

VII

In this chapter we have examined a particular conception of social justice that seeks to defend class inequalities on the grounds that they are reflections of differential merit—with merit being identified with educational achievement. Merit-selection therefore requires that individuals holding equal educational credentials be treated alike.

In fact we find that, with respect to our indicators at least, equals are treated unequally. It seems to be the case that, in modern Britain, class of origin (and sex) can, at least in some measure, undermine the principle of equality of opportunity through educational merit-selection in terms of which some theories of justice seek to legitimate inequalities of outcome. We also argued that this conclusion could be applied more or less equally well to the public and private sectors of the economy alike. In short, even if one accepts the suggestions that unequal educational achievements reflect genuine differences in ability and talent across classes, and that justice requires that such differences be rewarded in class terms, it is still far from obvious that one could, by appeal to these claims, defend existing class inequalities as just.

Arguably the weakest of our claims relates to the cross-national comparative analysis offered towards the end of the chapter. It may be wise, as some earlier commentators (e.g. Ishida et al. 1995) have claimed, to eschew attempts at constructing a single measurement of the extent to which class inequalities in mobility chances are mediated by educational qualifications in different countries. That effect will vary in strength across mobility trajectories and nations (although it should also be noted that all the evidence suggests the overall pattern of associations, if not their relative strengths, is the same in each country). Unfortunately, because of the relatively small sizes of the ISJP samples, we ourselves were able to do little more than fit the global model of merit-selection by education in each country and compare the resulting degrees of fit in a generalized way. However, both the more complex models and our simpler analysis point clearly to the same conclusion, which is that, when seen in cross-national comparative perspective, the logic of industrialism does not seem to imply a general or secular trend towards merit-selection by education. In summary, even when educational attainment is taken into account, class mobility chances in Britain are certainly as unequal as those to be found in other countries across the industrialized world—and, in the case of mobility between the salariat and working classes, probably more so.

Viewed in this cross-sectional way, therefore, the pattern of our results does not bode well for those who would seek to defend existing inequalities in class mobility chances on the grounds that they are consistent with the principle of merit-selection through education. Of course, it might be countered that we have constructed the meritocratic argument in too strong a way, as a proposition about the wholesale achievement of educational merit-selection during the present day. What *can* plausibly be claimed, it might be said, is that there is a tendency for merit-selection to increase over the years. It is to the issue of trends in merit-selection that we turn our attention in the following chapter.

NOTES

1. Bell (1976: 409, 426, 41). For a concise summary of the many other (mostly American) writers who write in similar vein, see Rehberg and Rosenthal (1978: ch. 1). Reviewing the American literature in the late 1980s, Hallinan (1988: 251) concluded that 'the central research question in the sociology of education since World War II has been the relationship between schooling and social inequality. Researchers have been deeply concerned with the factors that prevent students from attaining academic success and subsequent occupational status by merit alone ... This emphasis ... stems from the pervasive influence of progressivism at the start of the twentieth century—the social and intellectual movement that advocated public education as one of the means to social progress.'

   American functionalist sociologists of the 1950s and 1960s were not the only sponsors of the thesis which bracketed together educational achievement, equality of opportunity, and meritocracy. This argument also has an affinity with the liberal ideals behind the mid-nineteenth-century reform of the British civil service, which aimed at abolishing patronage and nepotism in public service in favour of selection to positions of responsibility on the basis of proven competence—in practice educational attainment, as demonstrated both in competitive examinations and in the completion of prescribed forms of training. Similarly, during the early decades of the twentieth century, the development of systems of mass education in Western societies was accompanied by the emergence both of an egalitarian impetus to make educational opportunities available to children from poorer backgrounds and of a Darwinian concern to avoid undue wastage of the national 'stock of ability'. The concomitant development of the various techniques of mental testing provided a convenient and seemingly scientific basis for the new policy of selecting for further training those children who would be most likely to benefit from continuing education. On these diverse origins of the concept of meritocracy, see Goldthorpe (1996a).

2. See Goldthorpe (1996a: fig. 8.1). It is important to note that there are two distinct propositions advanced here. On a narrow reading, the ideal of

meritocracy suggests that the allocation of individuals to positions in the class structure is based solely on educational attainment, without reference to the relationship (if any) between social origins and educational achievement. In other words, attention is focused squarely on the relationship between credentials and class destinations. However, in practice, many empirical studies of merit-selection have also documented certain class differentials in educational attainment—and then disputed the extent to which these could be justified in meritocratic terms. We pursue this point below.

3. Halsey (1977: 184). Of course, Halsey's inference that an increase (or no decrease) in the association between class origins and educational attainment counts against the thesis of increasing meritocracy would be contested by critics such as Peter Saunders and Charles Murray, who would argue that a tightening of the link between class origins and educational achievement need not indicate a move away from merit-selection—if, that is, one assumes talent to be unequally distributed across the classes, with the most gifted people being found in the highest social positions, and passing on their endowments (genetically or otherwise) to their children. This issue is pursued in Ch. 7 below.

4. Dronkers (1993: 263) also demonstrates, rather convincingly in our view, that one major weakness of the status-attainment tradition of research is that the linear models that typically are used to estimate changes in the parameters of path or LISREL analyses of the Wisconsin type 'cannot distinguish between the decreased effects of parental occupation and education that are due to the increased participation of more pupils, on the one hand, and "real" changes in the effects of parental occupation and education, on the other'. Dronkers himself uses survival ratio techniques to show that the creation of more educational opportunities all round did not result in a redistribution of relative chances for educational attainment across classes. Failure to separate out these two effects is analogous to that of not distinguishing changes in absolute mobility rates from changing relative mobility chances.

5. For technical details of the General Election Surveys, see Heath et al. (1985; 1994). When the data are merged in this way, no significant interaction effects can be found across the three surveys.

6. See e.g. the analysis of the CASMIN data reported by Hiroshi Ishida, Walter Müller, and John Ridge (1995: 171), who conclude: 'The reproductions of the petty bourgeoisie and the farming class are not affected by qualifications. Among our 10 nations, the reductions in the extent of class reproduction for class IVab and class IVc + VIIb after controlling for qualifications are small, the highest being only 11% in Japan. The tendency for the petty bourgeoisie and the farming class to inherit their fathers' positions is independent of qualifications and, therefore, is more likely to be the result of direct transmission of fixed capital, whether in the form of land or private business.'

7. Of course, it might still be argued that children from salariat origins score more highly *within* our educational levels than do sons and daughters from working-class backgrounds, and that this properly meritocratic criterion explains (if only in part) their relative advantage in terms of destinations. This is a difficult claim either to establish or to refute, at least without scaling educational attainment as a continuous variable (and our objections to this will already have been noted in Appendix D), but even if it were true it can only mitigate, not completely subvert, any inferences about lack of merit-selection by education. Furthermore, since it might be argued that some of the discrepancy in the fit between credentials and class destinations could be due to the fact that education is included in a clearly hierarchical way but destination less so (the CASMIN version of the class scheme distinguishes routine clerical employees from a collapsed category of supervisor and skilled manual worker), it is worth recording here that we have repeated the analysis reported in Tables 5.1 and 5.2 using a more obviously hierarchical 3-category (working, intermediate, service) class collapse and find substantially the same results. It is perhaps also worth reporting that the inclusion of *petit bourgeois* class destinations does not alter the import of these findings. See also the results reported in Marshall and Swift (1993: table 2).

8. The three random samples with which we are working, when pooled and analysed in this way, yield a table containing over 4,000 white but only 87 Afro-Caribbean and 78 Asian respondents. Because of the small numbers in the minority ethnic groups, it is then necessary to revert to a more highly aggregated version of the Goldthorpe class schema, distinguishing between the familiar salariat, intermediate, and working-class destinations. The findings suggest that, towards the lower end of the educational scale, Afro-Caribbeans are less successful than their white educational counterparts in terms of gaining salariat and other non-manual employment. All but two of the most lowly educated Afro-Caribbeans have had to settle for manual work—and (although the table does not show this) the overwhelming majority have manual jobs of the unskilled variety. However, in terms of their allocation to class destinations, individuals from Asian backgrounds would seem to be broadly comparable with whites having similar qualifications. Unfortunately, at the highest educational level, the fact that our sample contains so few respondents from ethnic minorities prevents us from drawing any firm conclusions. It is difficult to ascertain whether, at this point, ethnicity becomes unimportant (as qualifications almost guarantee access to the salariat) or whether some racial disparities do remain. The full results are shown below.

9. See e.g. Dex and Shaw (1986). The same argument can of course be made in relation to ethnicity (see Braham et al. 1981).

10. Although we are not here primarily concerned with the question of equality of opportunity as between the sexes, the following points arise by analogy with our discussion of class and merit-selection, and are worth noting. First,

Class Distribution in Britain by Educational Attainment and Ethnicity (Respondent's Class Determined by Reference to Own Employment): Percentage by Row

Ethnic group	Educational level	Class destination			N
		Salariat	Intermediate	Working	
White	1	11	10	79	1,435
	2	25	27	47	1,533
	3	60	19	21	774
	4	88	8	4	488
(N = 4,230)					
Afro-Caribbean	1	0	5	92	39
	2	13	26	52	31
	3	55	36	9	11
	4	83	0	17	6
(N = 87)					
Asian	1	15	11	78	27
	2	19	26	56	27
	3	60	20	20	10
	4	93	0	7	14
(N = 78)					

Notes
1. Classes are salariat (I, II); intermediate (IIIa, V); working (VI, VII, IIIb).
2. Asian includes Indian, Pakistani, Bangladeshi, Chinese; Afro-Caribbean includes black-Caribbean and black-African.
3. Since it is usually argued that ethnic minorities are at a relative disadvantage (as compared to their white counterparts), not only within the labour market but also in terms of opportunities to enter into paid employment at all, the analysis includes unemployed respondents as well as those currently in paid labour. The former have been assigned a class position on the basis of their most recent employment.

even if we suppose (for the sake of argument) that the differential distribution of educational attainment between men and women of similar class origins reflects differences in intelligence and motivation, still we cannot, by appeal to this supposition alone, defend the differential allocation of men and women to class destinations as being consistent with merit-selection by education. The significance of the SED interaction term shows that there is an association between sex and destination even when we control for educational achievement. Second, it is of course possible to argue that the differential allocation of similarly qualified men and women to places in the class structure reflects aspects of merit that are not embraced by educational qualifications. If men are more likely to work hard in their jobs, or less likely to leave their jobs (even temporarily, to raise a family) than are women with similar levels of education, then it might be claimed that their superior rewards in the labour market are indeed merited. However, it is not necessary to pursue these thoughts here, since neither relates directly to our central finding that there is, for both men and women alike, an association between origins and destinations that is unmediated by education.

11. In fact, however, as Jonsson's subsequent testing of this proposition in modern Sweden also suggests, labour markets are heterogeneous, and stratification within them is contingent upon organizational settings and negotiations, so that simple generalizations about education as a principle of allocation governing the public and private sectors in their entirety are unlikely to find empirical support. Larry Griffin and Arne Kalleberg (1981: 19) state that they 'had no expectation as to which sector (if either) would be characterized by more meritocratic processes', and report that their data 'suggest that allocation processes are quite comparable across sectors', and that 'meritocratic influences . . . are . . . observed to be, at best, quite modest'. It should be noted, however, that their sample is small and badly skewed. (Numbers for the private sector and public sector are 541 and 173 respectively.)

12. Readers who are familiar with the details of the Goldthorpe class scheme will be aware that his service-class category embraces a number of self-employed professionals and large proprietors. The private sector, as defined in the above analysis, therefore includes a relatively small number of self-employed individuals (in fact 182) alongside the majority who are employees. (Note that our earlier elimination of the *petite bourgeoisie* as a class destination has already excluded most of the self-employed from the analysis.) Since some of these remaining self-employed people are professionals, while others are entrepreneurs, it is not clear whether educational qualifications or the inheritance of property and capital has played the larger part in shaping their class trajectories. Nevertheless, from the point of view of our argument about sectoral differences in merit-selection, it is worth noting that the inclusion of such self-employed persons in no way distorts our analysis of the private sector—since the same pattern of results is obtained even when they are excluded.

13. In a separate but related investigation of the same data-set (and employing different techniques of analysis), Ishida et al. (1995) arrive at substantially the same general findings, but do then extend their analysis to examine directly the ways in which patterns of class reproduction via social mobility are mediated by means of educational qualifications. Having examined the effects of education in relation to (a slightly modified version of) Erikson and Goldthorpe's model of 'core social fluidity', they report detailed findings for each of 5 distinct effect matrices in their model. The gist of their argument is that, although there is an impressive cross-national similarity in the overall role played by qualifications in social mobility, there are significant variations in the component effects which generate this result. These occur, not only in relation to the effects of class origin on educational

achievements and educational achievements upon class destination, but also in relation to the direct effect of class origins on destinations. In other words, qualifications play different roles in class reproduction, according to the particular mobility trajectory in question.

Specifically, it was found that the reproduction of the *petite bourgeoisie* (Goldthorpe classes IVa and IVb) and farming class (IVc and VIIb) is not much affected by qualification, with sons from these backgrounds tending to inherit their fathers' positions as the result (the authors assume) either of direct transmission of fixed capital or of some such cultural property as a 'desire for independence' or 'attachment to the land'. The tendency for sons of the skilled working class to stay in their class of origin also appears to be largely independent of qualifications in all nations. The relatively low propensity for intergenerational mobility in either direction between the salariat and unskilled working or farming class is only partly explained by qualifications, which reduce this 'hierarchy' effect by between 23% and 39%, depending upon the nation concerned. By contrast, the other hierarchy effect (which implies barriers to mobility between the service and intermediate classes) is largely unaffected by a control for qualifications, suggesting that these barriers do not necessarily arise out of differential educational attainment. Finally, the relatively high propensity for mobility between the salariat and routine clerical classes is strongly affected by educational credentials, whereas that between the *petite bourgeoisie*, farming, and working class is largely independent of such qualifications.

What all of this suggests is that, although class reproduction and social mobility involve processes which are affected differently by the attainment of qualifications in different countries, nevertheless the net result is that there is a basic similarity in the overall effect of qualifications on processes of intergenerational social mobility across all industrial nations. Furthermore, because the extent to which education mediates the overall relationship between class origins and destinations varies according to the mobility process and nation in question, the role played by education in the processes of class reproduction and intergenerational mobility is not easily captured by any single measure of association. On this last point, see also Logan (1983) and Yamaguchi (1982).

14. Moreover, although our modelling techniques may be relatively simple, they do have the virtue of being easier to interpret sociologically. For example, the complex topological model proposed by Ishida and his colleagues yields a large number of statistically significant effect parameters relating to the different design matrices included in the model, but the sociological processes which might explain these effects are often opaque. Towards the end of their analysis, Ishida et al. (1995) report a series of percentage reductions in the estimates for the origin–destination effect matrix, after controlling for educational qualifications. These are repro-

duced in the table below. It will be seen from the table that e.g. in the cases of Hungary, Sweden, and West Germany, the tendency towards class reproduction among the salariat is no longer significant when a control is introduced for educational attainment. In England, Poland, and Scotland, this control has the effect of reducing class inheritance among the salariat by more than 40%. In Ireland and Northern Ireland, the role of education in the reproduction of the salariat is less pronounced, since the % reductions after controlling for qualifications are very small (at 10% and 22% respectively). The problem is that here, as elsewhere in the table, it is sometimes difficult to explain the observed effects. Why should it be that, specifically in both parts of Ireland, the service class does not use educational qualifications to pass on its privilege from one generation to the next? Similarly, how do we explain the fact that class reproduction among routine clerical workers (class IIIa) is significant only in Ireland, Northern Ireland, and Hungary, or that a control for education exerts a different effect on this association across the three countries? Why should the second hierarchy (HI2) effect—which indicates a low propensity for sons of the salariat to be downwardly mobile into the unskilled working or farming classes (and vice versa)—be significant in all nations except Northern Ireland; or become non-significant

Percentage Reduction in the Estimates of the Origin–Destination Effect Matrix, in Ten Countries, after Controlling for Educational Qualifications

	ENG	FRA	HUN	IRE	JAP	NIR	POL	SCO	SWE	FRG
DIG (I + II)	67	35	ns	10	*	22	67	46	ns	ns
DIG (III)	*	*	32	ns	*	24	*	*	*	*
DIG (IVab)	− 3	0	− 5	− 2	4	− 5	0	− 2	− 3	7
DIG (IVc + VIIb)	0	− 1	9	4	11	2	2	2	2	2
DIG (V + VI)	14	1	− 28	− 5	− 5	1	1	9	16	3
DIG (VIIa)	33	*	ns	0	*	11	− 17	− 6	*	*
HI1	4	19	24	*	8	ns	*	*	1	15
HI2	23	24	35	ns	37	*	ns	ns	23	39
AF2A	ns	ns	48	ns	*	ns	51	*	33	ns
AF2B	25	− 3	*	− 7	*	12	− 4	15	*	ns
AF1	na	na	na	na	22	na	na	na	na	− 7

Notes
1. Table adapted from Ishida et al. (1995: table 8).
2. DIG = direct inheritance effect parameter for each class.
3. HI1, HI2, AF2A, AF2B, AF1 = hierarchy and affinity effects adapted by Ishida et al. from Erikson and Goldthorpe's 'core model'.
4. na = not applicable.
5. * = parameters were non-significant in the original 2-way (origin by destination) table.
6. ns = parameters became non-significant after controlling for educational qualifications.
7. Countries are ENG (England), FRA (France), HUN (Hungary), IRE (Ireland), JAP (Japan), NIR (Northern Ireland), POL (Poland), SCO (Scotland), SWE (Sweden), and FRG (West Germany).

after controlling for educational attainment in some other nations (Ireland, Poland, and Scotland); and reduce the direct class inheritance effect differentially by between 23% and 39% in England, France, Hungary, Japan, Sweden, and West Germany?

One could multiply the examples, but sufficient have been cited to illustrate the general point, which is that neither we nor Ishida and his colleagues can offer meaningful sociological explanations for these specific effects at such a level of detail.

15. It is, however, difficult to achieve exact comparability between our results and those obtained from similar previous studies.

For example, in analysing the British data we have used the same 4-category collapsed version of the CASMIN educational schema as was employed by some of the earlier researchers, notably Heath et al. (1992). However, Ishida et al. (1995) use a less sensitive 3-category collapse, which does not distinguish between lower tertiary certificates (CASMIN level 3b) and university-level degrees or equivalent (level 3c). In Britain, for example, this has the (in our view undesirable) effect of treating City and Guilds Certificates, Higher National Diplomas, technical school diplomas, and university degrees as functionally equivalent in the labour market. By contrast, although they use the same CASMIN data-sets, Müller et al. (1990) fit in stepwise fashion a series of simple log-linear models (rather than adopting the more complex topological approach favoured in the paper whose lead author is Ishida), and so are able to work instead with the full 8-category version of the education schema.

Similarly, although all of these analyses are based on Goldthorpe class categories, that pursued by Müller et al. uses a highly differentiated 9-category version, collapsing only classes IIIa and IIIb, and IVa and IVb (cf. Table 3.1 above). By contrast, the paper co-authored by Ishida employs a 6-category schema, which differs from the standard CASMIN 7-category version used by Erikson and Goldthorpe in that it amalgamates the farming classes IVc and VIIb (cf. Table 4.1 above). In Jonsson's analysis of the Swedish data, a variety of different class collapses are used, including on occasions the perhaps questionable merging of classes II and IIIa, and of all three 'white-collar' classes.

Because of the ISJP sample sizes, we have been compelled to use a less detailed 4-category collapse, the nature of which is explained in the notes to Table 5.7. Most earlier studies (including all of those discussed here) incorporate the *petite bourgeoisie* as a destination class. While we ourselves can see no good reason for involving classes IVa and IVb (cf. Tables 5.2–6 above), there are some grounds for not excluding class IVc, in so far as it is sometimes difficult in practice, especially in the former state socialist societies, to distinguish small peasant farmers from agricultural labourers (especially if they are enmeshed in varying degrees of collectivization with private plots). For the sake of comparability, we therefore follow the practice of Jonsson, Ishida, Müller, and their associates, so that the results shown in Table 5.7 include the relevant data for a unified (IVc, VIIb) agricultural class destination (in addition, of course, to an agricultural class of origin).

Finally, we should explain that the Estonian and Japanese cases are excluded from our analysis, because of small numbers and the distribution of cases (which results in too many empty or nearly empty cells in some of the tables).

6

Education: Trends

I

In the previous chapter we argued that those who have proposed or tested meritocratic interpretations of mobility regimes have conventionally done so by reference to the role played by education in class reproduction. We then reported evidence which shows that educational attainment does not explain the relationship between class of origin and class destination in modern Britain—or, for that matter, in other advanced industrial societies. An unmediated association between origins and destinations is readily apparent. This is found among both males and females and those employed in the public and private sectors alike. These findings would seem to cast doubt on the claim that class inequalities in this country can be justified on the grounds that they simply reflect merit-selection through educational achievement.

Of course, this picture includes individuals who completed their education and entered the world of paid employment during different decades spanning the last half-century or so, since our respondents ranged between the ages of 18 and 80 (or thereabouts) at the time of interview. In this period educational systems have been subject to a number of major reforms. In Britain, for example, the 1944 Education Act established universal and free secondary schooling, defined a standard transition from primary to secondary education at around age 11, and raised the minimum leaving-age from 14 to 15 (later increased to 16 in 1973). The postwar tripartite secondary system erected by the Act—which channelled children of different abilities into grammar, technical, and secondary modern schools—was then replaced after a quarter of a century or so by a system of comprehensive secondary schools catering for children at all levels of ability (although a minority of schools continued as selective grammar schools). Selective education was also available throughout this period (and still is), for those prepared to pay for private tuition in the independent sector, which includes the (ironically titled) public schools.

Higher education has also undergone dramatic expansion, perhaps most notably during the 1960s and 1980s. Postwar reforms encouraged the growth of separate institutions of further education offering post-secondary schooling for those unable to obtain entry to the colleges and universities. This so-called alternative route provided further opportunities for the attainment of (largely technical and vocational) qualifications. As the various school reforms took effect, so the volume of students eligible for tertiary education (via the conventional or alternative routes) was substantially increased. The availability of state subsidies, notably through the introduction of a national system of student grants in the 1960s, encouraged wider participation, regardless of financial means, in the tertiary sector.

It is evident, when seen against this background of sometimes dramatic reform, that respondents will have experienced different educational as well as occupational opportunities during the years of their adolescence. These changes might therefore be expected to have influenced the relationship between class origins, educational attainment, and class destination during the decades spanned by the lifetimes of our interviewees. Is this influence apparent in our data? Has the association between social origins and educational attainment changed over the years; and, if so, how has this affected the trendless correlation of origins and destinations that is evident in our own and other studies of intergenerational social mobility?

In answering this question, we will extend our pooled data-set for Britain to include two further surveys, from the 1983 General Election Study and 1984 Essex Class Project. Together with the surveys from the 1991 British Social Justice Project, and 1987 and 1992 General Election Studies, this yields a sample of more than 11,000 individuals for whom the relationship between class trajectories and educational attainment can reliably be assessed in terms of the Goldthorpe class and CASMIN educational categories. Respondents have been grouped into six cohorts according to year of birth: those born before 1920, during each of the four subsequent decades, and in 1960 or later.[1]

Using these data we will attempt in this chapter to determine how (if at all) the relationship between class origins and educational attainment has altered throughout the course of this century. Has the steady expansion in education, which has provided greater educational opportunities for all, also succeeded in reducing class inequalities in educational outcomes? We then turn to investigate the relationship between educational achievement and class destination, before finally examining the

direct influence of class origins on occupational outcomes (net of education) over time.

II

Table 6.1 shows how overall levels of educational attainment have
improved during the decades captured by our cohorts. The proportion
of people educated to only the most basic level has steadily declined.
The proportions obtaining qualifications at each of the three higher
levels has risen. It is true that these improvements would seem to be
somewhat less evident among the youngest cohort. We suspect, however, that we are here simply underestimating the achievements of our
youngest respondents. The analysis excludes all individuals aged under
25, on the grounds that people younger than this may not yet have

TABLE 6.1. *Educational Attainment in Britain, by Cohort, and by Sex and Cohort:
Percentage by Row*

Cohort		Low	Ordinary	Advanced	Degree	N
Pre-1920		72	17	7	4	1,703
1920s		61	22	11	6	2,020
1930s		50	28	13	8	2,104
1940s		41	34	14	11	2,576
1950s		32	35	19	14	2,441
Post-1960		26	42	19	13	677

Cohort	Sex	Low	Ordinary	Advanced	Degree	N
Pre-1920	M	62	25	5	6	713
	F	78	12	8	2	991
1920s	M	54	27	10	9	1,010
	F	68	16	12	4	1,011
1930s	M	44	33	12	11	1,058
	F	57	24	15	5	1,046
1940s	M	36	34	15	15	1,206
	F	46	33	15	6	1,370
1950s	M	29	35	20	17	1,141
	F	36	37	17	10	1,300
Post-1960	M	22	41	20	17	322
	F	30	42	19	8	355

completed their education, but still includes a number of respondents aged 25 or over who are in the process of obtaining futher (especially degree-level and professional) qualifications.

It is apparent, from the lower part of the table, that these educational improvements are to be found among both sexes. But it is also evident that differentials between males and females have been maintained. Males continue to out-perform their female counterparts—even among our youngest cohort—when it comes to gaining educational credentials. Females are consistently more likely to acquire only the most basic (level 1) education and are, throughout, less likely to attain degree-type (level 4) qualifications. The sexes are more similar with regard to inter-mediate levels of attainment, particularly among recent cohorts, so that although ordinary (level 2) qualifications are more commonly held by men in earlier cohorts, this differential has tended to disappear over time.

Log-linear analysis of these data (see model 4 in Table 6.2) confirms both the marked improvement in overall educational standards (EC) and also that females perform less well than males (ES). However, the fact that the three-way association term (although relatively weak) is also required (since model 4 fails to fit the data) indicates that the improvements in educational standards have not been uniform over time for both sexes. For example, it is evident from Table 6.1 that females tend to have made greatest gains in respect of intermediate (level 2 and 3) qualifications, while males have gained more at the higher–tertiary (degree) level. Clearly, however, the attainment of

TABLE 6.2. *Educational Attainment in Britain, by Cohort and Sex: Models*

Model	G^2	df	p	rG^2	delta
1. E + C + S	875.9	38	0.000	—	12.7
2. EC + S	220.3	23	0.000	74.8	5.9
3. EC + CS	185.2	18	0.000	78.9	5.7
4. EC + CS + ES	46.6	15	0.000	94.7	2.9

N = 11,523.

Notes
1. Education (E) has 4 levels: low (CASMIN level 1), ordinary (CASMIN level 2), advanced (CASMIN level 3), and degree (CASMIN level 4): see Table D.1 for details of CASMIN categories.
2. There are 6 cohorts (C): those born before 1920; during the 1920s, the 1930s, 1940s, and 1950s; and during 1960 and after.
3. G^2 = log-likelihood ratio; rG^2 = % reduction in G^2 (treating the main effects model as baseline); delta = % of misclassified cases.

educational credentials has become more widespread throughout the course of the twentieth century. With some (relatively minor) differences these improvements have been common to British men and women alike. How then does the issue of class background fit in to this story?

Fig. 6.1 illustrates how sons and daughters from the different class origins have fared, over successive decades, in terms of obtaining education to the lowest level only. It is clear that there has been consistent improvement among children from each of the five origin classes over time. Among those from unskilled manual backgrounds, the proportion educated to only this level has decreased from 87 per cent, in the case of the oldest cohort, to 40 per cent of those born during the 1960s. Similarly, there have been reductions from 75 to 28 per cent among those from skilled-manual backgrounds, and from 39 and 41 per cent to 12 per cent among children from salariat and routine non-manual homes re-

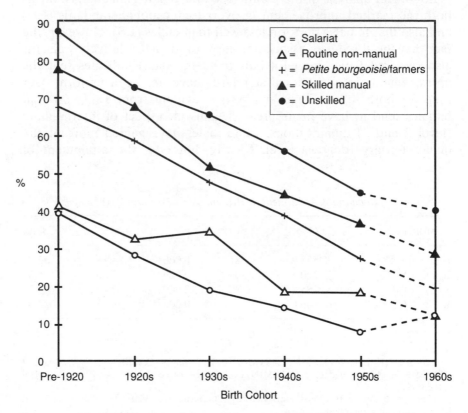

FIGURE 6.1. Attainment of Low Educational Qualifications, by Class of Origin and Cohort, Britain (Outflow Percentages)

spectively. Clearly, the less advantaged classes have had the greatest scope for improvement over time, and this is where the largest absolute gains have been made. But the trend-lines relating to each of the five origin classes are roughly parallel. This suggests that there has been no clear narrowing of class inequalities in terms of gaining qualifications above this lowest level.[2]

The picture at the intermediate levels of educational achievement is perhaps not so clear-cut. Fig. 6.2 shows the trend in attainment of ordinary-level qualifications for each of the five class origins over time. The proportion of individuals from salariat and routine non-manual families educated to this level has, with fluctuations, remained fairly stable over the years. Certainly there is no evidence of a monotonic trend in either direction. This is also true of advanced (level 3) qualifications (see Fig. 6.3). By contrast, the proportions from the different manual backgrounds who gain ordinary-level qualifications has increased considerably, over successive decades. There is also evidence of an increase, although much smaller, in the proportion of respondents with working-class origins who successfully gain advanced-level credentials.

What can be concluded from these results? Most obviously, overall educational standards have risen dramatically during the decades repre-

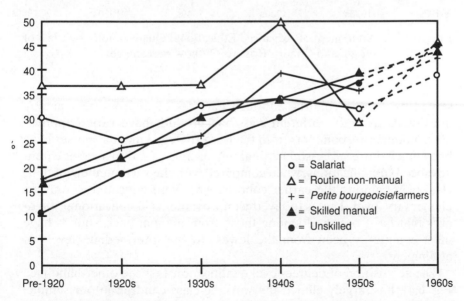

FIGURE 6.2. Attainment of Ordinary Educational Qualifications by Class of Origin and Cohort, Britain (Outflow Percentages)

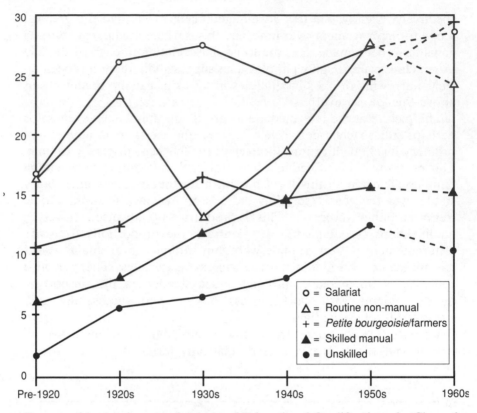

FIGURE 6.3. Attainment of Advanced Educational Qualifications, by Class of
Origin and Cohort, Britain (Outflow Percentages)

sented by our six cohorts, although patterns of improvement among
individuals from the different class backgrounds have varied appreci-
ably. Younger respondents from the less privileged manual classes have
been much more successful in obtaining ordinary (and to a lesser extent
advanced) qualifications, when compared with the vast numbers of their
class peers among the earlier cohorts, who were educated to only an
elementary level. That is to say, the improvements in educational standards that have occurred among those from manual backgrounds have
most commonly been from the lowest to the intermediate levels of
attainment.

The acquisition of degree-level qualifications, on the other hand (see
Fig. 6.4), has largely eluded the working-class children in our sample.
The percentage of those from unskilled origins gaining level 4 creden-
tials has not risen above 6 per cent. Among children from skilled manual

homes, the proportion obtaining degree-level qualifications remained below 9 per cent until the cohort born after 1960, among whom it rose to 13 per cent. This pattern contrasts greatly with the improvements among the more advantaged non-manual classes. Sons and daughters from these backgrounds have become increasingly more likely to gain university-type qualifications and to avoid the lowest levels of educational achievement. Among the offspring of the salariat, attainment of degree-level qualifications has increased from 14 per cent in the oldest cohort to 33 per cent of those born during the 1950s. Among those from routine clerical homes, the corresponding increase has been from 6 to 24 per cent. The proportions achieving intermediate levels of attainment have remained trendless (see Figs. 6.2 and 6.3), while those educated to the lowest level only have fallen (Fig. 6.1).

It would seem that, throughout the course of this century, a widening gap has developed between the social classes in terms of the proportions completing a higher–tertiary education. While it is evident that the number of individuals from manual backgrounds who obtain degree-level qualifications has gradually risen, it is those from the non-manual classes who have had by far the greater success, and increasingly so. As

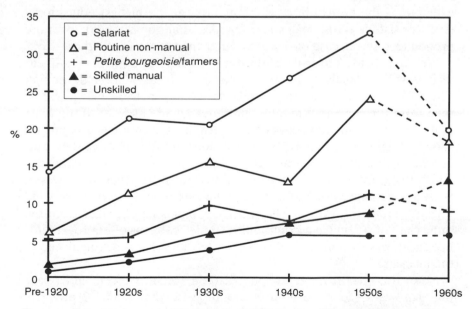

FIGURE 6.4. Attainment of Degree-Level Educational Qualifications, by Class of Origin and Cohort, Britain (Outflow Percentages)

we shall see shortly, these degree-level qualifications are particularly, and increasingly, important when it comes to the competition for service-class employment, especially for obtaining the higher-level (Goldthorpe class I) positions within this class.

We have also seen that there is no clear widening or narrowing of class inequalities in terms of attainments at the lowest educational level. At the intermediate levels the pattern is more complicated. In other words, children from non-manual backgrounds have enjoyed increasing success in gaining the highest qualifications and avoiding the poorest, with no clear increase or decrease at the middling levels. It is at these intermediate levels, and in particular at the lower end (level 2), that the manual classes have made the greatest gains in relation to their less educated predecessors. Fig. 6.2, for example, indicates some convergence of class inequalities in the attainment of level 2 qualifications. However, again as we shall see shortly, this level of educational attainment also constitutes a waning asset in the labour market. Arguably, it is degree-type qualifications that are of greater relevance for obtaining advantaged conditions of employment, and at this level we find widening rather than narrowing differentials between the classes.

Finally, it is worth addressing the issue of possible sex differences in the trends described above. (Most of the previous research in this area has either treated both sexes together or analysed males alone.) For example, is the growth in class inequalities at the highest educational level consistent across males and females alike, or is it perhaps more pronounced in the case of one sex rather than that of the other?

We can provide a formal test for this possibility by applying log-linear techniques of analysis to our data on educational achievement. The results, and the relevant models, are shown in Table 6.3. It will be seen from the table that model 3 provides an adequate fit to the data. Note that the four-way association between educational attainment, class of origin, birth-cohort, and sex is not required. This can be interpreted as evidence that class inequalities in educational attainment, which (as we have seen) vary over time, do not further vary by sex. Broadly speaking, therefore, the conclusions reached above are valid for both men and women. That is to say, males and females from the same class of origin have experienced similar patterns of improvements in educational attainments, across the various cohorts distinguished in the analysis.

Note also that the interaction between origin, cohort, and sex is not significant (compare models 2 and 3), so that model 2 provides an acceptable fit to the data. This model posits, first, an association between origins, education, and cohort, which reflects the class-

TABLE 6.3. *Educational Attainment in Britain, by Class of Origin, Cohort, and Sex: Models*

Model	G^2	df	p	rG^2	delta
1. O + E + C + S	2,931.0	226	0.000	—	20.1
2. OEC + OES + ECS	98.7	80	0.077	96.6	3.1
3. OEC + OES + ECS + OCS	75.8	60	0.082	97.4	2.5

N = 10,184.

Notes
1. Class origin (O) has 5 levels: salariat (I, II); routine non-manual (IIIa); *petite bourgeoisie* and farmers (IVa + b + c); skilled manual (V, VI); and unskilled manual (VIIa + b, IIIb).
2. Education (E) has 4 levels, as in Table 6.2.
3. There are 6 cohorts (C), as in Table 6.2.
4. G^2 = log-likelihood ratio; rG^2 = % reduction in G^2 (treating the main effects model as baseline); delta = % of misclassified cases.

distinctiveness of the improvements in education over time. (For example, those from the more advantaged backgrounds have been making the greater gains at the highest levels of attainment, as seen in Fig. 6.4.) Secondly, the education–cohort–sex term is required, denoting that educational improvements over time have not been the same for both sexes: as a whole, females have made greater gains at intermediate levels of education, while males have benefited more at the higher–tertiary level (see Table 6.1). Finally, the OES interaction is included, and indicates a sex differential in attainment among individuals from the same class background. Females have often been less successful than their male class peers throughout. Importantly, however, the class-distinctive patterns of improvement over time have been broadly similar for both sexes. Class inequality in educational attainment has remained more or less constant across the sexes throughout most of the twentieth century. Here, as elsewhere in this study, we find clear evidence that class processes remain resolutely sex-blind.

III

So much for the relationship between class origins and educational attainment. What then of the second leg of the meritocratic triad—the association between educational attainment and class destination?

Much of the previous research into this aspect of the debate has relied on a comparison between two (or more) cross-sectional surveys which were conducted at an interval (or intervals) of several years. These are viewed as snapshots of the class structure at different moments—from which, in turn, the relationship between educational qualifications and the destination of individuals in a structure can be assessed during each of the periods in question. This is the approach that we ourselves will pursue in due course, when we compare the association between educational qualifications and class destinations, as it is found in the recent surveys within our pooled data-set, against that observed in the data from the Oxford Mobility Survey of 1972.

However, before examining changes (if any) in the association between educational qualifications and class destinations in these earlier and later surveys, we will first consider the relationship, across successive birth-cohorts, between qualifications and class at time of entry into the formal labour market (here defined in terms of the respondent's first full-time job after completion of his or her full-time education). If the hypothesis of increasing merit-selection by education is indeed sound, then the evidence should be readily apparent in the progressively greater role played by educational qualifications in distributing respondents to their classes of first occupation.

These are, of course, two rather different ways of looking at trends in the relationship between educational attainment and class outcomes: on the one hand, as indicated by patterns of entry into the labour market, across successive birth-cohorts and, on the other, in terms of the distribution of class destinations (present job) revealed in samples taken at two different points in time. However, both strategies are entirely complementary from the point of view of testing the IMS hypothesis, and it is presumably for this reason that some earlier researchers have pursued both together (although most have tended to favour either one approach or the other).[3]

Figures 6.5–8 therefore illustrate the proportional allocation of individuals to the salariat, routine non-manual, skilled, and unskilled working classes, at time of first job, within each of our birth-cohorts, according to the level of education attained.[4] It will be seen from the first of these figures that, across all cohorts, the majority of those educated only to the lowest educational level enter the labour market via the unskilled working class. Individuals holding these low-level qualifications have in fact become increasingly likely to begin their working lives in unskilled manual employment. Approximately one-fifth of each cohort, at this educational level, secure skilled manual positions. The proportion entering routine non-manual occupations is also relatively small, varying between 7 and 16 per cent, although this figure has been reducing noticeably among the more recent cohorts. Finally, labour-market entry direct into the service class is an even rarer

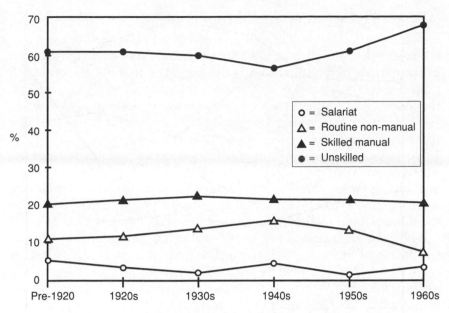

FIGURE 6.5. Class of First Job of Those Attaining Low Educational Qualifications, by Cohort, Britain (Outflow Percentages)

occurrence at this modest level of educational attainment, with fewer
than 6 per cent of each cohort succeeding in securing these advantaged
positions.

Consider the shifts in the class structure that form the background to
these figures. As we saw in Chapter 4, because of the growth in white-
collar work and the decline of manufacturing, the proportion of
men and women in working-class employment has been shrinking
over recent decades. We have now identified a modest decrease in the
proportion of individuals holding low-level credentials who succeed in
entering non-manual employment as a first job. Our evidence also suggests that, among those at the lowest educational level, labour-market
entrance rates to the skilled working class have not decreased, while the
rate of first entry into the unskilled working class has steadily increased.
These changes in the pattern of labour-market entry are therefore taking place at a time when sectoral employment shifts in Britain have
favoured the expansion of non-manual occupations at the expense of
manual work. This is a complex picture, but when both processes are
considered together they point to one obvious conclusion: that a minimum education makes for increasingly poor first-employment prospects
in modern Britain.

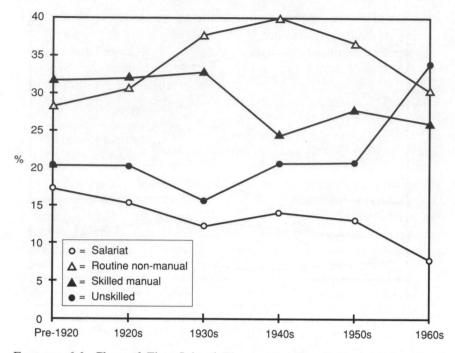

FIGURE 6.6. Class of First Job of Those Attaining Ordinary Educational
Qualifications, by Cohort, Britain (Outflow Percentages)

Similarly, among those holding ordinary (level 2) qualifications, entrance rates into the more desirable salariat and other non-manual
positions have declined over time (Fig. 6.6). Entry into unskilled manual
employment has, at the same time, become increasingly common. This
picture of declining access to service-class and (to a lesser extent) other
non-manual positions is then repeated among individuals who gain
advanced (level 3) credentials (see Fig. 6.7). Such qualifications have
become an increasingly ineffective safeguard against entry to the labour
market via working-class employment. Of those born before 1930, fewer
than 30 per cent entered via blue-collar jobs, a figure which had risen to
well over half (some 56 per cent) among those born during the 1960s
and 1970s.

Higher–tertiary (degree-level) qualifications alone have emerged as
the level of education needed for an individual to have a high probability of entering the labour market via the desirable occupational positions to be found within the salariat (see Fig. 6.8). Across all cohorts,
over 60 per cent of individuals holding such credentials entered the
labour market via the service class, with a further 10 to 20 per cent going

into routine clerical employment. Even at this level of educational attainment, however, entrance via unskilled manual employment has become more frequent. Roughly 5 per cent of those holding degree-level certificates among the earlier cohorts commenced their working lives in unskilled manual jobs, a figure which rose to 12 per cent among those born during the 1950s, and almost 15 per cent among those born in 1960 or more recently.

In summary then, and doubtless unsurprisingly, it is evident from these data that educational qualifications have a strong bearing on people's class of first employment. Individuals gaining low-level qualifications most frequently enter the labour market via unskilled and skilled manual jobs. Those born since 1960, and with an education as high as the lower tertiary level, have—for the first time during the period under review—become more likely to enter manual jobs than employment in the salariat, despite concurrent shifts in the class

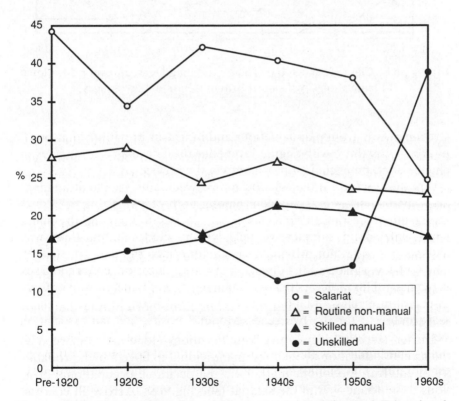

FIGURE 6.7. Class of First Job of Those Attaining Advanced Educational Qualifications, by Cohort, Britain (Outflow Percentages)

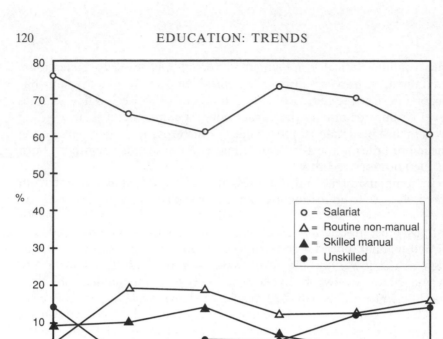

FIGURE 6.8. Class of First Job of Those Attaining Degree-Level Educational
Qualifications, by Cohort, Britain (Outflow Percentages)

structure away from manual labour and in favour of white-collar occupations. Only those with degree-level education have a better than even
chance of commencing employment via the service class.

Are these trends in the relationship between educational attainment
and labour-market entry evident among both sexes? Table 6.4 shows
the results of testing the relevant models separately among the males
and females in our samples. Model 3, which includes all four three-way
associations, does not provide a satisfactory fit to the data (p = 0.030).
The four-level association between first class, education, cohort, and sex
is required. This indicates that the changing role of education, over time,
in determining class of labour-market entry has been, to some extent at
least, different for the two sexes. Model 3 posits, first, an association
between education, initial occupation, and sex. This is evidence that
males and females, with comparable educational credentials, often enter different first employments. For example, of those with ordinary-
level qualifications, 58 per cent of females but only 13 per cent of males
enter employment via routine non-manual occupations. Males are,
throughout, more likely to enter via the skilled manual and salariat

TABLE 6.4. *Class of Labour-Market Entry (First Full-time Occupation) in Britain, by Educational Attainment, Cohort, and Sex: Models*

Model	G^2	df	p	rG^2	delta
1. E + F + C + S	3,990.9	179	0.000	—	32.8
2. EFS + EFC + ECS	85.8	60	0.016	97.9	3.2
3. EFS + EFC + ECS + FSC	64.5	45	0.030	98.4	2.7

N = 6,046.

Notes
1. Class of first (labour market entry) employment (F) has 4 levels: salariat (I, II); routine non-manual (IIIa); skilled manual (V, VI); and unskilled manual (VIIa + b, IIIb).
2. Education (E) and cohort (C) are as in Table 6.2.
3. G^2 = log-likelihood ratio; rG^2 = % reduction in G^2 (treating the main effects model as baseline); delta = % of misclassified cases.

classes. Secondly, model 3 includes an association between education, cohort, and sex. As was demonstrated earlier in this chapter, the improvements in the attainment of qualifications across the six cohorts have been different for the two sexes, with males making greater gains at the higher–tertiary stage and females gaining more at intermediate levels. Also included in model 3 is an association between first employment, cohort, and sex. This can be interpreted as showing that, regardless of educational attainment, the class of first employment has changed differently for the two sexes over time. However, note that the removal of this association from model 3 confirms it to be unimportant, as can be seen by comparing the results for model 2. The more complex third model reduces the deviance by only 21, for the sacrifice of 15 degrees of freedom, which is a statistically non-significant improvement (p = 0.128). Finally, model 3 includes an association between education, first employment, and cohort. In other words, the relationship between education and class of first employment has changed across the cohorts, as indeed we observed above. However, and to reiterate, the fact that we need the four-way EFCS association to fit the data adequately suggests that these changes have been slightly different for the two sexes.

These data on labour-market entry tend to undermine the thesis of increasing merit-selection through education. The bond between educational attainment and class of first employment has not been tightening. Indeed, to the contrary, even tertiary (level 3) qualifications have proved to be an increasingly ineffective safeguard against commencing one's working life in some form of manual employment. However, while the relationship between educational credentials and class of first employment is of substantive interest in its own right, it cannot provide a conclusive component in our test of the IMS hypothesis. Most obviously, the expansion of higher and tertiary education in Britain (particularly via the alternative route) has meant that increasing numbers of individuals return to gain qualifications after an initial spell in employment, or obtain certificates through part-time study whilst already in work. The qualifications gained are therefore of possibly questionable relevance to the first employment of these people.[5]

With this possible drawback in mind, therefore, we must now turn to compare the relationship between educational attainment and class of destination, as this is apparent in cross-sectional surveys of the British class structure at two different points in time, in our particular case some twenty or so years apart.

IV

The first of these surveys is provided by the Oxford Mobility Study of 1972. It will be remembered that the researchers drew a representative sample of adult males only in England and Wales. Our second data-set has again been obtained by pooling, and comprises the British General Election Studies of 1987 and 1992. In essence this provides a 'current' class distribution. In order to maintain comparability we have excluded all females and inhabitants of Scotland and Northern Ireland from the election studies. No relevant interaction effects are detected when the two General Election Surveys are combined in this way.[6]

The results reflect the changes in British society that were emphasized above: occupational shifts away from skilled manual labour towards the professional, administrative, and managerial positions of the salariat class, coupled with a proliferation in the attainment of educational qualifications. Table 6.5 illustrates both processes, and shows how the distributions of educational qualifications and class of destination have changed during the years between our two surveys. The percentage of employed male respondents educated to the lowest level only has dropped from 55 to 33 during these two decades, while all levels of educational attainment above this minimum have become more widespread. The changing class structure (among males at least) is evident in the lower section of the table. The salariat and routine non-manual classes have greatly expanded, while other forms of male employment (most notably skilled manual) have declined. Given these changes, both in the labour market and the attainment of educational qualifications,

TABLE 6.5. *Percentage Distribution of Educational Qualifications and Class of Destination, among Males in England and Wales, 1972 and 1987–1992*

	1972	1987–1992
Educational level		
Low	55	33
Ordinary	31	38
Advanced	10	18
Degree	4	11
Class destination		
I	13	20
II	12	17
IIIa	9	6
V/VI	33	23
VII, IIIb	23	21

N = (1972) 9,250; (1987–92) 1,915.

has the relationship between the two tightened or weakened during the past twenty years?

Table 6.6 shows the percentage outflow from each of the educational levels to class destinations at the time of the surveys. Clearly, both in 1972 and more recently, education has exerted a great influence upon the type of occupation obtained. The higher the level of qualification held, the greater the prospects of attaining the more desirable salariat positions, and of avoiding working-class employment. The great majority of males with degree-level qualifications are found in salariat occupations. Those with low-level education usually occupy manual positions. How, if at all, has this pattern changed over time?

The employment experience of those males gaining degree-level qualifications has remained remarkably constant over the past two decades. In both surveys, roughly 90 per cent are found in salariat positions, with a further 5 per cent in routine non-manual employment and 1 or 2 per cent in the working class. This level of education still appears to be as effective in securing the most desirable salariat employment as it was two decades ago. The increased numbers of males educated to degree level would seem to have been offset by an expansion of the salariat class.

Among the most poorly educated there is also some degree of constancy over time. The percentage reaching the salariat class despite low educational attainment has risen slightly, from 11 to 13 per cent. The

TABLE 6.6. *Outflow Percentages from Different Educational Attainment Levels to Class Destinations, among Males in England and Wales, 1972 and 1987–1992*

Educational level	Class destination					N
	I	II	IIIa	V/VI	VII/IIIb	
1972						
Low	5	6	9	33	36	5,067
Ordinary	12	12	10	45	11	2,892
Advanced	44	32	9	10	2	940
Degree	57	33	5	1	1	351
1987–92						
Low	5	8	3	24	44	626
Ordinary	13	16	7	33	14	721
Advanced	37	23	10	17	7	349
Degree	58	35	5	0	1	219

N = (1972) 9,250; (1987–92) 1,915.

proportion engaged in working-class employment is also fairly stable over time (69 per cent in 1972 and 68 per cent currently)—although unskilled manual work has become more common at the expense of skilled working-class occupations. At this particular educational level, the percentage of respondents engaged in unskilled manual jobs has risen from 36 to 44, while skilled workers have been reduced from 33 to 24 per cent of the male workforce.

These results neither refute nor confirm the argument that there has been a tightening bond between educational attainment and class outcomes. It is among males with middling levels of educational attainment that evidence against the IMS hypothesis emerges. Those holding advanced (level 3) qualifications have become markedly less successful in obtaining salariat employment and avoiding manual work. Among this group, there has been a reduction from 76 to 60 per cent in the take-up of salariat positions, while the percentage found in manual work has doubled from 12 to 24. Clearly, therefore, the employment prospects of males educated to this level have deteriorated considerably. Those with the inferior ordinary (level 2) qualifications have, in contrast, had marginally increased success in the labour market. The percentage reaching salariat positions has risen from 24 to 29 per cent as the manual participation rate has dropped from 56 to 47.

In summary, therefore, these findings also would seem on balance to count against the thesis of increasing merit-selection. They point to a substantial degree of constancy over time in the association between the highest or lowest qualifications and the likely class of destination. However, the expanding room at the top of the class structure seems increasingly to be occupied by growing numbers of individuals educated to degree level or equivalent, so that whereas 14 per cent of males found in salariat (class I and II) positions in the 1972 survey were educated to this level, the proportion so qualified twenty years later had precisely doubled. Men holding advanced (level 3) qualifications have become progressively disadvantaged, over the years, in the competition to secure desirable positions in the salariat. Finally, the fact that those with the poorest qualifications (level 1 and in particular level 2) have also become marginally more successful in securing salariat employment tells most obviously against a steadily tightening bond between educational attainment and class outcomes.

V

What do our data indicate about the direct effect of social origins on class destinations—that is, the effect after controlling for educational attainment? This brings us to the third and last of the relationships that comprise the meritocratic triad.

The direct transmission of class advantage (or disadvantage) from one generation to the next would seem to go against the functional requirement for advanced industrial nations to utilize their human resources most efficiently. It also stands in apparent opposition to prevalent conceptions of social justice, including those of equality of opportunity and desert as the basis of reward. According to the meritocratic thesis, the association between class origins and class destinations should diminish over time, except in so far as that association is mediated by educational attainment. In order, therefore, to assess the net influence of class of origin on class destination, the effect of education must be controlled, and in this case—for reasons of clarity in exposition—we do so via a logistic regression analysis. (The technique of logistic regression is outlined briefly in Appendix B.)

The upper section of Table 6.7 shows the regression results for the effects of educational attainment on whether or not salariat employment is gained, separately for 1972 and 1987–92. Column 3 (labelled O.R.) gives the odds ratios for individuals educated to, respectively, ordinary, advanced, and degree-level, gaining salariat employment, when compared to individuals educated to the lowest educational level. In other words, educational level 1 is taken as the baseline, against

TABLE 6.7. *Logistic Regression of the Effects of Education on Gaining Access to Salariat and Higher-Salariat Employment, among Males in England and Wales, 1972 and 1987–1992*

	1972			1987–1992		
	B	S.E.	O.R.	B	S.E.	O.R.
Salariat						
Constant	−1.93	(0.05)		−1.73	(0.13)	
Educational level						
2	0.93	(0.06)	2.5	1.12	(0.16)	3.1
3	3.26	(0.10)	26.0	2.37	(0.18)	10.7
4	4.47	(0.21)	87.4	4.40	(0.30)	81.5
(N = 7,859)				(N = 1,507)		
Higher salariat						
Constant	−2.77	(0.07)		−2.89	(0.21)	
Educational level						
2	0.91	(0.09)	2.5	1.16	(0.24)	3.2
3	2.61	(0.09)	13.6	2.45	(0.24)	11.6
4	3.14	(0.13)	23.1	3.24	(0.25)	25.5
(N = 7,859)				(N = 1,507)		

Notes
1. B = parameter estimates; S.E. = standard errors for these estimates; O.R. = odds ratios.
2. Parameter estimates and odds ratios for ordinary (2), advanced (3), and degree-level (4) qualifications are relative to low (1) qualifications.

which the other odds ratios are then calculated. Thus the odds ratio of gaining salariat employment among individuals holding advanced-level (level 3) credentials as opposed to those with low-level (level 1) attainment, is 26.0. By the time of the second survey (1987–92) sons educated to this advanced level have become 10.7 times more likely to obtain salariat positions than are those educated to the lowest level. This illustrates the devaluation of these advanced-level qualifications that was noted above. It is also evident that the benefits of degree-level qualifications (relative to low-level) have decreased very slightly, and that those holding ordinary-level certificates have had slightly increased success in gaining salariat positions, when compared with the most poorly educated.

The lower section of Table 6.7 then gives regression results for access to the higher salariat (Goldthorpe class I) in particular. It is here that the most privileged professional, administrative, and managerial positions are to be found. Comparison of the results from the two surveys indicates that access to positions in the higher salariat is increasingly associated with degree-level qualifications (albeit only slightly so). Over the twenty or so years between the surveys, the odds ratio for degree-level qualifications in relation to low-level qualifications has increased from 23.1 to 25.5, although the devaluation of advanced-level qualifications is not so marked as it is in the case of the salariat as a whole (the relevant odds ratio here decreases only from 13.6 to 11.6).[7]

These results reinforce our earlier analysis of the relationship between educational attainment and class destinations—although the findings are here presented more parsimoniously. The direct effect of class origins on access to salariat destinations can be assessed in similar fashion (see Table 6.8). From the upper section of the table we see that, both in 1972 and 1987–92, an individual's class of origin has a substantial net influence on whether he or she arrives at a salariat destination. That is, regardless of qualifications obtained, individuals from the more advantaged class backgrounds tend to have greatest success in gaining salariat positions. However, this influence has (with one exception, relating to sons from routine non-manual backgrounds) become somewhat less important over time.

The reduction is most obvious among those from salariat (and in particular higher-salariat) backgrounds. For example, the results suggest that, after controlling for educational attainment, the odds on securing salariat employment for those respondents whose origins lay in the higher salariat, relative to individuals from unskilled manual backgrounds, declined from 6.0 to 2.2, during the years between the Oxford and later surveys. Among sons from lower salariat homes, the corresponding odds declined from 3.8 to 2.0. Of course, these findings mean that it is still the case that males having social origins in the salariat are more than twice as likely to arrive at salariat destinations than are males with equivalent qualifications who were born into the working class. Nevertheless, while the direct effect of class origins on one's chances of obtaining salariat employment remains significant, it has declined over the past twenty or so years—at least according to the information available in these particular data-sets.

The picture is similar among those employed in the higher salariat. A substantial net class-of-origin effect is evident throughout (see the lower panel of Table 6.8). In 1972, sons from class I and class II origins were respectively almost six and three times more likely to arrive at higher-salariat destinations than were their unskilled and semi-skilled working-class peers, after controlling for educational achievement. Comparison with the corresponding odds ratios for the 1987–92 survey also suggests

TABLE 6.8. *Logistic Regression of the Effects of Education and Net Effect of Class of Origin on Gaining Access to Salariat and Higher-Salariat Employment, among Males in England and Wales, 1972 and 1987–1992*

	1972			1987–1992		
	B	S.E.	O.R.	B	S.E.	O.R.
Access to the salariat						
Constant	−2.31	(0.07)		−1.97	(0.17)	
Educational level						
2	0.79	(0.07)	2.2	1.03	(0.16)	2.8
3	2.98	(0.10)	19.6	2.17	(0.18)	8.7
4	4.02	(0.21)	55.6	4.13	(0.32)	62.4
Class origin						
V/VI	0.27	(0.08)	1.3	0.12	(0.17)	1.1
IV	0.81	(0.10)	2.2	0.72	(0.22)	2.0
III	0.79	(0.11)	2.2	1.02	(0.29)	2.8
II	1.33	(0.13)	3.8	0.69	(0.23)	2.0
I	1.79	(0.13)	6.0	0.79	(0.19)	2.2
(N = 7,859)				(N = 1,507)		
Access to the higher salariat						
Constant	−3.15	(0.10)		−3.12	(0.25)	
Educational level						
2	0.76	(0.09)	2.1	1.06	(0.24)	2.9
3	2.26	(0.10)	9.6	2.23	(0.25)	9.3
4	2.61	(0.14)	13.5	2.94	(0.26)	18.9
Class origin						
V/VI	0.27	(0.10)	1.3	0.03	(0.21)	1.0
IV	0.71	(0.13)	2.0	0.80	(0.25)	2.2
III	0.79	(0.14)	2.2	0.84	(0.30)	2.3
II	1.07	(0.14)	2.9	0.55	(0.26)	1.7
I	1.72	(0.13)	5.6	0.91	(0.24)	2.5
(N = 7,859)				(N = 1,507)		

Notes
1. Parameter estimates and odds ratios for ordinary (2), advanced (3), and degree-level (4) qualifications are relative to low (1) qualifications.
2. Parameter estimates for the skilled manual (V/VI), *petite bourgeoisie* and farming (IV), routine non-manual (III), lower salariat (II), and higher salariat (I) classes are relative to the unskilled working class (VII).

a decreasing direct influence of class background. Furthermore, in the case of both surveys, class of origin would appear to be no more influential in securing access to Class I than to the wider salariat as a whole. In short, and taken together, these findings point to a still substantial—but significantly weakening—direct effect of class background on class destination.

VI

In this chapter we have examined, in turn, changes over time in the influence of social origins on educational attainment; in the relationship between qualifications gained and class of labour-market entry and destination; and, finally, in the direct effect of social origins on class destinations after allowing for educational achievements.

The evidence itself seems complex but clear. Although the attainment of qualifications above the basic educational level has become more common over successive birth-cohorts, differentials relating to class origins have been maintained, and among both sexes alike. Inequalities in the attainment of degree-level qualifications have actually widened, so that whereas the gap between those gaining such qualifications from unskilled manual and salariat backgrounds was some 13 percentage points among those born before 1920, this differential has more than doubled by the time we reach the cohort born during the 1950s.

Moreover, and turning to the relationship between educational attainment and occupational outcomes, it is precisely these degree-level qualifications that provide the best guarantee of securing employment in the service class. Both the Oxford Mobility Study and the more recent General Election Surveys show that 90 per cent (or more) of men holding such qualifications arrive at destinations in the service class. At the lowest levels (1 and 2) of educational achievement, the proportion of men securing salariat employment has marginally increased, while the corresponding percentage has been considerably reduced among those holding lower tertiary and high-school (level 3) certificates. This is an uneven pattern that is hard to reconcile with the hypothesis of a tightening bond between educational attainment and class outcomes.

Finally, and allowing for changes over time in both of the associations involving educational attainment, the evidence does seem to suggest that the net influence of class origins on class destinations remains substantial but has declined during the past twenty or so years. Given the same level of educational attainment, the odds of a man reaching the salariat from a class I or class II background have been approximately halved, relative to those for a man from an unskilled manual background. In other words, as a corollary of the greater mediating role played by education, the direct (partial or net) influence of origins on destinations has diminished. Of course, as we have seen in earlier chapters, this does not imply a weakening in the overall association between origins and destinations. Our analysis of intergenerational mobility rates in Britain (and several other countries) confirms the findings obtained in most earlier studies, and demonstrates that social fluidity (that is, relative mobility chances, or the association between origins and destinations, net of the effects of structural change) shows a high degree of constancy over time.

These results can be set alongside those reported by the various studies that were summarized early in Chapter 5. On that occasion we noted a substantial measure of disagreement among previous researchers. At least some of the apparent contradictions can now be resolved by reference to our more detailed analysis.

For example, like Anthony Heath and his colleagues we find a generally unchanging association between class origins and educational achievement, although our data also show that class differentials in the attainment of degree-level qualifications have indeed widened—and to that extent A. H. Halsey is not incorrect when he suggests that there has been *some* increase in the association between social origins and educational achievement. Similarly, like Heath and his associates we too find that middling-level educational credentials are a declining asset in labour markets, although this may then also explain Halsey's claim that there is a tightening bond between education and destinations—since degree-level qualifications are, it seems, increasingly a requirement for specifically service-class employment. In short, there are interaction effects over time in both relationships, so that the association between class origins and educational attainment on the one hand and between educational attainment and class destinations on the other has indeed changed—but only with respect to certain levels of educational qualification.

At least some of the earlier disagreements may therefore be due simply to different researchers looking at distinctive elements of each association—perhaps because of the variety of statistical techniques that have been employed. Heath and Halsey were possibly describing different aspects of what are now revealed to be uneven associations about which it is hard to generalize across all four educational levels. These sorts of (largely undetected) interaction effect might then also explain apparent contradictions elsewhere in the existing literature.

Empirical complications such as this certainly do help explain why the seemingly straightforward problem of determining the extent to which unequal class mobility chances reflect merit-selection through education invokes such a complex sociological analysis. More fundamentally, however, as we made clear at the outset, the interpretation of findings even as measured as our own raises further—theoretical—issues that earlier researchers in this field have tended to ignore. Put most broadly, these concern the extent to which it is legitimate to identify 'merit' with education, and hence what conclusions about meritocracy can be inferred from data about the role of education in mediating the intergenerational transmission of advantage. It is to this difficult and complex issue that we devote our next chapter.

NOTES

1. Textual sources giving technical details of all but one of these surveys have been indicated in previous chapters. On the 1983 General Election Survey, see Heath et al. (1985). The surveys from 1983 (General Election Study) and 1984 (Essex Class Project) were excluded from the previous chapter, which concentrates on the patterns to be found in the 'snapshot' picture available from the (more or less contemporaneous) surveys fielded in 1991–2, but are here included since the focus in this chapter is on the changing experience of birth-cohorts over time.
2. Note that, in this and subsequent graphs, broken lines have been used to draw attention to the youngest cohort (born during the 1960s). The attainment of higher–tertiary qualifications among these individuals is, especially in the case of the salariat and routine non-manual classes, greatly reduced from that witnessed among the previous cohort (see Fig. 6.4). However, this is an artefactual rather than a substantive finding, and due simply to the fact that some people aged 25 and over had not completed their (higher–tertiary) educational careers at the time of interview. This would appear to have affected the salariat and routine non-manual classes disproportionately. The effects of this on the proportions ultimately attaining the lower educational levels should also, therefore, be borne in mind. This would explain the recent upward trend in the proportion of children from salariat homes apparently reaching only the lowest educational level (as indicated in Fig. 6.2).
3. Cf. e.g. Jonsson (1991), who considers both class of first job and present class separately; Breen and Whelan (1993), who focus upon first jobs; and Heath et al. (1992), who examine the meritocracy thesis in relationship only to class destinations (current jobs). In large part the sociological dispute here hinges upon the role played by educational qualifications at point of entry into the labour market. Some have argued that educational attainment exerts its most importance influence during the time at which an individual obtains his or her first formal employment: beyond this point, other criteria become more significant in securing successful job-shifts and promotions, so it follows that the thesis of merit-selection through education can most appropriately be tested in relation to first jobs. However, this argument neglects the

substantial numbers of qualifications that are obtained by means of part-time education secured concurrently with employment, via the alternative route—qualifications which may or may not then be important for subsequent occupational attainment. Because controversy about this issue continues, we have followed the conservative strategy of analysing the relationship between educational achievement and both first job and class destination.

4. Goldthorpe class IV (the *petite bourgeoisie*) has been excluded from the analysis, as a class of first job, and for the same reasons as were explained in Ch. 5.

5. One recent account (Kerckhoff 1990: chs. 1, 2, and 6) has suggested that qualifications obtained via part-time further education are of increasing importance for explaining the transition from school to work in Great Britain in particular. Kerckhoff's findings are consistent with those reported in earlier studies, and show both that credentials gained after labour-force entry have a substantial effect on later levels of occupational prestige among British males (over and above the effects of educational attainment before commencing employment) and that the importance of this alternative route to educational qualifications is much greater in this country than in the US. Note, in this context, that the surveys referred to in our own exposition did not collect 'educational histories' of respondents. Typically, information was obtained about only the 'highest qualification held', a limitation in the data which helps explain our rather different analytical strategy.

6. Readers may recall that our earlier analysis of the 'current' class distribution for Britain, as reported in Ch. 4, was based on data from the 1991 British Social Justice Project as well as the two election surveys. Unfortunately, the BSJP survey does not distinguish between residents of England and Wales on the one hand and Scotland on the other. We have therefore omitted these data in order to facilitate comparison with the Oxford study.

7. Of course, the findings for the higher salariat also show that the odds ratios at educational level 4 tend to be smaller than those found among the salariat as a whole; but this merely reflects the fact that, whereas in the upper section of the table the odds demonstrate different chances (at varying levels of educational attainment) of gaining access to the whole salariat as against all other class positions, those in the lower portion of the table show the chances of gaining access to the upper salariat as against all other class positions (including the lower salariat itself). Since 'other class destinations' now incorporates Goldthorpe class II—individuals in the lower service class of whom many hold degree-level qualifications—the odds will be diminished in comparison with the earlier analysis contrasting the salariat as a whole with other class destinations.

7

Meritocracy

I

It may be helpful, before tackling the difficult question of how exactly the empirical findings reported in previous chapters relate to issues of meritocracy, to remind readers of the structure of our book thus far.

We began by noting that matters of inequality and social justice are hotly contested in both political and academic debate. We then attempted, in Chapter 2, to identify the different principles of justice in terms of which one might seek to defend class inequalities as just. Distinguishing between equality of outcome and equality of opportunity, we indicated that our focus in this study would be on the latter, and in particular on the question of whether class inequalities can be justified on meritocratic grounds. Chapter 3 explained the conception of class that we would be using, and Chapter 4 proceeded empirically to assess patterns of social mobility, as between the various class positions so identified. Making clear the difference between absolute and relative mobility rates, we explained why the latter are particularly relevant to an investigation of issues of equality of opportunity, and we found, in line with a number of previous similar studies, that in a wide variety of advanced societies (including Britain) the chances of achieving advantaged class positions are distributed unequally—and, seemingly, unchangingly—between children born into more or less advantaged classes of origin.

Where some have considered such findings as evidence of inequality of opportunity, and therefore as testimony to social injustice, we were concerned to take seriously the possibility that they might be consistent with social justice understood in meritocratic terms. Might not the association between origins and destinations reflect the unequal distribution of meritorious attributes between those born into the various social classes? In that case, inequalities in class mobility chances need not indicate any inequalities of opportunity, as between those possessed of similar capacities and abilities.

Accordingly, in Chapters 5 and 6, we looked at the role of education in the intergenerational transmission of advantage. We reported, in Chapter 5, that a person's class of origin substantially influences his or her class of destination, even when the role of education has been taken into account, implying that class-related processes operate independently of education to play a significant role in the selection of people for more or less desirable occupations. Then, in Chapter 6, we examined, for the case of Britain, the changing role of education in this intergenerational transmission of advantage. We considered, in turn, the three associations that constitute the meritocratic triad. We found, first, that the direct effect of origins on destinations has declined somewhat over the past twenty or so years. Second, class inequalities in educational attainment have widened, over the same period. Finally, and in broad terms, the association between educational achievement and class destinations has remained more or less constant over time.

In sum, the main story of the book thus far is one of basically unchanging inequality in class intergenerational mobility chances, although rather more of the association between origins and destinations has, in recent years, been mediated by educational attainment.

In telling this story we have drawn on a variety of different survey data-sets, paying special attention to issues of reliability and comparability of the relevant variables (recoding these, where necessary, by means of our own specially developed algorithms), and also examined a number of related issues in class analysis. For example, we have intervened in the contemporary debate about the relationship between class and gender, and explored the implications of non-vertical social mobility for arguments about social justice. In passing, we replicated—twenty years on—the classic Oxford Social Mobility Study, and extended the range of countries examined as part of the subsequent CASMIN Project.

In other words, even without going into the minefield that surrounds the question of how our empirical findings can be interpreted in relation to matters of meritocracy, we can claim to have contributed in other ways to the existing sociological literature on class generally and on the role played by education in social mobility in particular.

II

That minefield can, however, no longer be avoided. Unlike previous researchers, who in our view have tended to overlook, or at least to underestimate, the problems involved in any attempt to interpret data of the kind reported in previous chapters, we think it important to address the complexities inherent in any such interpretation. As the above summary makes clear, we were ready to acknowledge the invalidity of inferences from data on class mobility to conclusions about social injustice and inequality of opportunity; indeed, it was that acknowledgement, and our taking seriously the possibility of a meritocratic defence of mobility patterns, that motivated the introduction of data on education into our analyses. It would be convenient if, having thus described the role of education, we could present our results as decisive. We fear, however, that matters remain unhappily inconclusive.

The problem, of course, and as we made clear when we started to investigate the role of education in mobility processes, is that one cannot straightforwardly identify education with merit. If one could, then the implications of our findings for arguments about meritocracy would be fairly straightforward, since any association between origins and destinations that was not mediated by the influence of social origins on educational attainment would indicate a lack of meritocracy. Our findings could then readily be taken to show that mobility processes in Britain are far from meritocratic; and, moreover, that opportunities for those with similar levels of education to acquire advantaged class positions are distributed considerably less equally in Britain than in most of the other industrialized societies for which we have comparable data. Our finding that the association between origins and destinations, net of educational achievement, has tended to reduce over a twenty-year period would, however, indicate that Britain has (in these terms at least) been getting more meritocratic. That is, although the overall influence of origins on destinations has remained almost constant, the fact that more of this influence has operated via the *ex hypothesi* meritocratic channel of educational achievement means that the educationally equal are increasingly being treated alike. To the extent that one regarded meritocratic principles as sufficient to justify class inequalities, with social justice achieved by a meritocratic allocation of individuals to class positions, one might conclude that Britain is not just—but is gradually becoming more so.

There would, of course, still be a good deal of room for haggling over details and nuances of emphasis. On the one hand, some would doubtless stress the extent to which the inequalities that constitute the British class structure remain unjustified, even when so many assumptions are granted to the meritocratic defence. They would insist, for example, on the overwhelming significance of our finding that individuals with low levels of educational attainment from service-class origins are four times more likely to achieve service-class employment than are similarly educated people born into the working class. Likewise, they would emphasize that, in modelling the data on class mobility and educational attainment, the association between origins and destinations (the OD term in the model) reduces by more than two-thirds the deviance in our baseline model of merit-selection by education (OE + ED), and almost halves the proportion of misclassified cases. When these results are generalized to the population of Britain as a whole, they imply that there are many individuals whose class destiny is influenced by their class origins in ways that interfere with the conversion of educational into occupational achievement.

On this account, the important lesson from our research would be that class inequalities in Britain cannot be defended as just, even if one equates social justice with meritocracy and regards education as an adequate indicator of merit.

On the other hand, those concerned to reconcile our findings with meritocratic claims would perhaps point to the relative crudity of some of our analyses, and seek to emphasize the extent of the changes over time that we have identified. As regards the former point, for example, our strategy has been to group manifold educational qualifications into four levels, each of which necessarily contains a range of attainments. It may be that more of the variation in destinations would be explained by education, and less attributable to origins alone, in models that had a more nuanced approach to the measurement of credentials. Perhaps people from service-class origins are disproportionately achieving quali-fications at the top end of our categories? It could then be this properly meritocratic criterion which goes some way towards explaining their relative advantage in terms of destinations. This would, in effect, be to object that we do not compare people from different class backgrounds with sufficiently similar levels of educational attainment. Since there is an overall association between origins and education, it is at least plaus-ible to think that there will be an association between them within the educational categories that we distinguish, and this may mitigate— although it cannot completely subvert—any inferences about lack of meritocracy.[1]

Those who sought to cast doubt on or to diminish our argument that meritocratic processes remain far from complete would doubtless also make much of our observations regarding changes in such processes over time. They would point, for example, to our finding that, given the same level of educational attainment, the odds of a man reaching the higher salariat from a higher-salariat background, relative to those of a man reaching the higher salariat from an unskilled manual background, were approximately halved between 1972 and 1987–92. Alternatively, they might point to the apparent convergence of class inequalities at the middling levels of educational attainment, especially among those who obtain qualifications of what we have characterized as an intermediate vocational and general (level 2) type. Here is evidence, they would insist, that Britain is steadily becoming a genuine meritocracy.

These are the kinds of minor skirmish and variation of emphasis that would survive even among those who were agreed in identifying education with merit. The real and important arguments that have now to be addressed are, however, those that dispute precisely this identification.

One helpful way to divide up the various issues raised by such arguments is to locate them in terms of the three associations that together form the meritocratic triad which we introduced as Fig. 5.1. First, and with regard to the association between origins and education (O–E), note that to treat people's formal qualifications as a satisfactory indicator of their merits is to assume that the unequal distribution of educational attainments between those born into different classes accurately reflects the distribution of merit. Second, and with regard to the association between education and destination (E–D), observe that to welcome any increase in the linkage between people's credentials and their occupational destinations as a move in the direction of meritocracy is to assume that educational qualifications are an adequate indicator of those meritorious attributes relevant to the performance of different occupational roles. Finally, and with regard to the association between class origins and class destinations (O–D), notice that to deem unmeritocratic any effect of origin on destination that does not go via people's educational achievements is to assume that there are no class-related meritorious attributes other than those that manifest themselves in educational terms. We shall consider these assumptions in turn. As we will see, the arguments concerning the interpretation of these three associations tend to invoke different conceptions of merit, so that the term 'merit' comes to be used in quite diverse senses by different people.

III

In the context of arguments about meritocracy, it is the interpretation of the association between people's class background and their educational achievements that is most obviously problematic. Sociologists have devoted a great deal of effort to the empirical study of this association, and there is fairly widespread agreement both that inequalities in educational outcomes between those born into different classes are substantial, and that they have not changed much over the years in most industrialized societies. That is, although the average level of educational attainment has risen overall within advanced societies, especially in the half-century since the Second World War, if the effects of this expansion are allowed for, then class differentials in educational attainment can be seen to have changed little across successive cohorts throughout most of the twentieth century.[2]

Against this background many sociologists have concluded that such persistent inequalities of outcome reflect a variety of class biases that are entrenched within national systems of schooling. Class differences in educational attainment are the result, not of an unequal distribution of meritorious attributes, but of forms of discrimination along class lines— in terms of access to, provision of, selection for, and treatment within educational regimes. It has been argued, for example, that class disparities in educational achievement are the result of one (or some combination) of the following: labelling, by middle-class teachers, of working-class children as 'under-achievers' in the classroom; prejudice, again on the part of the educational authorities, in tracking working-class children into less ambitious and less adequately resourced streams, schools, or colleges; the culturally loaded organizational ethos of schools, which includes a (sometimes 'hidden') curriculum and examinations that favour children from middle-class homes, or having middle-class verbal and other skills; residential segregation or zoning, which—together with the catchment-area policies practised by schools—serves to isolate working-class children from their middle-class peers, invariably in financially disadvantaged establishments; and, perhaps most obviously, the continued provision of private education for those whose parents are able to pay. This list is, of course, far from exhaustive.[3]

Others have pointed, not to mechanisms by which the educational system discriminates against working-class children, but rather to the way that the relative material disadvantages of those born into working-class homes manifest themselves as handicaps to educational achievement. Children with bedrooms of their own, those who do not need to undertake casual work for financial reward, and those with access to books or (increasingly) computers may find it easier to do homework, and in other ways to concentrate upon and make progress in their studies, than do those without these advantages. In so far as educational institutions quite properly reward children who are better prepared to take exams, it would be hard to argue that there was any discrimination involved here, but to the extent that one accepted that factors such as these influence how children perform at school and develop academically, it would also be difficult to sustain the claim that there was genuine equality of opportunity.[4]

From these sorts of standpoint, any analysis that regards education as an adequate indicator of merit is over-charitable, since it ignores the ways in which class-related factors enter into and distort the process by which people's abilities are rewarded in educational terms. This rejection of educational achievement as a sufficient measure of merit necessarily then affects the interpretation of any changes that may be observed in the relation between origins and education. For example, it is because he assumes that people's formal qualifications do not accurately convey their actual merits that Halsey (1977: 184) is able (as we have seen) to interpret his finding of a strengthening association between an individual's class origins and his or her level of educational attainment as evidence that parents from advantaged class backgrounds are 'playing the education game' with increasing success, rather than as proof of a genuine expansion in the process of merit-selection through education.

Against this view, however, it has been argued by some that the inference from inequality of educational outcome to a lack of meritocracy, or to inequality of educational opportunity, is invalid. The association between origins and education may be the result, instead, of an unequal distribution of attributes that are quite properly rewarded by educational systems and reflected in educational outcomes. Perhaps working-class children are less intelligent, on average, than are those born into the service class? Or perhaps, though equally intelligent, they are less motivated to achieve educationally, choosing not to apply their natural abilities to the acquisition of educational credentials? In either case, class inequalities in educational outcomes cannot be attributed to inequalities of opportunity, and (it has been concluded) do not therefore point to the lack of meritocracy. Let us consider these two suggestions separately and in reverse order.

IV

First, there is the possibility that the explanation for class inequalities in educational achievement lies, not in discrimination or material disadvantages of the kind outlined above, but in differential tastes for education or differential motivation to succeed educationally. According to James Murphy (1990: 41–2) at least, this view has become so widespread that 'most commentators now see aspiration and disposition as critical', and 'seem to regard the historic indifference of the disadvantaged as of at least equal significance to the more traditional rigidities in access and the like'. In these newer accounts, attention is focused instead upon such dispositional attributes as fatalism, inability to defer gratification, and indifference towards education.

There remains widespread disagreement as to the origins of these motivational and aspirational characteristics. For example, early cultural deprivation theorists (such as Herbert Hyman) attributed class differentials in educational outcomes to the various pathologies that were said to follow from poverty, including the absence, among lower-class groups, of supposedly middle-class traits like need for achievement, competitiveness, and willingness to innovate. A somewhat different subcultural twist was given to these arguments (most obviously in the work of Albert Cohen and David Hargreaves) by researchers who proposed that working-class children did in fact share the same goals as their middle-class peers, but being deprived (by externally imposed opportunity structures) of the means to achieve conformist ends, were motivated instead to develop oppositional (anti-educational) subcultures that offered alternative sources of status.[5]

Others have pointed instead to what Stephen Ball (1986: 41–2) describes as 'a realistic adjustment on the part of the working class to their circumstances'. One such interpretation, offered by a number of prominent rational-action theorists, suggests that, because of the dissimilar opportunities and constraints facing children from working-class and middle-class backgrounds, they (and their parents) are involved in different calculations of the possible costs and benefits of particular educational strategies. As children reach distinct transition points in the educational system, families must make choices (for example, to encourage sons and daughters to leave school or stay on, or to take vocational rather than academic courses) that are influenced by the structural constraints arising from the relationship between their different class origins and the destinations they envisage for their offspring. From this point of view, aspirations (say) to attend university on the part of working-class children are rather more ambitious than would be those same desires when expressed by their middle-class peers, and also involve the increased risks implied by the attempt to travel a greater social distance. Any tendency among working-class children to pursue less demanding courses of study, or to obtain more modest qualifications and credentials, might therefore be the result, not of pathologies in the proletarian subculture, but of a rational evaluation of the probable gains and losses to be made from different educational strategies.

Thus, for some skilled working-class families containing bright children, the best option might appear to be a vocational course leading to a skilled manual job, offering relatively high initial wages, a fairly low risk of relegation into the ranks of the unskilled or unemployed, and a high probability of early promotion to a supervisory position—rather than an academic course, requiring not only continued investment in the child's education but also investment of a more hazardous kind (since downward mobility is perceived to be a likely consequence of a failed attempt to obtain academic qualifications). By comparison, middle-class families confronting the same decision about the future of their children would perhaps be more likely to choose the more ambitious option, since they have access to greater resources that might mitigate the consequences of educational failure—for example the ability to purchase extra tuition, or links into personal networks that could offer direct access to the labour market at a reasonably attractive level, despite the lack of formal qualifications.[6]

What all such accounts have in common is that they seek to explain differential motivations externally, as in some way adaptive, or as the product of relative social disadvantage or cultural deprivation.[7] In contrast to this kind of approach, Murphy (1990: 48–51) argues that such differences should be regarded simply as differences; that is, as 'another manifestation of difference in a culturally differentiated society', since not only is there no evidence for the claim as to the causal priority of structure over culture but, in his view, such evidence is in principle unavailable. For Murphy, indeed, the unsupported and unsupportable assumption that working-class indifference to educational success needs to be remedied by social policy involves the illiberal imposition of middle-class values on members of the working class. This precludes the possibility that the working class might simply, and without anything pathological being involved, see the world, and the place of education in it, in a rather different light.

V

So much for arguments that seek to account for unequal educational outcomes in terms of contrasting motivations or choices. What of the rather different explanation that those born into the various social classes differ systematically in their possession of natural intelligence?

This is a proposition with a long and disputed academic pedigree. Intelligence, in this context, is normally measured by an Intelligence

Quotient (IQ) test. One of the first such tests was developed by Alfred Binet, in early twentieth-century France, for the purpose of identifying schoolchildren in need of remedial attention. The test attempted to gauge intellectual ability by measuring an individual's capacity to reason, identify patterns, and draw analogies. A large number of similar such mental tests have subsequently been devised, including for example the Lorge–Thorndike and Kuhlmann–Anderson Intelligence Tests, and most of these seek to provide a unitary indicator of each person's general intelligence. The results obtained from these tests tend to be highly intercorrelated.[8]

Almost from the outset, critics have argued that (among other things) it was unreasonable to assume that any such measure of intelligence could be objective, since the tests were in practice both culturally specific and class-related, for example tending to favour formal (and middle-class) linguistic abilities rather than other (perhaps artistic or informal) skills. Some later advocates suggested, controversially, that a battery of such tests measured a general intelligence which was genetically transmitted and consequently immutable. Critics replied that the technique had not been designed with the intention of providing an absolute measure of intelligence that was unamenable to improvement; and that, in any case, average IQ (as measured by the tests themselves) had demonstrably risen over the years in several countries, confirming that this supposedly innate characteristic was in fact (at least in part) open to social manipulation, for example by expanding the provision of education across populations. Estimates of the heritability of IQ ranged (and still range) between zero and 80 per cent. Various studies—all hotly contested—have since claimed that IQ is associated with class background (and, even more contentiously, with ethnicity and race).[9]

The relationship between IQ and social class in particular has recently become a focus for renewed academic discussion after being many years in abeyance. For example, in his critique of the class analysis tradition of research, Peter Saunders starts by pointing to Michael Young's (1958: 94) classic definition of merit as 'intelligence and effort', deduces that one might therefore expect research on social mobility to include evidence on these two characteristics, but observes that the question of ability has been largely overlooked in earlier studies (our own included). For Saunders, at least, measured intelligence is a good indicator of people's abilities—indeed, by ignoring data on real education and including simulated IQ scores in his analysis, he seems to imply that it is a better indicator of merit than is educational attainment. Furthermore, according to Saunders, many studies of class mobility arrive unwarrantably at conclusions about inequality of opportunity because researchers fail to take IQ into account. Much of the apparent 'class bias' in mobility outcomes might simply be 'a function of differences in average levels of measured intelligence between the classes'. Finally, while suspending judgement on the strong claim that as much as 80 per cent of the variance in IQ scores is due to hereditary factors, Saunders insists that 'it is difficult to avoid the conclusion that . . . IQ tests . . . do to some extent measure these variations in genetic endowments between different individuals'. Class differentials in educational (and occupational) outcomes do not therefore testify to lack of meritocracy; they may, rather, reflect 'differences in innate ability reflecting the different genetic endowments of different individuals'.[10]

There are two issues here, in principle distinct, but in practice interrelated when the matter of social class comes to the fore. One is the extent to which IQ tests (whether of general intelligence or of more specific mental characteristics such as vocational aptitude) improve upon educational attainment (qualifications or certificates obtained) as an indicator of 'merit'. The other concerns the degree to which intelligence is or is not a hereditary characteristic. Both are complex, although in the present context we can do little more than simply raise them as issues, given that each is already surrounded by a substantial literature.

On the one hand, for example, Richard Herrnstein and Charles Murray's recently controversial account of the relationship between class and intelligence in America (*The Bell Curve*) is only the latest in a long line of studies which argue along the same lines as does Saunders: that IQ is a good indicator of natural ability, and appears to be a largely inherited trait. On the other hand, sceptics have assembled no little evidence which casts doubt on both of these propositions, and concluded that educational attainment and IQ scores are both products, not only of putatively natural or genetic origins, but also of socially determined influences. Most obviously, the results of intelligence tests are (at least in part) a reflection of attributes such as miscellaneous information picked up at home and on television, and of the inclination (mainly instilled by school teaching) to try harder at this particular task than at any other. In other words, test results are partly a function of socialization, substantial aspects of which are already influenced by existing inequalities in the class distribution of resources. The argument here is that, as John Miner long ago observed, 'no test item that has ever been devised taps native potential directly, independent of the past life and learning of the respondent'.[11]

However, even if one rejects this reasoning and continues to regard

IQ as the more appropriate measure, there is evidence that leads critics to suggest that differences in measured intelligence do not in fact account for those class differences in the transmission of advantage and disadvantage which researchers such as Saunders have claimed might be justified in meritocratic terms. For example, the longitudinal data gathered over almost half a century in Britain by J. W. B. Douglas and his colleagues seem to show clearly that, during the years of tripartite selective secondary education, there were substantial social class-of-origin effects on the proportion of children entering grammar schools, even after controls were introduced for measured intelligence. Similarly, and again irrespective of test scores, children from non-manual backgrounds were more than twice as likely to stay on at school after the minimum leaving age had been reached.[12]

The association between origins and education is, then, a matter at once of widespread agreement and of intense disagreement. Few dispute that people's class of origin has a substantial influence on their educational achievements, but there is little agreement about the mechanisms by which this influence is effected. Discrimination in the education system, inequalities in relevant material and cultural resources, differences in attitudes to education, and the unequal possession of natural ability are perhaps the most important of such possible mechanisms. We do not claim to have provided more than a brief survey of the kinds of causal process that might be located within each of these categories. Our real purpose is to consider the implications of such explanations for issues of equality of opportunity, meritocracy, and social justice, a task we pursue in the following chapter. Before considering these implications, however, we must also address, albeit in similarly schematic fashion, the other two components of the meritocratic triad: the links between education and destination, on the one hand, and between origin and destination on the other.

VI

Suppose we granted, against the sociological orthodoxy, that the distribution of educational achievements as between those born into different classes reflects the distribution of actual abilities and real (that is, non-adaptive or in some other way pathological) motivations. With education accepted as a proper measure of merit in this sense, would it then follow that we could interpret any association between education and destination as meritocratic, and any lack of association as not so? In that case, after all, it might seem unproblematic to welcome as meritocratic a tight fit between the qualifications that people achieve and the jobs that they do (and hence the class positions that they occupy).

The reason why things are not so straightforward has to do with a crucial duality in the notion of merit as that concept is used in the meritocratic argument. When we discuss the association between origins and educational attainment, and how this relationship affects the question of meritocracy, we naturally have in mind the issue of whether the educational system properly rewards with educational qualifications those who are more rather than less able or motivated (non-adaptively) to acquire them. That was the issue to which we devoted the previous two sections of this chapter. But to equate the meritocratic distribution of individuals to occupations with an allocation on the basis of educational achievements is to take it for granted that educational qualifications provide an adequate indication of people's merits in a significantly different context. Here, what counts as a meritocratic allocation is, presumably, one in which people get jobs on the basis of their possession of the abilities and motivations to do those jobs (let us call these 'relevant competences'), rather than to acquire educational certificates. It is then an open and empirical question as to the extent to which educational qualifications accurately reveal these competences.

Of course, there are many types of job for which people's formal educational attainments can be regarded as a good indicator of their relevant competences, and in those cases we would indeed consider a close fit between education and occupation as being meritocratic. But there are many jobs for which the abilities certified by a person's school or college qualifications are much less relevant than are other possibly independent attributes—such as displaying a pleasant manner, being sensitive to the feelings of others, or having a willingness to take risks.

For example, there is a growing range of personal-service occupations (such as those involving sales or public relations) for which cognitive abilities may be less important than are a number of social skills, including (say) the ability to display a certain demeanour or communicate using a particular manner of speech. Bartenders are an obvious case, since the most valued members of staff are not necessarily those who can operate the beer-pumps and cash-tills most efficiently, but those whose honesty curtails their pilfering and whose conviviality brings custom into their particular establishment rather than any other. Arlie Hochschild has also identified a number of occupations (such as that of flight attendant) for which the ability to do 'emotional labour'—to manage the feelings of oneself and others—is especially important.[13]

Similarly, as large-scale businesses and public corporations move away from bureaucratic to more 'flexible' or 'adaptive' forms of organization, there may be an increasing need for professional and managerial employees having a range of personal competences that go beyond those rewarded by formal qualifications. As Phillip Brown and Richard Scase (1994) have observed, in the post-Fordist enterprises of the 1990s, the demand for academic credentials is perhaps giving way to the nurturing of wider motivational and attitudinal (or even charismatic) qualities among employees—on the grounds that creative and entrepreneurial individuals are better placed to cope with ambiguity and change.

In a wider sense, the range of attributes that might merit a job but might not be picked up by education is potentially huge, and could include willingness to comply with the just orders of an employer, acceptance of a moral obligation to perform work diligently no matter how menial the task, or the ability to work companionably as part of a departmental group.[14] This list could be extended to embrace such idiosyncratic factors as having good hand–eye coordination, a muscular physique, or even an attractive face. In other words, once we start to think about the particular qualities relevant to the performance of specific jobs, it soon becomes clear that it is hardly less problematic to equate education with merit when discussing its links to occupational outcomes than it is in discussions of the association between class origins and educational attainment.[15]

It would, however, be throwing the baby out with the bathwater to pursue this train of thought to such an extent as to dismiss information about educational achievements as simply irrelevant to the issue of whether selection processes in the labour market are meritocratic. Doubtless, it is true that employers sometimes use educational qualifications merely as a filtering device for processing employees, rather than as a reliable indicator of the accumulation of human capital or of different relevant competences.[16] But it is surely also undeniable that the kinds of intellectual or cognitive skill to which the achievement of educational qualifications does attest are relevant competences for a great many of the jobs that constitute the relatively advantaged positions in the class structure. It is not as if the qualities that the education system rewards are altogether useless when it comes to the real world of work: employees generally need the relevant technical and other abilities that are recorded by their respective educational certificates in order successfully to perform their various occupational tasks (as physicians, computer programmers, or whatever).[17]

It is the level of analysis that is of critical importance here. While many non-educational considerations may indeed be crucial when it comes to thinking about which of two people with similar educational credentials (*ex hypothesi* indicating similar levels of cognitive skills and knowledge) is likely best to do a particular job, they are less likely to be of sufficient importance to make the difference as between two candidates whose levels of skills and knowledge are markedly unequal, or in the case of jobs sufficiently different as to occupy different places in the class structure. It remains, of course, possible that someone who lacks badly the skills properly rewarded by the educational system should none the less possess those necessary for the successful carrying out of a well-rewarded job. We can think, perhaps, of entertainers or athletes whose relevant competences may be altogether different from those that the education system seeks to certify. But the point is that these are exceptions: it is surely more likely that those who are competent to do advantaged jobs will also possess the kind of skill and ability that are indicated by a decent measure of educational attainment. So it is consistent with these observations about the way in which education cannot be equated with merit, when it comes to processes of occupational selection, that it can none the less be regarded as a reasonably adequate indicator at a sufficiently generalized level of analysis—such as we ourselves have utilized in Chapters 5 and 6 above.

VII

Before we go on to consider the third leg of the meritocratic triad, the direct association between origins and destinations, it may be helpful to summarize and clarify the main points of our exposition thus far by contrasting two examples. In the paragraph above, we acknowledged the possibility that somebody could get—and merit—a job at the top end of the class structure, while possessing hardly any of the abilities or motivations that the education system seeks to reward with qualifications. This is a separate case from that in which somebody gets a good job (Prime Minister?) despite doing very badly at school but where the reason why they did badly at school is of the kind discussed in section V. In that case, their educational qualifications do not accurately convey the extent to which they possess the abilities that those qualifications are supposed to indicate.

There are, then, two distinct kinds of doubt one might entertain here. On the one hand, there are doubts about the extent to which people's educational attainments actually reflect their ability to achieve them, while on the other there are doubts about the extent to which people's ability to achieve in educational terms is relevant to the successful performance of those jobs that constitute the relatively advantaged positions in the class structure. When we take on board the fact that both these doubts can apply simultaneously, or in combination, it becomes clear that the issue of how we should interpret the role of education when assessing claims about meritocracy is complex indeed.

One way of summarizing this story is to point out that we have in play no fewer than three conceptions of merit and meritocracy. For some, merit refers to something like 'real natural ability and motivation', and a meritocracy is a society in which people get jobs on the basis of these attributes. While on some accounts this conception of merit might accurately be indicated by people's educational achievements, most sociologists who work with it would dispute the claim that it can be equated with education, and would argue, rather, that the link between origins and destinations does not result from the distribution of merit but from class-related processes that distort the real picture.

For others, merit refers straightforwardly to educational achievement. On this view, what matters about meritocracy is that the most educationally qualified people get the best rewarded (and, it is usually assumed, most intellectually demanding) jobs. Advocates of this relatively straightforward conception may not worry about whether people's educational qualifications reflect their real natural ability and motivation; a society is meritocratic to the extent that there is a good fit between people's level of education and the kind of job they do.

The third view understands merit in terms of what were earlier referred to as relevant competences. Here, a meritocratic society is one in which people get jobs on the basis of their ability to do them well, and it may or may not be the case that educational achievements are good indicators of people's abilities to do well those jobs that make up the more advantaged positions in the class structure. On this view, there may be nothing unmeritocratic about giving a job to someone on the basis of their good looks or engaging personality, since this will depend on whether or not these attributes are relevant to the successful performance of the job. The only thing that would count as unmeritocratic on this third view would be giving a job to someone who was not thought the most likely of the candidates to be able to do it best.

It should be clear that these complications make the interpretation of the findings reported in earlier chapters problematic to say the least. What do they imply for the association between origins and destinations—the effect of people's class background on their class position that is not mediated through the effect of that background on their educational attainments?

On the straightforward view that identifies merit with education—either the version that holds people's educational achievements adequately to indicate their real natural abilities and motivations or the version that is simply not interested in the question of what leads some people to have superior educational qualifications to others—such an unmediated effect is clear evidence of a lack of meritocracy. However, now that we have introduced the possibility of meritorious attributes that are not adequately operationalized by education, we can envisage arguments that would explain this direct effect in terms consistent with meritocratic principles.

Such arguments would have not only to invoke the observations of the previous sections but further to claim that the meritorious attributes not detected by our measures of education were systematically and unequally distributed between those born into the different classes.[18] We are not aware of anybody who asserts that educational systems are biased in favour of working-class children, or that the pattern of educational achievement fails sufficiently to reflect the superior natural abilities or stronger motivation of service-class children. Nor can we think of plausible reasons why this should be the case. It is rather the suggestion that education may not adequately indicate those attributes meriting occupational success that might seem to give some hope to those concerned to reconcile the persisting direct effect of origins on destinations with the claim that Britain is a meritocracy.

For this hope to be realized, the claim would have to be sustained that the kinds of ability meriting occupational success, but not adequately identified by measures of education, are possessed disproportionately by those born into relatively advantaged class backgrounds. This is in principle an empirical issue, albeit one very difficult to research, given the sheer variety of jobs and context-specificity of what might be deemed competences relevant to their successful performance.[19] In this situation it is perhaps, therefore, legitimate to offer what can only be speculations.

It is by no means implausible to think that middle-class parents instil in their children values and attitudes that fit them well for the labour market, and it is surely likely that such children will tend to acquire social skills that will count as 'relevant competences' for a range of jobs, especially when we bear in mind the role of what we referred to earlier as 'reaction qualifications'. It is, however, important to keep clearly in focus the fact that we are now considering the influence of these factors over and above the effect they have on people's educational achievements. With this in mind, one obvious problem for such moves is that many sociologists of education would argue, along the lines laid out earlier in this chapter, that working-class children achieving the same educational qualifications as their middle-class peers will have to have worked harder and been more strongly motivated to succeed. In that case, it seems implausible to attribute to motivational factors the greater occupational success of middle-class children than working-class children, when we have controlled for education attainment. Of course, it may be that different kinds of motivation are relevant in educational and occupational contexts, and the middle-class schoolboy or schoolgirl not interested in doing well at school but intent on getting a good job or setting up a small business is not impossible to imagine. But this consideration surely dampens any temptation to accept the reconciliatory suggestion wholesale.[20]

Despite this sceptical observation, it is entirely possible that some educated working-class children who achieve levels of education that would fit them for service-class occupations may be less motivated to be upwardly mobile into the service class than are those sons and daughters who come from service-class backgrounds to stay there. There is some evidence (see Jencks et al. 1979: 70–1) that, among men with similar credentials and skills, those from advantaged backgrounds tend to seek jobs in higher-status occupations than do others having relatively disadvantaged social origins. Perhaps, even though they do perfectly well at school, some children of working-class parents prefer not to compete for the intermediate or service-class jobs that their educational qualifications would seem to make appropriate? For example, it may be that they simply like the idea of staying in the community with which they are familiar, so that the range of job opportunities available to them is substantially restricted. Alternatively, they may have a more active antipathy to the life-styles and values that they take to go with middle-class occupations, regarding office jobs as soft or in some other way alien. Perhaps they just enjoy and find satisfying the kinds of work that tend to be carried out by those doing jobs that our scheme would not categorize as intermediate or service class? In other words, it is important to recognize that people's jobs are not necessarily regarded by them merely as means to the achievement of material rewards, but may also be, to borrow a phrase coined by David Miller, 'vehicles of self-realization'. Clearly, it is by no means implausible that people should choose not to attain the highest class position of which they are capable, and there need be nothing irrational or pathological about such a choice. And since the desire to do a job must presumably be regarded as a competence relevant to the successful carrying out of that job, such an account could then help to explain the direct association between origins and destination, by appealing to mechanisms that cannot be regarded as unmeritocratic.[21]

VIII

By considering each of the three legs of the meritocratic triad in turn, we have acknowledged that there are different conceptions of merit, some of which would not regard it as adequately indicated by measures of education such as those that we have used in previous chapters. Some of these conceptions imply that Britain may be less meritocratic than our analyses would suggest—perhaps because the processes by which people's abilities convert into educational achievements favour those with relatively advantaged class origins. Others make available the possibility that it may be more meritocratic—perhaps because individuals from advantaged class origins are more likely to possess competences that are not captured by measures of education but are relevant to the performance of jobs located within relatively advantaged classes. We have, however, studiously avoided the issue with which we are primarily concerned: the normative question of how these various conceptions of merit relate to claims about social justice. That is the task of our next chapter.

NOTES

1. Much less plausible, though logically possible, would be the analogous attempt to soften our findings by pointing to the fact that each of our class categories embraces a range of occupations, characterized by slightly differing levels of advantage. While it is conceivable, for example, that children of working-class origins are achieving the relatively advantaged positions within their classes of destination, while children of service-class origins are tending to cluster among the less desirable occupations within theirs, we can think of no reason why this should be the case. On the contrary, our evidence on the continuing influence of non-meritocratic class processes suggests that we should expect the opposite. However, even if this logical possibility did turn out to be the empirical reality, the scale of non-meritocratic allocation that we have discovered is such as to make this a

very minor mitigating observation. At best it suggests that access to positions of relative advantage is not quite so unmeritocratic as our less fine-tuned picture alone would imply.

2. Evidence for some reduction in class disparities has occasionally been produced, but this has usually pointed only to temporary or minor shifts, often invisible in (or even contradicted by) other studies of these same cases. On this general point, and for a summary of the relevant studies, see Goldthorpe (1996b).

   Disagreement has often centred on matters of statistical method, with different techniques producing different results, as e.g. where sequential logit models suggest no real change, while an approach based on matching marginals—applied to the same data—claims to detect decreasing class differentials in educational achievement (cf. Kerckhoff and Trott 1993 and Blackburn and Marsh 1991). Sequential logit models, as well as requiring relatively large numbers of cases to guarantee reliability, make strong assumptions about hierarchical ordering (in this case of educational qualifications), by assuming that respondents progress from lower to higher certificates without skipping categories, for example by taking a university degree while holding O-levels but no A-levels. Marginal matching, on the other hand, confounds effects due to absolute changes in the distribution of classes and qualifications with those arising out of changes in relative class disparities. These sorts of consideration help explain our preference for the simpler log-linear and logistic regression techniques that were used in Chapters 5 and 6 above.

   Sweden seems to be one of the few exceptions to the rule that, despite expanding school systems, social class inequality in educational attainment has remained stable over time. The reduction in class differences that can be observed during the twentieth century has been explained in terms of reduced inequalities in living conditions in that country, which had the effect of levelling the costs of higher education, and of a comprehensive school reform that postpones early decisions about educational trajectories. On the extent of Swedish exceptionalism on this point, and for an account of the mechanisms by which the remaining class differences in educational attainment are generated, see the papers collected in Erikson and Jonsson (1996).

3. For a review of this literature, and an indicative bibliography, see Murphy (1981).

4. For an example and further discussion, see Marshall (1990: 45–6).

5. Despite the explicit link that was made, in most of these studies, between working-class cultural deprivation and material deprivation, some critics nevertheless argued that all such subcultural approaches neglected the structural constraints imposed upon the lower classes, and appeared therefore to 'blame the victims' for what were, instead, arbitrary middle-class biases in schools, evident in tracking, teacher expectations, and such like. Probably the best known of these exchanges was the debate about the

culture of poverty (see Valentine 1968). The so-called New Sociology of Education has more recently added reproduction theory, resistance through rituals, and post-Marxist interpretivism to this tradition. The first of these found its most vigorous expression in Samuel Bowles and Herbert Gintis's claim that schools served the interests of capitalism, by promoting passive adaptation and under-achievement among working-class children, so persuading them to acquiesce in predetermined subordinate roles. Paul Willis and other resistance theorists subsequently claimed that closer study of the processes generating unequal educational outcomes revealed that class disparities in attainment were the result of working-class children developing and expressing oppositional proletarian values in a nascent form of class struggle. Most recently, post-Marxists (such as Philip Wexler) have extended this analysis, adding gender and race to social class, so offering a more inclusive theory of youthful resistance to the dominant ideology as represented in schools. For a useful review of these (and other similar) accounts, see Davies (1995).

6. Good examples of studies in this general tradition of rational-action theory are Gambetta (1987) and Goldthorpe (1996b)—both of which develop, in rather different ways, the ideas of Raymond Boudon (see e.g. Boudon 1974). See also Erikson and Jonsson (1996: 55), who conclude from their study of twentieth-century Sweden that class inequalities in educational outcomes can be explained by five mechanisms: academic performance is better among children from advantaged class backgrounds; educational costs are higher for families in less advantaged class positions (which affects the transition to tertiary education); better-educated parents tend to teach school-related skills to their children (so increasing the probability of their successfully negotiating the educational system); children from advantaged backgrounds place a negative value on social demotion that outweighs the positive value placed on the corresponding social ascent by children from disadvantaged class backgrounds; and, finally, the perceived probabilities of success are lower, even at the points of earliest educational choice, among children from relatively disadvantaged class backgrounds.

7. This is not to deny that the differences between these explanations are also substantial. For example, rational-action accounts of class differentials in education explicitly challenge the thesis of 'cultural deprivation' among the working class, because they claim to be able to explain not only persisting differentials but also the greatly increased absolute rates of take-up of superior educational options by working-class as well as middle-class children. According to Goldthorpe (1996b), at least, culturalist ex-planations cannot cope with this increase—those from the right (Murphy) no more than those from the left (Willis)—since such accounts would have to predict *widening* class differentials in a context of educational expansion.

8. For additional examples and a discussion, see Herrnstein and Murray (1994: appendix 3).

9. For a comprehensive survey of the literature and issues surrounding intelligence testing, see Brody (1992). The history of mental testing in England,
   and of its relation to the educational system, is fully documented in Sutherland (1984) and Wooldridge (1994). On the substantial effects on measured
   intelligence of social factors in general, and class background in particular,
   see Anastasi (1988) and Fogelman et al. (1983).
10. Saunders (1995: 27–38). Saunders concludes, on the basis of a modelling
    exercise which examines the Oxford social mobility data in relation to
    simulated IQ scores, that Britain may well already be a meritocracy. Com-
    pare the arguments of Wooldridge (1995), who shares Saunders's enthusi-
    asm for meritocracy but would reject the claim that Britain today is
    meritocratic. In Wooldridge's view, schools currently select children not on
    the basis of ability, but on non-academic criteria such as living nearby,
    family connections, parental status, and academic records (which last he
    regards as favouring the well-taught rather than innately able). He advo-
    cates a meritocratic selective education system, but with a properly sys-
    tematic and rigorous testing of ability, on the basis of IQ tests and
    examinations, to be held not once and for all (as under the former 'eleven-
    plus' arrangement), but on a continuing basis.
11. See Miner (1957: 3–4) and, for empirical studies, Jencks et al. (1975: 54–5)
    and Nicholas Mascie-Taylor (1990: 134–5, 140). This last-mentioned author,
    after reviewing the literature on social class and IQ, concludes that since
    'we know that a large number of other variables also associate with IQ—for
    instance, extent of crowding—which is itself not independent of social
    class . . . it is unclear therefore to what extent the difference in IQ is due to
    class *per se* or to what extent it is confounded by other variables'. His own
    data, which are taken from the (British) National Child Development
    Study, show that the mean difference in IQ scores between classes is re-
    duced (though not eliminated) when other social, economic, and contami-
    nating co-variates of social class are controlled. Moreover, of the remaining
    association between social class and IQ, one can conclude only that 'such
    differences might reflect genetic differences between social classes. Equally
    the differences could reflect untested environmental variables and imper-
    fections in the measurement of variables that were analysed.' In other
    words, although social-class effects are not eliminated in a multiple regres-
    sion analysis, 'efforts to partition this remaining fraction among other envi-
    ronmental conditions, errors in measurement, and any underlying genetic
    differences remain so far largely unresolved'. The recent evidence and
    arguments against interpreting the results of intelligence tests as a measure
    of an immutable inherited IQ are also summarized in Gould (1995) and
    Gardner (1995).
12. Tests were taken in schools at ages 8, 11, and 15 years, and at home age 26.
    On each occasion, 4 tests were administered, in a mix of verbal and non-
    verbal forms. For details, see Wadsworth (1991: 224–6).
    Bringing class destinations into the picture appears to cast further doubt
    on Saunders's claims. If we look at the children who scored in the top,

middle, and lowest thirds on tests taken at age 8, and control also for the type of schooling each child received, there is still a substantial class-of-origin effect in class outcomes. Those from middle-class homes are much more likely to be found in the Registrar General's social classes I and II than are children from working-class backgrounds, who have much higher chances of arriving at manual class (IV and V) destinations (Wadsworth 1991: 80, 106, 145).

Summarizing these results, Wadsworth (1991: 144–7) concludes that, even with a high intelligence test score at age 8, 'whatever type of school had been attended a distinct career advantage was conferred by an upbringing in a family in which the father was employed in a non-manual class job'. Indeed, this class-of-origin effect was even more pronounced among those who scored in the middle and lowest thirds on the tests, again irrespective of the type of education actually received. As Wadsworth observes, 'a sifting out process occurred at a number of points', so that 'children from lower social class families, and those who went to non-selective schools had the lowest chance of professional or salaried careers, even if they had apparently high attainment potential'.

13. See Marshall (1986) and Hochschild (1983). It is worth emphasizing, in this context, that some of these relevant competences are what have been called 'reaction qualifications'—that is, 'personal attributes which contribute to job performance via the responses of other people, as opposed to straightforwardly technical qualifications'. This is obviously the case for certain social skills. Thus, for example, the pleasing manner that one quite properly and meritocratically looks for when appointing flight attendants is precisely the ability to evoke certain kinds of reaction from airline passengers. But this then raises an additional complication. Suppose passengers held racist views that led them to react unfavourably to black attendants. Would we be making our appointment meritocratically if we took this into account and ruled out all black candidates? We discuss the normative implications of this kind of case in the next chapter.

14. For a wider discussion of the many potentially relevant such competences, see Rose (1985). Much the same point has now been made in relation to debates about over-education, occupational mismatch, and the functioning of labour markets generally. For example, the literature on so-called overtraining poses the question of whether or not any disparity between workers' acquired education (usually measured as 'years of schooling') and the level of schooling typical of particular occupations is a valid indicator of either nominal 'over-education' of the workforce, on the one hand, or of a deficit of 'relevant skills', on the other. For a review of this material, and a good discussion of some of the measurement problems that apply equally to debates about skill and merit in matching persons to jobs, see Halaby (1994) and Witte and Kalleberg (1995).

15. Indeed, it becomes possible to think of ways in which the association between education and destination may actually indicate a lack of meritocracy. This might happen, for example, if those appointing people to jobs

paid particular attention to the educational qualifications of candidates, even where these could not be considered relevant competences, simply because they regarded such qualifications as likely indicators of their holders' having certain kinds of life-styles or socio-cultural backgrounds of which they approved. This is certainly one thrust of the literature on the growth of 'credential societies' and so-called 'diploma disease' (see Collins 1979; Dore 1982).

16. Cf. e.g. Berg (1971), Spence (1973), and Riley (1976).

17. Hardly surprisingly, therefore, most studies of occupational attainment continue to pay particular attention to the effects of educational qualifications on labour-market entry. And, despite their differing premises, theories of human capital, credentialism, signalling, and filtering all deal with the ways in which employers use educational attainment as a criterion for choosing between candidates about whom they otherwise have relatively little information. Educational and training certificates tend to be used as a basis for hiring personnel, even in the case of the least well-educated workers, entering unskilled manual occupations (see e.g. Lee et al. 1990). However, while educational credentials operate to get people through organizational gates and onto organizational ladders, there is some evidence that they are of possibly less value in promotions (especially internal promotions), since managers have direct access to other indicators of each person's performance, including e.g. the number of years each candidate has actually spent doing the job. On this last point, see Bills (1988).

18. We have already mentioned one version of this argument, when we acknowledged the possibility that people from service-class origins are disproportionately achieving qualifications at the top end of our categories, so that this properly meritocratic criterion might explain some of their relative advantage in terms of class destinations. At this point, however, we have in mind arguments that reject education as an indicator of merit in a rather more thoroughgoing way.

19. This is what we take to be the main thrust of Goldthorpe's (1996a) critique of the concept of meritocracy. It is perhaps worth noting, in this particular context, that there is no evidence to suggest that 'measured intelligence' is one such attribute—despite Herrnstein and Murray's (1994) recent claim that the allocation of jobs according to intellectual ability, and therefore the association between class and intelligence, has grown throughout the twentieth century (especially since the 1950s). Interestingly, although this is one of the central claims made by these authors, critics of their controversial book have concentrated almost exclusively on the issue of ethnic or racial differences in IQ (see e.g. the papers collected in Fraser 1995). One of the few attempts to test Herrnstein and Murray's proposition that classes in American society are increasingly stratified by measured intelligence shows fairly conclusively that, to the contrary, social class differences in intellectual ability have become smaller among people born after the Second World War—probably as a result of changes in the quantity and effects of

education. It follows, therefore, that the social problems which currently beset the US cannot be attributed to the growing concentration of low ability people in the lower classes (see Weakliem et al. 1995).

20. More speculatively still, it is perhaps also worth pointing out that the kinds of job for which social skills (of the sort that might plausibly be associated with class but not with education) are likely to be relevant competences are not obviously those located within the service class. The occupations that come immediately to mind are those of (say) waiter, receptionist, or sales assistant. At best, some such employment points only to an intermediate (and more probably a working-) class location, in the terms of the Goldthorpe scheme we have adopted for our study. So, while possession of relevant social skills might well provide the means by which service-class children who fail educationally can resist downward mobility into unemployment or into certain types of unskilled manual work (and resist doing so in ways consistent with meritocratic principles), it is less likely to explain the extent to which such children manage nevertheless to achieve service-class destinations.

21. It is perhaps worth emphasizing that what is needed to achieve this task is a claim about motivational differences that applies specifically to those from different class origins but having similar levels of education. To the extent that people's lack of desire to maximize class position will be reflected in their attitudes to education, and so (along the lines discussed earlier in the chapter) their educational achievements, the force of the attempt to render our findings compatible with meritocratic claims by appealing to class differentials in occupational aspirations would seem to be considerably weakened. On the substantial range of attitudes (or so-called orientations) to work, at least some of which would be consistent with the idea that people may not choose to obtain the most advantaged occupation for which they are educationally qualified, see Rose (1988).

8

Social Justice Revisited

I

The previous chapter identified a variety of different conceptions of merit that tend to arise in sociological discussion of the three legs of the meritocratic triad. Its central thrust was to point out the sheer fact of this variety, and how different issues arise when we consider the associations between origin and education, education and destination, and origin and destination. What people have in mind by 'merit' seems to vary according to these different contexts: sometimes it is natural ability, sometimes natural ability plus motivation, sometimes natural ability plus *non-adaptive* motivation, and sometimes what we have called relevant competences. The extent to which any of these can adequately be grasped by measures of educational attainment of the kind that we used in our analyses in Chapters 5 and 6 is far from clear. It is this failure of our measure fully to capture what is sometimes understood by merit that makes possible the claim that our findings are insufficient to demonstrate that Britain is not a meritocracy.

Might appeal to these different understandings of merit license the conclusion that the class structure of Britain—or more specifically the pattern of mobility that exists between the positions that constitute that structure—is consistent with social justice?[1] This is a rather different question, for it is by no means clear that the conceptions of merit that might allow us to judge that Britain is a meritocracy are of the right kind to warrant the claim that the mobility patterns which it manifests are just; indeed, it is not clear that any of the conceptions of merit that prevail in the sociological literature are of this kind.

To see what we mean, observe that any attempt to reconcile our findings on social mobility patterns with the proposition that Britain is just because meritocratic must involve appeal to the postulate that merit is unequally distributed across those born into different classes of origin.

This can in turn be broken down into two distinct claims. Whether the argument is put in terms of educational qualifications or innate intelligence, the motivation to work hard or the possession of relevant competences, it must be argued *both* that these attributes are unequally distributed by class of origin *and* that they can be regarded as meritorious in the sense of justifying inequalities of access to positions of relative advantage. Where the previous chapter focused almost exclusively on the first of these claims, being concerned simply to set out the variety of attributes that might be regarded as 'merit' in different sociological contexts, it is now time to move on to the second and rather more fundamental question of why we should regard these various attributes as being 'meritorious' in the required sense.

It must be remembered here that our overriding concern is with questions of social justice. What matters from this perspective is whether or not our data on social mobility are consistent with meritocratic claims of a particular kind—namely, those that invoke a conception of merit that will justify or legitimate the distributive phenomena indicated by those data. It will not then be sufficient to claim that there are ways of conceiving merit that might explain how our findings on mobility could be understood as meritocratic—by appeal, for example, to the differential distribution of natural ability or to the possibility that children of advantaged parents are more likely to possess social skills that are quite properly considered 'relevant competences' when it comes to selecting people for jobs. It will need further to be argued that such conceptions are able to support the claim that it is *just* that their possessors should be rewarded with the advantages—superior access to positions of relative advantage—that our findings show them to be enjoying. In short, to do the job required, a conception of merit must not only fit the data but must also allow us to understand those data as indicative of social justice.

In this context, it is important to distinguish between the criteria that do or should govern the allocation of individuals to occupations, on the one hand, and the criteria that do or should govern the allocation of rewards to individuals, on the other. The reasons why particular kinds of person should do particular kinds of jobs are in principle quite distinct from the reasons why particular kinds of person should enjoy unequal rewards of the kind indicated by our class scheme and the patterns of mobility within it. It is perfectly possible to argue for an allocation of individuals to occupations in accordance with their possession of relevant competences, whilst rejecting the view that social justice demands that people be rewarded for the possession of such competences.

Of course, in the real world occupations tend to play a dual role, since they both define the differing tasks that people perform in their work and can be characterized in terms of differing levels of advantage. Indeed, it is sociological (and economic) orthodoxy to explain the latter in terms of the former: to account for these differences in occupational advantage by invoking the differences in the tasks carried out by those who enjoy them. It is not our purpose here to dispute that orthodoxy. We do not challenge the explanation of inequality that sees it, in very broad terms, as the result of processes whereby labour markets reward people differently, depending on the supply of and demand for the competences that they have, and for the jobs that those competences enable them to do.[2] This may indeed be the right way to explain the inequalities that we have found—but does it also then allow us to regard those inequalities as manifestations of social justice?

II

Looking at dictionary definitions of merit, one finds clear connections with the notion of desert. The *Shorter Oxford* lists among its meanings the condition or fact of deserving, 'the quality of deserving well, or of being entitled to reward or gratitude', while *Chambers* refers to 'excellence that deserves reward'. These are not pedantic, or merely academic, connotations of the term, for it is surely the case that the link between meritocracy and justice is normally presumed to operate via the idea that, in a meritocracy, people are rewarded in accordance with their merits, precisely in the sense that they then get what they deserve.[3] Let us consider, then, the implications of the introduction of yet another conception of merit, one strikingly different from those outlined in the previous chapter, yet apparently central to the justification of inequalities, whether of access or outcome: the idea of merit as the basis of desert.

On the view now under consideration, the claim that merit is unequally distributed as between those born into different classes of origin means that children from different backgrounds tend to be differently, and unequally, deserving. Many will find this an unpalatable view because they take it to imply the judgement that such children tend to be more or less morally worthy or virtuous. This would be a mistake for two reasons. In the first place, as David Miller (1989: 158) has argued, while desert claims are, typically, moral claims—else they could not in the appropriate sense *justify* inequalities—'this is not to say that the properties in virtue of which people come to deserve things are necessarily themselves moral properties'. People can deserve rewards, and this can be a moral claim, on the basis of qualities other than the possession of moral worthiness or virtue. Secondly, it is important to be clear that the view in question holds only that children from different social origins tend to be unequally deserving of those advantages that characterize the different positions in the class structure. It need not be argued that they are unequally deserving of anything else—such as divine forgiveness, human sympathy, or respect for their life-plans. This second clarification is important. The question we need to address is whether or not those born into different classes might be differently deserving of the goods that our data on mobility show them differently to be enjoying.

To make that suggestion persuasive, it would be necessary only to believe that people deserve this kind of reward on the basis of their contribution to society, and that those with different class origins will tend to be unequally able to contribute. It should be clear that this is not the only way in which the claim about differential deserts might be spelled out. For example, it might be held that people deserve such rewards on the basis of their natural abilities alone, or (perhaps more plausibly) only on the basis of their own efforts, and that these are unequally distributed between those born into different classes of origin in a way consistent with our data. Considered purely formally, any of the conceptions of merit that we argued in the previous chapter would not be fully captured by our measures of education *might* be argued to be distributed in the right way, and to constitute a proper basis for the appropriate kind of desert claim. However, in our view it is the conception of merit that identifies it with people's relevant competences— understood now as their ability to contribute to society by performing valued tasks—that could most plausibly be invoked by those concerned to mount a meritocratic defence of our findings, so it is to this particular claim that we will devote our attention from here onwards. Since people's relevant competences will be in part a result of their natural abilities, partly a result of their past efforts to develop those abilities, and will also include their current motivation to contribute, this approach will in any case require us to address the normative aspects of the full range of issues discussed in the previous chapter.

How exactly we should measure people's 'contribution to society' is obviously a difficult question. Who is to say that the well-paid professional in advertising contributes more to society than someone who keeps the streets clean? Or that either contributes more than the unemployed man who spends his time doing voluntary work in a hospital? Identifying people's contribution to society with the market price of their work is problematic in various ways. Most obviously, perhaps, there is the issue of whether it is appropriate to consider the satisfaction of other people's preferences as a contribution—but without taking into account the content of those preferences. It may well be that a smiling cabin attendant, by satisfying the preferences of others, contributes more to society than would his sullen counterpart, so that rewarding one but not the other with the advantages gained by doing the job can be justified by the contributory principle. As we noted in the previous chapter, it may often be the case that relevant competences involve reference to other people's reactions. But what if customers want a white cabin attendant? Since he is better able to satisfy racist preferences, our measure of social value seems to commit us to saying that the white candidate for the job is better able to contribute value to society than is his black counterpart.[4]

Even if we set aside this problem, and accept that it is appropriate to measure people's contribution to society by the extent to which they satisfy the preferences of others, this then leaves the issue of whether labour markets actually do reward people in accordance with their contribution in this particular sense. One might accept that, in principle, perfectly competitive markets function so as to make the price of a skill reflect its value to others. (We need not, given our theoretical purposes, allow our exposition to be held up by the labour-market imperfections that economists quite rightly draw to our attention.) But without calling into question a conception of value that equates it with preference-satisfaction, and ignoring the extent to which actual labour markets fail to correspond to the perfectly competitive model, it remains pertinent to point out that what actually gets rewarded even in this hypothetical case is the ability to satisfy the preferences of those who have the money to pay to have their preferences satisfied. Only the prices arrived at by a perfect market, in which all had equal amounts of resources to devote to the satisfaction of their preferences, would genuinely reflect the 'value to society', understood in welfarist terms, of the various activities that individuals might undertake. The unequal distribution of market power means that wages or salaries can give only a distorted sense of what it is that others—all others—in their society actually want them to do.[5]

Clearly, there is a great deal of room for further discussion, and many ways in which it might be argued that class processes fail to reward people for their contribution to society. But let us leave aside such complications and accept, for the sake of argument, both that 'contribution to society' can, in this context, plausibly be measured in terms of preference-satisfaction and that labour markets at least approximate the pattern of rewards to occupations that reflects contributions in this sense. Let us grant also that the ability to satisfy other people's preferences might indeed be distributed unequally across those born into different classes of origin—along one or more of the various lines of argument that we considered in the previous chapter. The crucial question, then, is why people should deserve to be rewarded for this contribution. Why should the fact that one has (and exercises) the ability to satisfy other people's preferences make one more deserving of reward than somebody who does not have (and hence cannot exercise) that ability?

We do not deny that many people believe that it does make one more deserving. Indeed, in Appendix J below we report our own findings in respect of popular beliefs about social justice, which make it clear that there is a great deal of support for the web of ideas that might seem to underlie the principle of 'reward for contribution' (although we note also that these findings are unfortunately indecisive at key theoretical junctures). But whether people believe in a distributive principle is a separate question from whether they are right to do so, and it seems to us (and to many political theorists) at best deeply problematic to regard social advantage as being deserved by people on the basis of their superior contribution to the welfare of others.[6]

III

The problem here is that there seems to be a strong link between the notion of desert and that of personal responsibility. As David Miller (1989: 168) puts it, we want 'to see people as deserving on the basis of features for which they can be held responsible'.[7] However, since it is hard to deny that differences in people's ability to satisfy the preferences of others rest (at least to some extent) on factors for which they cannot be held responsible, it may seem difficult to see how those differences could be sufficient to ground the claim that they deserve unequal rewards. Market mechanisms are blind to questions of responsibility—they reward people unequally, in proportion to their differing capacities to provide what others want, and without reference to the source of the differences in that ability. Thus, it might be argued, labour markets cannot plausibly be thought to give people what they deserve, since luck or chance plays too great a role in influencing who gets what—even when those markets are perfectly competitive, and even in the ideal case where all have equal resources to devote to the satisfaction of their preferences.

There are at least four ways in which luck might be thought to play a role; that is, four factors that make individuals unequal in their ability to satisfy, and to get paid for satisfying, other people's preferences, but for which the individual cannot claim responsibility. The first two, though this may seem somewhat banal, are the preferences and abilities of others. The value of my skills and abilities will depend upon how much other people want them and how many other people have them. It is true that people may be responsible for their choices to develop particular skills, or to acquire new abilities, and that such choices may take into account precisely such factors as the demand for and supply of such attributes. It may not be an out-of-work actor's fault that he lives in a society that doesn't want the theatre enough to provide him with a job, but it may well be his fault that he has not then adapted to this situation, by making the effort to acquire skills and abilities that it does want. The ex-out-of-work actor who has become a computer programmer may quite plausibly claim to deserve his rewards for having done so—or at least to deserve greater rewards than the still-out-of-work actor who has not. But this will leave cases in which the individual has chosen as responsibly as he or she can, but still finds that the market changes so as to leave his or her skills comparatively worthless; and it will also leave untouched the point that there will be people who, whatever choices they make, would do better under different market conditions than they would under those that happen to exist and for which they cannot be held responsible.

The other two chance factors that influence a person's ability to satisfy, and get rewarded for satisfying, the preferences of others will perhaps be more familiar. First, individuals cannot claim responsibility for the talents that they are born with, any more than they can claim to have chosen their parents. Who is born with what natural advantages or disadvantages is entirely a matter of chance—at least as far as the individual is concerned. Second, there is the luck involved in whether or not the child is born into the kind of family (or other) environment that is able or inclined to provide the child with the conditions helpful to the development of those attributes that make the child able to satisfy the preferences of others, when he or she reaches adulthood. Without going into the difficult question of what exactly we should include among what James Fishkin (1983) calls 'developmental conditions', it would be hard to deny that there are some such conditions, and that whether he or she is provided with them is, in large part, a matter beyond the individual's control.[8]

Issues of responsibility, desert, and the relation between the two are notoriously complex, and have been the subject of a great deal of philosophical discussion. In this context, it may be helpful for us to make it clear that our suggestion that these various kinds of luck undermine the idea that the market gives people what they deserve is concerned quite specifically with the way in which luck affects people *differentially*. It does not, therefore, depend upon the strong and controversial view that a person can only properly be said to deserve reward for performing an action (such as doing a job) when he or she is responsible for the fact that they possess all the attributes that enable them to perform that action. We do not, that is, appeal to the idea that an individual's action can form the basis of a desert claim only if the individual is 'fully responsible' or 'responsible all the way down' for it—so that, for the claim to be justified, the role of luck must be entirely eliminated. Such a view would be unnecessarily controversial.[9] Our scepticism is focused more specifically on the idea that factors beyond people's control can ground claims to *unequal* deserts—that one person can deserve to be better (or worse) off than another due to factors for which he or she is not responsible. Luck *per se* may be ineliminable, and need not be argued to undermine desert claims. But why should it be just to permit the fact that some are lucky and others unlucky to influence the distribution of rewards in society?[10]

One further point of clarification is necessary, for it must be acknowledged that we have apparently conflicting intuitions in different contexts. When we ask whether Seamus Heaney, rather than some lesser writer, deserves to win a Nobel prize, we seem to be asking a question solely about the quality of his contribution to literature, and are not at all interested in the extent to which he can claim to be responsible for his ability to make it. He must, of course, be responsible for having written the poems that won him the prize—and in that very weak sense all desert claims depend upon the attribution of responsibility. But those who would reject people's claims to deserve superior reward on the basis of superior natural talent need not deny that the individual may be responsible for exercising that talent. What bothers them is the lack of responsibility for the fact that they, and not others, have it in the first place. Nor, more importantly, need the opponent of such claims deny that people may be responsible for their possession of the ability to provide what others want, for developing their natural talents in socially useful ways, *to some extent*. It can well be acknowledged that nobody's natural talent can be of value to others without some efforts having been made to cultivate and channel it in particular directions: the objection need not take the form of denying all responsibility for the possession of current abilities, but may quite coherently insist simply that the extent of someone's deserving reward cannot be a function of those abilities, since that extent depends on factors for which the individual is not responsible.

What is important about the Nobel prize example, however, is that this second kind of objection seems irrelevant. Although it matters that Heaney is responsible for having written the poems, it does not matter at all that his ability to do so may to a very great extent be the result of factors beyond his control. Even if Heaney's literary talent were overwhelmingly the result of natural genius in combination with a highly propitious upbringing, this surely would not affect our judgement about his deserving to be a Nobel prize winner. We would suggest, however, that this is because of the symbolic and reputational nature or meaning of the award. It would not be absurd to hold that he deserves to win, deserves the prestige and the admiration—simply because the prize is given for literary excellence, and his ability to write poems that display it is what matters, irrespective of where it might come from or how responsible he is for having it—but then to deny both that he deserves the money that goes with it and that people can deserve other rewards on the basis of attributes for which they are not responsible in other contexts. To extrapolate from this example (and there are many others with similar characteristics) to the labour market more generally would, it might seem, require strong and perhaps implausible assumptions about the symbolic nature of the occupational structure in our society.[11]

We must remember that what needs justification is unequal access to social positions characterized by unequal advantage—and advantage of a kind that has pervasive consequences for people's ability to pursue their life-plans, for their health, and for a host of other important things.[12] It may be right to observe that people can deserve to win prizes, or deserve applause, or deserve to get better exam marks than others, for exhibiting skills that they are lucky to have (and others unlucky not to have). But it does not follow from these cases that one can acknowledge the role of luck in determining people's abilities to fill the various occupational roles that make up the class structure, and plausibly argue that rewards (or the lack of them) of the kind attaching to those positions can themselves be deserved, on the basis of possession of those varying abilities.[13]

It is notable that David Miller (1996), who rejects our suggestion that people cannot deserve unequal rewards for achievements affected by contingencies which impinge unequally on different people, also worries about the fact that other benefits beside purchasing power—such as the size of one's pension, access to medical care, and the quality of education available to one's children—can become income-related. As he puts it, 'if all of these benefits are allocated, indirectly, on the basis of merit, then we have a system where far too much turns on whether you happen to be constituted in such a way that you can provide the goods that the market or the state will pay you to provide'. Building upon ideas most fully articulated by Michael Walzer, Miller argues that it would be justified to allocate jobs and income on the basis of economic contribution, but only if this were offset by an egalitarian distribution of goods such as education and health care, and only if social relations as a whole recognized and rewarded a plurality of different kinds of merit, not just economic contribution. Although perhaps more plausible than the view that factors which are beyond the individual's control can ground claims to deserve the full range of advantages that currently go to those lucky enough to be able to provide marketable goods and services, Miller's position still involves the claim that they can lead people to deserve more or less money, and thus the commodities that money can buy. And, since the amount of money a person has influences his or her capacity to lead the life of his or her choice, some may feel uncomfortable with the implication that luck can play a major role in determining something of such importance.[14]

Note that, once it is acknowledged that people can deserve *some* kinds of advantage for deploying attributes for which they are not fully responsible, it becomes hard to hold onto that focus on issues of access rather than of position that we have hitherto sought to sustain. In effect, it becomes necessary to consider arguments for or against the deservedness of particular forms of relative advantage or disadvantage, and so attention necessarily turns to the extent and content of those relativities. One might, of course, deny that any inequalities in income and wealth could be regarded as deserved on the basis of the exercise of attributes that some rather than others have merely by chance—and this might be the position of those who would say that Heaney deserves the prestige and the praise but not the money. But since the typical form of debate concerns the *extent* to which people are or are not responsible for their unequal possession of relevant competences, even this strong view leaves a great deal of room for disagreement as to which inequalities of position, and which inequalities in the chances of access to them, might be deserved. That is, it could be recognized that the extent to which people's class positions are a matter of chance does indeed undermine the validity of claims that the relative advantages currently enjoyed by those in superior positions could be deserved; but it could none the less be insisted that since people's possession of relevant competences is not altogether a matter of luck, some kinds of relative advantage (and advantage in financial terms) might be so.

In order to avoid these complexities, the rest of this chapter will discuss issues raised by either or both of the two claims in which we are primarily interested: that the inequalities of position and access described by our mobility data are deserved, or that a perfectly competitive labour market in which people are rewarded for their contribution to the satisfaction of other people's preferences will produce distributions in which individuals get what they deserve.

IV

It is surely undeniable that people's relevant competences depend to some extent upon attributes beyond their control. We shall see shortly that this is something emphasized by those who would defend our mobility data as consistent with social justice. But, as the previous section suggested, it might be argued that this extent is not very great. Is it not possible to distinguish between two aspects of a person's ability to provide what others want—namely, that which depends on factors beyond the individual's control, and that which results from his or her own efforts and for which he or she can thus claim responsibility—and then to identify how much of a person's ability to contribute stems from which source? The problem is that distinctions of this kind are notoriously hard to sustain. The efforts that people make depend to a great extent on their perception of how likely it is that those efforts will make a difference that is worth making. Thus, for example, it makes much more sense to try to do well at school if one believes oneself to possess the ability to do well if one tries. This means that inequalities in people's efforts are themselves likely to depend to a great extent upon factors for which they cannot claim responsibility.[15] There is also the familiar problem that people's ability to make an effort seems to be influenced by their socialization—that is, on whether they are brought up in a family or other immediate environment that instils in them the proper kinds of attitude and motivation, an issue to which we return below. And it is of course also the case that, even if one found a way of dealing with these worries in principle, it would still remain impossibly difficult in practice to distinguish between the contributions of the two kinds of factor to inequalities in people's actually existing capacities or competences, at least in the standard cases with which sociologists and political theorists are properly concerned.[16] Add to this the fact that it would be absurd (and perhaps even unjust) to reward people simply for their efforts in developing their abilities, without reference to the question of whether anybody would actually benefit from those abilities if developed,[17] and it may well seem that even if one believed that labour markets do unjustly reward people for the possession of attributes that they possess by chance, still they better approximate a just distribution than would any other practically feasible, and perhaps even theoretically conceivable, distributive mechanism (cf. Miller 1989: 169–70). This would be a justification of the patterns of rewards that such markets tend to produce—but it would fall significantly short of the claim that such a pattern was just.

We cannot hope to resolve these complexities here. Our purpose is primarily to bring them to the attention of those who would seek to justify the inequalities indicated by our evidence on mobility patterns by appealing to notions of merit. Even where one might argue for a meritocratic allocation of individuals to occupations, because one thought it sensible for people to be given those jobs that they are best able to do, it remains quite a different matter to argue that the distribution of rewards attached to those jobs should follow merit in this sense. If such an allocation of individuals to jobs reflects the possession of attributes for which the individual is only partially responsible, and if it is problematic to regard people as deserving of unequal rewards (of the kind indicated by our findings on class and mobility) on the basis of attributes which are theirs (at least to some extent) only by chance, it may seem that labour markets that operate to reward people for the exercise of such attributes are at best imperfect mechanisms for giving people what they deserve. Now, while it may of course be argued that responsibility for those attributes is no more necessary in this case than it is in the case of the Nobel prize or the exam grades, those who would maintain this position should be aware of its implications. It implies not only that the woman to whom the natural lottery has given stunning good looks deserves whatever others are prepared to pay her to stand in front of a camera. It implies also that the woman who has been so naturally unlucky that, however much effort she puts in, she will never be able to provide things that others are willing to pay for (and, who, had she had the other's good looks, would have been more than willing to put in the same or greater effort to render them productive) deserves her lowly and relatively disadvantaged economic position.

For those troubled by these implications, let us sharpen the issue a little further. If we suppose that it is difficult to regard people as deserving their class position on the basis of chance attributes, then this would seem to be particularly problematic for those who would view our mobility data as consistent with social justice. The irony is that those who would defend mobility patterns as just because meritocratic do so by appealing to propositions—about the unequal distribution of merits as between those born into different social classes—of a kind that many would take precisely to undermine the claim that justice is achieved by rewarding people according to their possession of merits in this sense.

Let us explain. In order to argue that it is meritocratically just that those of service-class origins are (say) four times more likely to achieve service-class destinations than are those of working-class origins, it is necessary to maintain that those of service-class origins are four times more likely to possess the relevant merits. When we take into account factors of the kind discussed in the previous chapter, and recognize that they are so far from being mutually exclusive as to be in some cases mutually reinforcing, it is by no means impossible to argue that competences relevant to the performance of service-class occupations might indeed be distributed in this way. But the suggestion that such competences are indeed distributed so unequally by class of origin might be thought to undermine the idea that they can form the basis of desert claims, since children can hardly claim responsibility for the class into which they happen to be born. The very claim that certain attributes are distributed unequally by class, which is necessary to defend mobility patterns as meritocratic, would seem to stand in some tension with the claim that such attributes are deserving of reward.

This is most obvious in the case of those who appeal to the unequal distribution of properties that they regard as natural or biologically given (such as intelligence) to justify such mobility patterns. By emphasizing the natural or biological basis of class inequality, those who argue this way seem particularly to emphasize the extent to which people's position in the class structure does indeed result from attributes that are no more than accidents of birth. As the Nobel prize example showed, it is not necessarily incoherent to believe that people deserve some kinds of reward on the basis simply of what they can actually do, and without reference to the question of how or why they came to be able to do what they can do. But it surely flies in the face of a deep-rooted intuition to believe that people can deserve advantage in class terms because they happen to have been born into the right class of origin—the class more likely to endow its children with particular genes.

To be sure, this kind of objection does not depend upon any claim about the class-related distribution of natural endowments, nor indeed upon any claim about the intergenerational transmission of such endowments. The suggestion that natural talents are distributed differentially by class of origin, or that they tend to be inherited, adds nothing to the objection that it is unjust for such attributes to be rewarded in class terms, for that objection applies against desert claims seeking to justify inequalities in advantage on the basis of chance inequalities in attributes, whether or not those attributes are differentially distributed by class, and whether or not they are statistically associated with parental characteristics. We would suggest, however, that emphasis on the relationship between class origin and any such attributes makes apparent the more general problems that surround attempts to justify inequality in such terms that are not so obvious, or of such sociological significance, without that emphasis. It may be psychologically easier to regard people as differentially deserving on the basis of what they can actually do (rather than on the basis of what they are responsible for being able to do) when it is assumed that natural talent, the component of what they can do for which they are not responsible, is randomly distributed across the population. Such ways of thinking might become harder to sustain, even if they become no more normatively implausible, if it were further understood that those born into different subgroups of the population—whether rooted in ethnicity, sex, or class—tend to be more or less naturally talented. In this sense, the attempt to legitimate class structures, and the patterns of mobility within them, by appeal to the distribution of natural endowments across classes of origin may tend to undermine what we acknowledge to be widely accepted ways of legitimatizing inequalities in general.[18]

Although it is easy to confuse points about arbitrariness and heredity with claims about the class-related distribution of people's biological make-up, it is not difficult to see why one might have doubts about the justice of rewarding people for the possession of some genes rather than others—doubts that persist in the face of the more careful and charitable formulation that recognizes that we do not deserve reward for the genes as such, but only for actively using them in valued ways (Kate Moss does not get paid just for looking good, she has to stand in front of a camera at the right time) and for having taken the trouble to develop them in socially useful directions (presumably Ms Moss has over the years made some efforts to make sure that she looks quite as good as she does). Let us turn now from nature to nurture, from heredity to environment, and consider how desert-claims fare in the face of the observation that not all children enjoy (or suffer) the same conditions in which to develop whatever it is that nature may have bestowed upon them.[19]

It is, of course, inequalities in developmental conditions that those who value equality of opportunity, and many of those who would defend meritocracy, have conventionally been concerned to rectify, or at least to ameliorate. On a reasonably standard view, equality of opportunity requires us to make sure that those who have similar natural

abilities are equally able to develop them, whatever their social circumstances or class background—and it is widely recognized that the social
and material advantages enjoyed by relatively well-off parents tend to
convert into the possession of what we are calling relevant competences
on the part of their children. James Fishkin (1983: 52) gives a fairly
typical list:

Consider, in our society, all the advantages that families from the higher strata
can give to their children: private schools, culture in the home, a secure home
environment, trips abroad, private lessons, an advantaged peer group, and
successful role models. These are only the most obvious examples of differential developmental opportunities affecting both competence and motivation so
as to give children from the higher strata systematic advantages in any system of
meritocratic competition . . .

As Fishkin suggests, even if individuals were not born with unequal
talents, these 'differential developmental opportunities' as between
children born into different classes would be likely to account for a
substantial part of the difference in the actual development of their *ex
hypothesi* equal talents into relevant competences.

Since we think it hard to deny either that developmental conditions
make a difference or that individuals cannot be regarded as responsible
for those conditions that they experience, it should be clear how the
logic of the previous argument applies no less to these considerations
than it did in the case of biological difference. The distinction that
matters, we have suggested, is not that between nature and nurture, nor
between heredity and environment, but that between factors for which
individuals can and cannot be held responsible. If we grant that people
cannot be held responsible for their class of origin, accept that this does
indeed tend to influence (through differential developmental conditions) the possession of relevant competences, and reject the claim that
people can deserve unequal rewards in terms of class advantage on the
basis of factors beyond their control, then we will have exactly the same
problem regarding class positions as deserved as that outlined in the
biological case.[20]

V

Although the general issue of differential developmental conditions is
adequately addressed by the thought above, there is one aspect that
demands slightly fuller consideration, or is at least worthy of emphasis.
It will be noted that Fishkin regards developmental conditions as influencing not only competence but also motivation; and it seems entirely

plausible to think that advantaged parents are more likely to instil in their children the kinds of motivation that will tend both to foster the development of their natural abilities into relevant competences, and themselves to count as relevant competences for the successful perform-ance of relatively well-rewarded jobs. We saw in the previous chapter the extent to which motivational or aspirational factors might be thought to explain both the unequal educational achievements as be-tween those born into different classes and, perhaps (though less plau-sibly if considered to operate independently of effects on education), their unequal occupational achievements also. We think it likely that future debate on social mobility will focus substantially on the role played by such factors in explaining mobility patterns, so it is particu-larly important that we give this difficult and controversial issue proper attention.

To do so, let us briefly remind the reader of where we have now reached in our exposition. In the previous chapter we explained how those who would defend existing mobility rates as meritocratic might do so by claiming that there is nothing unmeritocratic about a society in which people get jobs on the basis of their ability to do them well. For a variety of reasons that may be presumed to act in combination—inherited natural talent, socialization into valued skills, superior (or at least different) motivation—those born into service-class households could be argued to be more likely, when they grow up, to possess the ability to do service-class jobs than are those born into working-class households. In this chapter we have not challenged the claim that Brit-ain is meritocratic in this sense. We have discussed the question of whether, even if it were, the allocation of rewards to individuals that our mobility data represent could be regarded as indicative of social jus-tice—in the sense of giving people what they deserve. Noting that it is problematic to regard people as deserving of reward (at least of the kind of reward represented by our data) on the basis of attributes the un-equal distribution of which is a matter of chance, we suggested that this was particularly problematic for those whose own arguments empha-sized the extent to which natural talent (usually in the form of intelli-gence) tended to be distributed unequally, as between those born into different classes of origin. The same problem was shown to arise in the case of developmental conditions for which, again, the individual could not plausibly be held responsible.

We suspect that even those who are troubled by the idea that people can deserve reward in class terms on the basis of the deployment of attributes for which they cannot claim (full) responsibility will feel that people do deserve such reward for their motivations and aspirations.

While it seems impossible to regard people as responsible for their natural assets, it is surely more plausible to view them as able to decide whether or not to make an effort to cultivate those assets, or to deploy them in the ways that others would be willing to pay to have them deployed. Here, surely, is precisely the kind of class-related attribute that must be regarded as meritorious. Who would disagree that those who work hard deserve to earn more than those who do not? Very few—as we report in Appendix J. Who would disagree that those who have, over the years, made the effort to work hard to develop the skills and gain the qualifications that equip them to do a demanding job deserve rewards not deserved by those who have not made that effort? Again, surely, very few. Even if the argument for differential desert on the basis of chance attributes fails, and leaving aside the problem of how exactly we might identify the relative contribution of the differing factors, could we not justify the inequalities in mobility rates that we have found by appeal to the suggestion that those born into different classes are differently motivated and in this way differently deserving?

We have already suggested that the source of one kind of problem is the causal interdependence of natural ability and motivation. If it is right to think that people are more likely to be motivated to develop their abilities the more likely it seems to them that there will be some point in doing so, then the problem is not merely that it is difficult, perhaps impossible, to identify how much of any current ability can be attributed to natural talent, as opposed to effort in developing it. It is, further, that to reward on the basis of effort would be to reward some, and not to reward others, for doing something that it was much easier, and more sensible, for some to do and others not to do. These are important considerations which by themselves would constitute serious objections to the view that people deserve to be rewarded in proportion to their efforts. In addition to this, however, and setting aside the interdependence of ability and motivation, there is also the difficulty that people's aspirations and motivations are themselves (at least in part) the result of their environment. This raises the question of whether they can be held responsible for them in the way we suggest would be necessary if they are to ground claims to differential deserts.

Once more this question is particularly, and paradoxically, pertinent for those who would insist on the extent to which such motivational factors differ by class. For, in the most general terms, what such an insistence amounts to is the claim that whether or not people possess a particular kind of motivation is likely causally to depend upon something—their class of origin—for which they cannot be held responsible.

Again, then, the effect of the attempt to reconcile our findings with meritocratic principles might seem to undermine the claim that such findings are consistent with the view that people should be rewarded in accordance with desert—at least for those who reject the view that people can deserve class advantage (or disadvantage) on the basis of attributes the distribution of which is a matter of chance. As before, the pure point is one that stands quite independently of questions of class, and concerns solely the relation between environment and motivation. But, again as before, it is made all the more explicit and salient by claims that regard meritorious attributes to be unequally distributed between those born into different social classes.

Since we here approach fundamental issues of social determinism and individual freedom, it is important that we be clear about what kind of argument along these lines might be thought both defensible and subversive of a desert-based justification of rewarding people in proportion to their relevant competences. We are not proposing the strong view that the mere fact that people acquire their motivations by causal processes means that they cannot be held responsible for them. It is plausible to argue that what matters for the judgement of responsibility is not how they came by those motivations but whether they reflectively endorse them.[21] We do not, in normal cases, regard a wrongdoer as blameless merely because she was brought up in a family that encouraged wrongful behaviour—we think that she has the ability herself to reflect rationally upon her socialization and to endorse or reject it.[22] Similarly, it would at least be highly controversial, and contrary to our normal practice, to regard observations about the causal relation between class and motivation as undermining any and all attributions of responsibility for motivations that are differentially distributed across classes.

The thought under discussion gets its critical bite, however, from the observation that people's motivations tend crucially to influence their prospects *when they are children*; that is, at a time when those motivations *cannot* be regarded as the result of rational and critical reflection of the kind that would allow us to regard their possessors as responsible for them.[23] It is generally accepted that children will tend to adopt and mimic the values of their parents, rather than to develop their own independent attitudes, or that where they rebel against parental pressures their doing so cannot plausibly be regarded as the exercise of that reflective faculty which might license attributions of responsibility. To the extent, then, that it is differential motivations and aspirations in childhood that account for the possession of different relevant competences in adults, it seems to us hard to regard as deserved those inequalities in reward that result from the exercise of such competences.

It is, of course, an open question how much of the differences in adults' relevant competences can be attributed to differences in childhood motivations and aspirations. ('Childhood' here means simply 'before the development of that faculty which might permit us to regard people as responsible for their motivations'). We are not educationalists, and can only speculate that the cumulative and mutually reinforcing effects of motivation on achievement make it considerable. How infants and primary-school children regard school presumably makes a big difference to their progress, which in turn is likely significantly to affect how they develop subsequently. Without hazarding a view about the age at which it might be that people start to become responsible for their own motivations—and of course this may be different for different people—we can observe that once the non-responsible unmotivated have approached this age they will already, other things equal, be some way behind the non-responsible motivated. To achieve the same school results or personal development from that position of inequality would require not just the same but greater motivation on the part of the previously less motivated than on the part of those who were already enjoying the benefits of their success-oriented childhood socialization.

We cannot pursue these speculations here. Our basic point is simply that those who regard class-based differences in socialization as justifying class-based differences in access to positions of relative advantage should bear in mind that people are not responsible for their socialization. Even if we regard adults as responsible for their attitudes and motivations, it remains importantly the case that children cannot be so regarded, in which case our general scepticism about the appeal to inequalities in deserts on the basis of differences for which people are not responsible has plenty of room to take hold.

One further aspect of the motivational issue warrants brief discussion. It will be recalled, from the previous chapter, that a central sociological issue concerns the appropriate way to analyse the motivational and aspirational differences between classes—and in particular whether these are themselves the product of social inequality. It might be thought that this would affect how we should think about such differences in relation to questions of desert and social justice. For example, to the extent that low aspirations can properly be regarded as adaptive to the prevailing class structure itself, then it may seem particularly problematic to regard those who have such aspirations as deserving their relatively disadvantaged destinations in the class structure. If people's motivations are themselves to be explained in terms of the context of inequality that they confront, then it looks implausible to argue that social justice is achieved when those motivations result in actions that tend, across generations, disproportionately to leave the relatively disadvantaged and the relatively advantaged where they are, in terms of the class structure. It is hard to appeal to differential aspirations to justify unequal outcomes if those aspirations are themselves best analysed as responses to differences in people's conditions of action.[24]

Whether the explanation of differential aspirations makes a difference to their implications for judgements of justice seems to us to depend on whether we have in mind the childhood case of the kind discussed above or the adult case in which people are normally regarded as responsible for their aspirations. In the case of adults, the explanation of the differential aspirations does indeed seem to matter. There is a difference between the person who does not bother to invest in the acquisition of relevant competences because she thinks the likely costs and benefits make it a bad investment, or whose rejection of the pursuit of material advancement can be understood as part of a process of cultural adaptation to the context of inequality, and the person who does not bother because she is genuinely and non-adaptively happy in her current badly paid job and has no desire to be upwardly mobile. In the latter case, it seems appropriate to regard the choice as justifying the low rewards, whereas in the former two it is at least arguable that the structure of opportunities against which aspirations and values are formed tells against the justice of the outcome. In this sense, even in those cases where we regard individuals as responsible for their motivations, we may still think it inappropriate to appeal to differential motivations to justify the inequalities that they tend to produce.

In the childhood case, on the other hand, it seems that worries about the explanation of motivations and aspirations undermining claims that they can justify unequal rewards on desert grounds do not depend upon the suggestion that such origins lie in the fact of social inequality itself. Even if one agreed with Murphy that differential motivations and aspirations could not be explained as adaptations to background structures of inequality, but rather reflected genuinely and irreducibly different world-views as between those born into different classes, that would still not be sufficient to establish that children who held such attitudes were indeed responsible for doing so, and hence could be said to deserve the class positions to which those attitudes tended to lead—at least not in so far as their attitudes were things that they had come to by socialization processes of the kind apparently emphasized by those who regard

differential educational and occupational achievements as the consequence of differential childhood aspirations. All that is needed to get
our worry going in the childhood case are the assertions that a child's
parents influence his or her motivations and aspirations, that their
motivations and aspirations as children make a different to the relevant
competences that adults possess, and that people cannot be held responsible for who their parents are.

The analysis of differential motivations and aspirations seems to us
likely to constitute the terrain of much future research on issues of class
and inequality. That is why we have given the normative implications of
differing accounts such extended treatment. As usual, however, the
basic thrust of our discussion is rather straightforward. Those who, in
order to reconcile the facts about social mobility with ideals of social
justice, insist that psychological factors are differentially distributed by
class of origin necessarily raise the question of how exactly it is that class
exerts its influence. Our point is simply that they may also need to think
about whether it does so in ways that undermine the justification it was
intended to provide.

VI

We think it unlikely that readers will want to deny the significant role
played by chance in determining which people do and which do not
possess competences that others might want to pay them for exercising.
Even if one resists the more controversial of the suggestions set out
above, it is clear that factors for which individuals are not responsible
are very influential in terms of their prospects for success in life. This,
indeed, seems to be something emphasized precisely by those who
would defend mobility patterns and class outcomes in Britain as instan-
tiations of social justice.

It seems, then, that one is presented with the following choices. One
could argue that people can deserve class advantage (and disadvantage)
on the basis of exercising attributes that they are lucky (or unlucky) to
possess (or not to possess). Or one could claim that such patterns and
outcomes, though constituting a very rough and imperfect form of social
justice, are none the less the best practical approximation to it: that is,
nobody deserves exactly what they get, but given problems in identifying the relative contributions of different factors to people's marketable
abilities, we have to regard what the market will pay for those abilities
as the best feasible indicator of how much they do indeed deserve.
Alternatively, one could defend the distributions that labour markets

produce on grounds other than those of justice. Finally, one could argue that justice requires that people be rewarded in accordance with their relevant competences, even though those competences are not of the kind to justify the claim that the individuals who possess them *deserve* those rewards.

To see why these last two alternatives need not be very far apart, recall the distinction between the criteria that do or should govern the allocation of individuals to occupations, on the one hand, and the criteria that do or should govern the allocation of rewards to individuals, on the other.[25] It is relatively straightforward to see how one might defend a meritocratic allocation of people to jobs, where merit is understood in terms of relevant competences: there are obvious advantages to be had from a system in which jobs are done by those best able to do them. The difficulty arises when one tries to defend the allocation of rewards to people on the basis of their possession of relevant competences whilst rejecting the claim that such competences, because significantly the result of luck, deserve reward. At this point, as we suggested in Chapter 2, considerations of efficiency naturally arise, and it becomes plausible to argue that inequalities of reward may be justified since they are required to induce people to exercise their abilities in the ways that are most productive for the society as a whole.[26] While it is conventional to present such considerations as independent of justice, they might none the less be argued to be of the right kind to provide a moral justification of such inequalities, for it is surely morally desirable that people's talents be exercised so as to maximize the aggregate social product—if only to ensure that those who lack the ability to succeed in the labour market can be given the resources necessary for the meeting of their basic needs; or, if that could be done in a sub-optimally productive society, so that they can have as many resources as possible to devote to their life-plans. And, of course, if we took justice to require that basic needs be met, or (following Rawls's difference principle) that the least advantaged have as many resources as possible, then we would seem to have a justice-argument justifying the inequalities necessary for the production of the resources required to meet these conditions.[27]

This last argument is, however, not without difficulties. One problem, as we noted, concerns the motivation it attributes to agents. If people are assumed to care about maximizing the position of the worst-off group, why do they need incentives to induce them to do that which will do so?[28] Another concerns obvious conflicts between the idea that justice requires the maximization of the well-being of the least advantaged and the value of self-realization. How many would-be poets are to be forced into more productive lines of business by the requirement that they exercise their abilities in the way that is optimal for the worst off?[29] A full exploration of the issues raised would involve careful consideration of the difference between rewarding people for possessing scarce and valued abilities *tout court* and rewarding them for undergoing long periods of training, or taking on particularly burdensome kinds of work, or perhaps for not doing something else (such as writing poetry) that they would very much like to do.

This perhaps prompts the thought that the justification of inequalities we have in mind here—that which appeals to their beneficial consequences for the least advantaged—gives grounds for rehabilitating the notion of desert after all. There are, in fact, various ways in which this rehabilitation might be effected, and it is important that they not be confused with the conception of desert that we have been considering in the bulk of this chapter. First, it seems to make sense to say that, other things equal, those who do unpleasant jobs—or whose socially useful work requires them to incur other forms of disadvantage—deserve to earn more than those who do not. Those attracted to this particular move should, however, be aware both that it involves a closet egalitarian claim about the justice of compensation for disadvantage—the unequal reward is deserved only in so far as it is required to equalize the balance of burdens and benefits—and that it is extremely implausible to regard claims of this kind as justifying the inequalities of access and outcome indicated by our empirical findings. The British labour market is far more plausibly regarded as rewarding people in accordance with their unequal possession of relevant competences than with their unequal bearing of work-related burdens.

Secondly, we may well think that those who invest in years of training because they understand that doing so will fit them for highly paid work deserve the high pay they get for so doing, but on the specific grounds that they have a legitimate expectation of such reward. Here the brute (or pre-institutional) notion of desert as reward for some activity or quality possessed by a person is confused with a claim about people's legitimate expectations given current institutions and practices. It is quite coherent to recognize, on the one hand, that people making choices about what to do in an institutional structure that is known to reward some activities over others deserve to be rewarded for those choices whilst, on the other, rejecting the view that the institutional structure of rewards for activities can be justified as giving people what they (really) deserve. Finally, and involving a more serious confusion, it seems to us likely that some people regard as desert-based justifications of inequality what are actually consequentialist and incentive-based arguments of the kind that we have been careful to distinguish from questions of desert properly understood. People may perhaps think that brain surgeons deserve to earn more than hospital orderlies, but take as their grounds for this belief the consequentialist view that if they did not earn more, then nobody would want to be a brain surgeon. Here we might be tempted to say that such people *think* that they believe that the brain surgeon deserves more, but in fact what they believe is not really a claim about desert at all.[30]

With these complexities out of the way, the justification of class-related inequalities that appeals to the necessity of incentives can clearly be distinguished from the justification that appeals to the idea that people born into different classes are unequally deserving of class-related rewards. We hope that this chapter has raised some serious doubts about the latter—doubts that apply at a general theoretical level as well as to more concrete attempts to justify the actual inequalities of access that characterize modern Britain. And although we have outlined the possibility of an alternative defence of the justice of meritocracy—understood as a distribution in which people are rewarded in proportion to their ability to satisfy the preferences of others—this should not be taken to indicate that we regard that defence as unproblematic. However, it would be inappropriate for us to pursue our critique at greater length, and we would doubtless lose yet more of our readership should we try to do so. No matter. G. A. Cohen (1995: 332) has wryly observed that 'economic inequality is no new thing in capitalist society, so there has been plenty of time for a lot of arguments to accumulate in favor of it'. If we have persuaded the reader that these arguments are too often confused with one another, and that the argument from desert in particular is deeply problematic, we will have fulfilled our aim.

NOTES

1. We distinguish between the justice of the class structure and the justice of the pattern of mobility within it only because, as we pointed out in Ch. 2, issues of access and opportunity do not necessarily exhaust the concept of social justice. Individuals could arrive at different class positions by whatever processes one might wish—however meritocratically, or through a competition characterized by however much equality of opportunity—and it would still be a further question as to whether the inequalities between the positions themselves were just.

2. Strictly speaking, only some of the inequalities between class positions are properly thought of as resulting from labour-market processes, since some

of the advantages enjoyed by those who hold particular occupational roles may result, not from the market situation, but from the work or employment situation that characterizes the occupation. It is not simply a function of supply and demand that academics enjoy a kind of autonomy and security of tenure not available to those who work on assembly lines or to small shopkeepers. There are what we might think of as aspects of advantage that are intrinsic to certain kinds of occupational role and that do not result merely from the operation of market forces. While it is instructive to bear in mind the differences between the kinds of advantage enjoyed by occupations placed in different classes by our categorization, and in another context it might be appropriate to consider whether these different kinds of advantage have different kinds of explanation, it will simplify our discussion if, for present purposes, we regard all inequalities between class positions as the result of market processes. We are also, of course, aware that some sociologists (including many who write about segmented labour markets) would reject the view that differences even in such apparently market-driven phenomena as pay are the result either of supply and demand or even of the different tasks that people perform. On these alternative views, such inequalities are better explained in terms of social exclusion, power, and suchlike.

3. Daniel Bell (1976: 451–5), for example, defines a 'just meritocracy' in precisely these terms, linking merit to individual achievement, earned status, and desert.

4. Miller (1996) argues that racist preferences can be ignored by those concerned with meritocracy, because they are not mere preferences, but are rather 'informed by theories or beliefs that directly contravene the principle of merit—for instance the belief that there is a whole category of persons who are unfit to take on work of a certain kind'. In his view, there is thus nothing paradoxical in excluding such preferences from consideration, when deciding who is best able to perform a job. But even if we regard this response as satisfactory, Miller acknowledges that there are other borderline cases where the issues are less straightforward.

    Such cases may well be directly relevant to the issues of class that we are investigating. Suppose it helps people do a job well that they get on with the others in the workplace and that others get on well with them. This might involve a willingness to socialize together, a shared set of norms easing communication, and so on. Here it could clearly be the case that someone would be able better to do the job, and so to contribute to the satisfaction of the preferences of others, just because they shared a subcultural milieu with others already employed in the business. Suppose now that we make one such group a chambers of barristers and another a building-site of manual labourers. When the barristers hire someone who comes, like them, from a certain social class, has been to a certain kind of school and university, and so on, they may not have in mind anything other than the need to appoint someone who will be able to do the job well, taking into account all the relevant considerations, including how he or she will get on with colleagues. The same applies to the labourers. It is easy to see how tendencies to class self-recruitment are likely to result and might be defended by appeal to the contribution principle. But it should also be clear that 'reaction qualifications' may stand in some tension with the ideal of meritocracy. On this issue, see also Wertheimer (1983) and Fishkin (1983: 25–7).

5. We ignore here complications arising from the fact that some people's preferences may be more or less expensive to satisfy than others. If I need champagne and caviar to get the same welfare that you get from beer and crisps, then our having equal amounts of resources to devote to the satisfaction of our preferences would yield us unequal amounts of welfare. Properly to specify what might be meant by 'value to society' would, of course, take us into issues concerning not only the distribution of money but also the distribution of welfare itself: if our goal were simply that of maximizing aggregate welfare, it would make sense to give extra resources to those most efficient at converting those resources into welfare, resulting in an unequal distribution of both. The definitive pieces on this kind of issue are those by Dworkin (1981a; 1981b).

6. We have discussed elsewhere the question of whether it should matter to political philosophers that most people appear to disagree with them on matters of desert—or, indeed, whether they have any reason to take popular beliefs about distributive justice into account at all (see Swift et al. 1995). On the discrepancy between political philosophers and popular opinion, see Scheffler (1992).

7. Notice that this is different from saying that people must deserve the very attributes that justify their claims to deserve something. As Nozick (1974: 213–27) has pointed out against Rawls, who is often regarded as arguing in this way, this would generate an infinite regress. For a good discussion of this issue, see also Zaitchik (1977).

8. Note that neither of these factors is beyond everybody's control, so they are not merely a matter of chance *tout court*. Even in the hereditary case, it is quite possible to imagine people attempting to influence the kind of children that they are likely to have by choosing co-parents on the basis of the attributes that they are likely to pass on to those children. Indeed, it is possible to imagine societies using political means to encourage or discourage certain sectors of the population from procreating, on similar grounds. In such cases, it would not be entirely a matter of luck what kinds of children were born, but it would still remain something for which the individual child could not claim responsibility—a matter of chance as far as the child is concerned. Similarly, it may of course be the case that parents are responsible for whether or not they provide, or are able to provide, their children with non-biological conditions of development. But, again, this does not tell against the role of luck in determining the individual's destiny.

9. For a valuable discussion of what she calls 'the regression principle' and its problems, see Hurley (1993: 179–92).

10. We are grateful to Andrew Williams for helpful discussion on this point. Notice that our focus on the comparative issue might seem to leave non-comparative desert claims untouched, and it is no objection to our argument that this should be so. But if desert claims, by their nature, imply that people should, as a matter of justice, *get* what they deserve, and if resources are scarce, then it seems to us problematic to suppose that we could assert that some individual (non-comparatively) deserves a particular reward. Whether he should in fact get what he is claimed to deserve would seem to depend upon what other people deserve, and how their deserts compare with his, in which case it is not clear that the comparative issue can be avoided. Cf. Feinberg (1980: 267): 'When the occasion for justice is the division of divisible but limited goods or the assignment of divisible but limited chores, *how much will be left for the others* is always pertinent to the question of how much it would be just for any particular individual to get.'

11. David Miller (1992*a*: 167–9) discusses various problems of regarding jobs as prizes in his essay on 'Deserving Jobs'. For an illuminating discussion of the issue of voluntariness in desert claims generally see Lamont (1994).

12. In different ways, the extent of the unequal advantages enjoyed by those in different class positions are documented in e.g. Reid (1989), Goldthorpe and Marshall (1992), and Bartley et al. (1996).

13. Cf. Thomas Nagel (1991: 113): 'Like beauty, talent and excellence also attract recognition, admiration, and gratitude, and such responses are among the natural rewards of human life. But the economic rewards which some talents are able to command, if properly developed, are another story. They cannot be said to be merited just because the recognition of excellence on which they are based is merited. To try to sever the connection between talent and admiration would be wrong. But to sever the connection between talent and income, if could be done, would be fine. Those with useful talents do not naturally deserve more material benefits than those who lack them.'

14. See also Walzer (1983). Miller and Walzer's edited volume on *Justice, Pluralism and Equality* (1995) offers a fuller statement of Miller's development of Walzer's ideas along these lines.

15. This, rather than any dehumanizing denial of the idea that people can control whether or not they make an effort, would seem to be what Rawls (1971: 312) has in mind: 'The effort a person is willing to make is influenced by his natural abilities and skills and alternatives open to him. The better endowed are more likely, other things equal, to strive conscientiously, and there seems to be no way to discount for their greater good fortune. The idea of rewarding desert is impracticable.'

16. We do not deny the commonsense conviction that there will be cases where it is possible to attribute to people responsibility for their being more or less

productive than others. We need think only of genetically identical twins with the same upbringing. The problem of attribution arises at the macro-level where we are concerned with very large groups, with markedly unequal endowments of genetic and social luck.

17. One might deal with this last problem by claiming that people should be rewarded, not for their actual ability to provide what others want, but for their efforts to do so. On this view, two people who try equally hard to cultivate valued skills would deserve equal reward, even if one succeeded and the other failed in acquiring them. But this still seems insufficient, since we surely want people to take into account the likelihood of their acquiring the skills if they try, in which case we are back to the earlier problem of the dependence of effort on chance attributes—but with the added twist that not merely is it the case that people's efforts do depend upon natural abilities but it is also quite right that they should.

18. One way of putting the point that does tie the general objection from arbitrariness to the specific issue of class origin as a determinant of reward would be to observe that any attempt to talk about meritocracy whilst arguing that natural endowments can properly play a role in determining who gets what seems to blur the distinction between achievement and ascription upon which meritocratic theory conventionally relies for its normative appeal. It makes sense to value the idea of people being rewarded on the basis of what they have achieved rather than on the basis of ascribed characteristics such as class, race, or gender, but it makes less sense to do so if one simultaneously asserts that such ascribed characteristics significantly influence people's possession of those attributes necessary for such achievement. The stronger the claim about the significance of hereditary and hence ascriptive factors for individual achievement, the less morally significant any attempt to distinguish between the two. Here class does come into the story, because it is one of the ascribed characteristics that those who would argue for meritocracy are particularly keen to see replaced by achievements.

19. Our turning from nature to nurture should not be taken to imply any acceptance of a clear or sharp distinction between the two. Since the development of the foetus in the womb is itself affected by the conditions of the mother—including conditions that we would normally regard as environmental—it is clear that what people are born with, and thus have as if from nature alone, is itself in part socially conditioned. On this point, see Gardner (1995).

20. In an interesting comment on a draft of this chapter, David Miller suggests that our treating as equivalent differences in natural ability and differences in developmental conditions misses the point that the former, and not the latter, are integral to personality. It makes sense to think about what a particular child might have achieved if he or she had had a more encouraging home backgound or better schooling, whereas if we think about someone with different natural abilities we are thinking of a different person.

This would explain why people react differently to the two kinds of factor, even when both are acknowledged to be a matter of luck. It is certainly more usual to worry about unequal luck in developmental conditions than about unequal constitutive luck, and it is generally considered more acceptable to seek to mitigate the former than the latter. Miller is doubtless right about why. But he himself goes on to point out that we cannot equate 'constitutive of personality' with 'given by nature rather than by environment'. (What about cultural factors such as being raised a Catholic?) And even if we accept that the chance factors constitutive of personality are in important ways different from those that constitute a person's environment and developmental conditions—which would explain why we might be more willing to intervene to compensate for inequalities in developmental conditions than to do so in the case of brain cells—that does not itself touch our claim that differences in constitutive factors that are a matter of luck cannot ground claims to unequal deserts of the kind manifested by the class structure and the patterns of mobility within it.

21. Cf. Tim Scanlon (1995: 64): 'Aside from external impediments to bodily motion, what is required for moral appraisal on the view I am presenting is the "freedom", whatever it may be, which is required by critically reflective, rational self-governance. . . . What is required is that what we do be importantly dependent on our process of critical reflection, that that process itself be sensitive to reasons, and that later stages of the process be importantly dependent on conclusions reached at earlier stages. But there is no reason, as far as I can see, to require that this process itself not be a causal product of antecedent events and conditions.' For a book-length defence of this kind of compatibilist position, see Wallace (1994).

22. We might, however, regard someone subject to emotional deprivation in childhood as having been unable to develop the appropriate faculties and hence as less than fully responsible for his or her wrongdoing. For an analysis of reponsibility that takes this thought seriously, and interestingly suggests that justice requires that we should regard such deprivation as itself 'payment-in-advance' for the wrongdoing to which it leads, see Klein (1990).

23. Those who take a compatibilist line on issues of responsibility are happy to recognize that childhood should be regarded as an excusing condition. Or, in Wallace's (1994: 118) more nuanced approach, 'We may distinguish two kinds of conditions that are acknowledged to block or inhibit responsibility: excuses, which function locally (examples include physical constraint or coercion); and exemptions, which operate more globally (such as insanity, childhood, or perhaps addiction).'

24. Notice that this remains the case even if the background inequalities are not themselves unjust. What matters, on this account, is not the injustice of the structure in the context of which aspirations and motivations are formed. All that is needed to subvert the claim that differential aspirations can justify differential and unequal outcomes is the view that the structure is such that those differential aspirations are adaptations to it.

25. Norman Daniels (1978: 218–19) identifies no fewer than 6 different reward schedules—ranging from 'unbridled meritocracy' to 'socialist meritocracy'—that are consistent with meritocracy understood solely in terms of the former.

26. For Daniels (1978: 207), 'claims of merit, in the restricted sense of that term relevant to meritocracies, are derived from considerations of efficiency and productivity and will not support stronger notions of desert'.

27. This is not, of course, to say that the size of the inequalities in the rewards attaching to different jobs that we find in contemporary Britain are of the order that would be needed on incentive grounds. Our point here is simply that some inequalities of this kind might be defended in this way. Note also that, to be precise, an allocation of individuals to occupations could be maximally productive even though nobody was actually doing the job that they were best able to do—since what matters is the best fit overall, not the best fit between any particular person and his or her job. For a discussion of this issue, see Daniels (1978).

28. As Cohen (1995: 336–7) puts it, Rawls's difference principle 'can be used to justify paying incentives that induce inequalities only when the attitude of talented people runs counter to the spirit of the difference principle itself: they would not need special incentives if they were themselves unambivalently committed to the principle. Accordingly, they must be thought of as outside the community upholding the principle when it is used to justify incentive payments to them.' For an excellent discussion of this issue, see also Van Parijs (1993).

29. Rawls's theory prevents such conflicts by listing freedom of occupation as among the basic liberties that are lexically prior to the difference principle.

30. That the compensation and consequentialist approaches to questions of desert are 'not the genuine article but a surrogate' is emphasized by Miller (1991: 378–9). The books reviewed by Miller that give particular attention to these analyses of desert are by Sher (1987) and Sadurski (1985).

9

Conclusion

The concept of meritocracy has two aspects. In one sense of that term, to ask whether a society is meritocratic is to ask a question about the fit between jobs and the characteristics of those who do them. To answer it fully requires both a thorough empirical investigation of the processes by which individuals come to occupy their occupational roles and a careful analysis of the concept of merit. We hope that our empirical findings on the role played by education in the intergenerational transmission of class advantage constitute a contribution to this first task— although, as we recognized when we turned to the second, it is clear that people's educational attainments are only one amongst many factors that may explain, and quite properly be regarded as fitting them for, their occupational destinations. In the other sense of the term, to ask whether a society is meritocratic is to ask about the justice of the distribution of rewards to its members. The two senses are sufficiently independent for this to be a quite separate question. However meritocratic the fit between people and jobs might be, it remains a further issue whether the conception of merit invoked in support of such a claim is capable of justifying inequalities in access to positions of relative advantage. To address this fully requires consideration of issues in moral and political theory that are no less complex and perhaps more controversial.

We do not claim to have provided definitive answers to these questions—although the reader who has come with us this far will be aware that we find the claim that Britain is meritocratic in the sense that people get jobs on the basis of their ability to do them well (or what we have called their relevant competences) rather more plausible than the claim that this ability is justly rewarded in class terms. Our analysis suggests there is something of a paradox here. This may most clearly be brought out by a brief reminder of our argument as a whole.

We started by documenting the unequal mobility chances enjoyed (or suffered) by those born into different social classes. Ready to acknowledge that any immediate inference from these findings to a claim about social injustice or inequality of opportunity would be invalid, we pursued the suggestion that such mobility patterns might be consistent with social justice understood in meritocratic terms, for they might simply reflect the differential distribution of merit. While our analysis of the role played by education suggested that those with similar levels of educational achievement in fact had unequal chances of acquiring well-rewarded jobs, we went on to recognize that there were ways of thinking about merit that might rescue the meritocratic claim, in particular the view which identified merit with the possession of relevant competences. It is at this point that the paradox arises, since this conception of merit—the one that has to be invoked to render at all plausible the claim that our mobility data are consistent with a meritocratic fit between people and jobs— is unable to justify claims about inequalities in access to positions enjoying unequal rewards of the very kind indicated by those same data. Having thought hard about many of the processes by which those born into different classes come to possess different relevant competences—whether these be genetic inheritance, access to educational resources, socialization into marketable social skills, or childhood acquisition of the will to succeed—we find it difficult to see how it could be just for people to be differentially rewarded for having or not having those competences. In this sense, we would suggest, the claim that the fit between people and jobs is meritocratic can be sustained only by highlighting those very considerations that show why a meritocratic allocation of rewards to individuals would be unjust.

Even if this argument about the relation between social class and social justice does not persuade, we trust that we have at least clarified the range of issues at stake, and brought together and made clear the interrelations between these sociological and political-theoretical matters which are too often treated quite separately. We hope that we have given a sense of the difficulties involved in gathering and interpreting empirical data on class and education, in relating these data to various conceptions of merit, and in connecting those various conceptions to issues of justice and desert—difficulties that are usually overlooked by those who come to easy judgements on issues of class inequality and justice, on both sides of the political divide. But we hope also to have made sufficient progress in addressing such difficulties to suggest that they are not altogether insurmountable, and to provide the kind of foundations on which others (including perhaps our future selves) might proceed to build, whether by the collection of relevant empirical evidence or by engagement with the normative issues that underpin judgements about social justice.

APPENDIX A
Technical Details of Data-Sets

Country	Inquiry	Field date	References for survey details	Survey organization	Ages	Mode	Response rate (%)	No. of cases
Bulgaria	ISJP	1991	Kluegel et al. (1995)	Academy of Sciences	18+	face-to-face	90	1,405
Czechoslovakia	CASMIN	1984	Boguszak (1990)	•	15+		91	18,829
Czechoslovakia	ISJP	1991	Kluegel et al. (1995)	STEM	18+	face-to-face	83	1,181
England + Wales	CASMIN	1972	Goldthorpe (1980)	Mary Agar	20–64	face-to-face	82	10,309
Estonia	ISJP	1992	Kluegel et al. (1995)	Saar Poll	18+	face-to-face	93	1,000
Federal Republic of Germany	CASMIN	1976–8	Erikson and Goldthorpe (1992)	ZUMA	18+	face-to-face	61–74*	18,990
Federal Republic of Germany	ISJP	1991	Kluegel et al. (1995)	ZUMA/INFAS	18+	face-to-face	71	1,837
German Democratic Republic	ISJP	1991	Kluegel et al. (1995)	ZUMA/INFAS	18+	face-to-face	71	1,019
Great Britain	BES	1983	Heath et al. (1985)	SCPR	18+	face-to-face	72	3,955
Great Britain	Essex Class Project	1984	Marshall et al. (1988)	SCPR	16–59/64	face-to-face	64	1,770
Great Britain	BES	1987	Heath et al. (1991)	SCPR	18+	face-to-face	70	3,826
Great Britain	ISJP	1991	Kluegel et al. (1995)	RSGB	18+	face-to-face	71	1,319
Great Britain	BES	1992	Heath et al. (1994)	SCPR	18+	face-to-face	73	3,534
Japan	ISJP	1991	Kluegel et al. (1995)	Chuo Univ	20+	face-to-face	52	777
Poland	CASMIN	1972	Erikson and Goldthorpe (1992)	CSO	15–19	face-to-face	90 approx.	74,551
Poland	ISJP	1991	Kluegel et al. (1995)	ISS	18+	face-to-face	88	1,542
Russia	ISJP	1991	Kluegel et al. (1995)	VCIOM	16+	face-to-face	76	1,734
Slovenia	ISJP	1991	Kluegel et al. (1995)	ISS	18+	face-to-face	95	1,375
United States	CASMIN	1973	Featherman and Hauser (1978)	DSD, US Census Bureau	20–65	face-to-face	88	33,613
United States	ISJP	1991	Kluegel et al. (1995)	ISR/SRC	18+	telephone	72	1,414

*ZUMA Superfile is an aggregation of selected relevant variables from 9 different surveys.

APPENDIX B

Guide to Statistical Techniques

Class analysis is among the technically more sophisticated specialisms in modern sociology. Readers who are new to the literature on social mobility may therefore be unfamiliar with some of the statistical methods used in this volume—most notably those of log-linear modelling and logistic regression. The short explanations that follow are intended as a—distinctly non-technical—aid to understanding the tables that appear in earlier chapters.

The Odds Ratio

In the hypothetical situation shown in Table B.1, we have simple mobility tables for two societies, in which men can be mobile from working-class or middle-class origins to working-class or middle-class destinations. In society A, three-quarters of men from middle-class origins arrive at middle-class destinations, while the remainder are downwardly mobile, Similarly, three-quarters of those born into working-class homes are to be found in working-class destinations, while one-quarter are upwardly mobile. If one then calculates the odds of being mobile using the formula shown—that is, the chances of someone born in the middle class arriving at a middle-class rather than a working-class destination, relative to the chances of someone born into the working class achieving a middle-class position rather than remaining in the working class (or, in other words, the ratio of the former to the latter set of odds)—then simple arithmetic shows that the odds ratio in this particular case is approximately 9. That is to say, in the competition to achieve middle-class and avoid working-class destinations, the chances of someone who starts from middle-class origins are nine times greater than those for someone having a working-class background. This odds ratio is then a measure of the unequal mobility chances of individuals having these different class origins.

Now compare the data for society B. Here too, three-quarters of those born into each of the two classes remain there, while one-quarter are socially mobile. However, it should be noted that the working class is relatively much larger in society B, which has also undergone an

TABLE B.1. *The Odds Ratio*

Society A (N = 2,000)

		Destinations					
		Middle	Working				
Origins	Middle	750	250	(1,000)	$\dfrac{f_{11}:f_{12}}{f_{21}:f_{22}}$	$\dfrac{3:1}{1:3}$	$\dfrac{3}{.33} = 9$
	Working	250	750	(1,000)	=	=	=
		(1,000)	(1,000)				

Society B (N = 3,000)

		Destinations					
		Middle	Working				
Origins	Middle	750	250	(1,000)	$\dfrac{f_{11}:f_{12}}{f_{21}:f_{22}}$	$\dfrac{3:1}{1:3}$	$\dfrac{3}{.33} = 9$
	Working	500	1,500	(2,000)	=	=	=
		(1,250)	(1,750)				

intergenerational shift in the class structure that is evident in the marginal totals of the table: the middle class comprises 33 per cent (1,000/3,000) of all class origins but almost 42 per cent (1,250/3,000) of class destinations. If one then considers the inflow rate from working-class origins into the middle class, in comparison with that to be found in society A, it appears that society B is less closed. Some 40 per cent (500/1,250) of the middle class in this society are from working-class origins. In society A this is true of only 25 per cent (250/1,000) of those to be found in middle-class destinations. This straightforward consideration of absolute inflow rates alone suggests that society B is the more open. Furthermore, the working class is twice as large in this society, and greater numbers are upwardly mobile. However, as will be seen from the table, the chances of mobility for the working class, relative to those of the middle class, are in fact the same in both societies (the odds ratio is approximately 9 in each case). This apparent contradiction is simply a consequence of absolute (inflow) rates failing to take into account structural differences in the sizes of classes in the two societies in question.

Odds ratios, in the context of a social mobility study, therefore allow us to appreciate *comparative* mobility chances—regardless of how class structures may vary across societies merely because of structural processes which have altered the relative sizes of the classes. In other words, they facilitate a clear distinction between absolute (or total observed) mobility rates, and relative mobility chances (or social fluidity). From the point of view of social justice (at least when considered as equality of opportunity), this is of course both crucial and convenient, since our interest lies precisely in determining the comparative chances of mobility and immobility of those born into different social classes—rather than documenting mobility chances as such (which will be partly a function of the changing class structure).[1]

As was noted in the text, equality of opportunity is an inherently comparative concept, because it refers to equal opportunities rather than the absolute chance of mobility from any particular class. If, therefore, changes in the class structure create more 'room at the top', as for example happens in society B, we are interested in the chance of someone from working-class origins moving there as compared to the chance of someone from middle-class origins staying there. Clearly, it is necessary to adopt this comparative approach (and therefore the technique of odds ratios), in order to address the issue of equality of opportunity that lies at the heart of debates about meritocracy.

Log-linear Modelling

For ease of presentation, the fictitious example used in the previous section to demonstrate the properties of the odds ratio depicts societies having simple dichotomous class structures, whereas in reality mobility tables commonly include half a dozen or more social class locations. To assess the degree of openness in such cases would require the calculation of large numbers of odds ratios relating to each competing pair of origins and destinations.

A five-class mobility matrix, for example, generates no fewer than 100 odds ratios derived in this fashion. Often these are not without interest. Survey data from the British Social Justice Project suggest that the salariat versus working-class odds ratio for intergenerational mobility among British men is about 5.5; or, in other works, that the chances of a man from service-class origins arriving at a service-class rather than a working-class destination are between five and six times greater than those for someone starting from a working-class background. This is a measure of the advantage held by service-class men over their working-class counterparts in the competition to achieve service-class and avoid working-class destinations. This can be compared with the corresponding odds ratios based on mobility matrices relating to other industrialized societies, as was done in Table 4.5 of our text, which also shows the results of this calculation when applied to data for females.

Similar odds could be determined for all other pairs of competing origins and destinations—salariat versus routine clerical, routine clerical versus *petite bourgeoisie*, and so forth—but it may well then become difficult to perceive any systematic differences in the patterns of relative mobility chances across societies as a whole (or across cohorts or sexes within a particular society). Moreover, odds ratios are sensitive to the effects of sampling error, and become unreliable if the numbers in the cells of the mobility matrix are particularly small. Fortunately, a more robust and concise approach to this problem is readily available, via log-linear techniques for the analysis of cross-tabulated data.

Log-linear models are in fact based on the calculation of odds ratios, but provide a further, simple statistical test for whether or not the results observed are consistent with a number of hypotheses relating to the associations found in contingency tables—in this case those between origins, destinations, and the absence or presence of changes in this association across (say) nations, birth cohorts, or sexes. The technique allows researchers to compare the expected cell frequencies resulting from a given model (hypothesizing, for example, an association between origins and destinations which remains constant across nations) with those which have actually been observed for the real world (as reported in the relevant contingency tables). By moving through a hierarchy of models embracing no association, two-way association, three-way association, and so on between variables, and testing at each stage the goodness of fit between the cell frequencies obtained from the model and those actually observed, we can determine whether or not significant improvements are gained by allowing for more complex associations between the variables involved. In this way we can find the model that best fits—or predicts—the observed values. For this reason, log-linear techniques are now standard in mobility research involving trajectories between social classes, where relative rates—comparative mobility chances or equality of opportunity—are of substantive sociological interest.[2]

There is no agreed 'industry standard' by which the results of such analyses are set out for publication. In part, this is because there are both several ways of doing the modelling, and also a large variety of statistical packages which offer log-linear methods as an option (all tending to produce output in somewhat different forms). Furthermore, however, there are genuine and unresolved disputes among practitioners about (for example) which criteria should guide the selection of models; what constitutes an acceptable degree of fit for a model; and about how the results are affected by limitations of the data, such as the sample size in relation to the number of cells in the tables, or the distribution of cases across the cells themselves.[3]

Our own analyses tend to follow the format shown in Table B.2. Here we report the results of fitting a model of common social fluidity (CmSF) to intergenerational class mobility data (taken from the ISJP) for Polish and West German males. These particular countries have been chosen simply for ease of exposition—specifically because their respective class distributions are rather dissimilar. (The comparison itself forms part of the larger eleven-country test reported in Table 4.4.) The top panel in Table B.2 gives

TABLE B.2. *Results of Testing the Model of Common Social Fluidity in West Germany and Poland (Males Only)*

Model	G^2	df	p	rG^2	delta
1. O + D + N	469.30	24	0.000	—	24.15
2. ON + D	349.71	21	0.000	25.5	20.65
3. ON + DN	231.11	18	0.000	50.8	18.59
4. ON + DN + OD	12.76	9	0.174	97.3	2.50

Notes
1. Class origins (O) and destination (D) class each have 4 levels: salariat (I, II); intermediate (IIIa, IVa + b, V); working (VI, VIIa, IIIb); and agricultural (IVc, VIIb).
2. Independence model = ON + DN.
3. Common social fluidity model = ON + DN + OD.

Class Distribution by Class of Origin (Percentage by Row)

Origins	Destinations				Total
	Salariat	Intermediate	Working	Agricultural	
West Germany					
Salariat	62	18	20	0	100 (138)
Intermediate	39	34	27	0	100 (113)
Working	29	20	51	0	100 (225)
Agricultural	28	6	49	17	100 (53)
Column % total	40	21	38	2	N = 529
Poland					
Salariat	40	30	27	3	100 (60)
Intermediate	26	32	36	6	100 (47)
Working	12	19	64	4	100 (186)
Agricultural	11	9	44	36	100 (166)
Column % total	17	18	49	16	N = 459

the results of the log-linear analysis. The bottom panel shows the cross-tabulated data from which these have been derived.

If we look first at the cross-tabulation, it is clear from the marginal totals that the distribution of both origin and destination classes is different in the two countries, since (for example) the salariat forms a relatively larger proportion of class destinations in West Germany (40 per cent of the total) than in Poland (17 per cent)—whereas the opposite is true in relation to agricultural classes (2 per cent of all class destinations in the German case but 16 per cent in the Polish). It is also evident that, in both countries, there is some association between class origins and destinations. In West Germany for example, 62 per cent of sons from salariat backgrounds arrived at salariat destinations, as against 29 per cent of sons from working-class backgrounds who did so. The corresponding percentages in Poland are 40 and 12. However, what is harder to see—at least from the cross-tabulations alone—is whether or not this association between origins and destinations remains constant (or varies) across the countries, once the differences in the marginal distributions have been taken into account.

The log-linear analysis shown in the upper panel of the table provides a test for this proposition by fitting a model of common social fluidity. The first line in the table reports the relevant statistics when only the so-called main effects are taken into account. This is the model of no association. In essence, the computer, having been given the real figures reported in the cross-tabulation, here creates an imaginary world (or model) in which the cases within the various cells of the tables are redistributed, so that none of the three variables (origins, destinations, nation) is associated with any other—although the marginal totals for each individual variable are constrained to be the same in the imaginary and the real data tables alike (hence 'main effects' model). The cells of the model table are filled with the frequencies that would be obtained if this hypothesis were true.

Model 2 then redistributes the cases again, but this time allowing (in addition to the main effects) for an association between origins (O) and nation (N); or, in other words, not only constraining the marginal totals in the model to be the same as those in the real world, but stipulating further that the association between these two variables should also be identical in the model and in reality—while maintaining the condition of no association between the other variables. The third model then adds the further requirement that the association between destinations and nation is the same in both model and data. Finally, model 4 constrains the association between class origins and destinations in this way, so that the constructed table now corresponds to the real table with respect to the associations found between all three pairwise relationships (ON, DN, and OD). There is an implicit fifth—or saturated model—that is crucial to this analysis (and which we will come to shortly).

At each stage we can measure the goodness of fit between the model and the real data by looking at the statistics shown. Reading from left to right in the table, these are: the log-likelihood ratio statistic (or G^2)—which is a summary measure of the (aptly named) 'deviance' of the model (describing the 'gap' between the cell frequencies expected under the model and cell frequencies as observed in the real world); the number of degrees of freedom in the model (which decrease as a function of the constraints that are imposed on the model—and so represent, as it were, the number of ways in which the imaginary world is allowed to vary from the real world); a test of statistical significance (which calculates the probability that the 'gap' between the model and real tables might be due to sampling error); the percentage reduction in the G^2 achieved by each model when compared with that which we have chosen as our baseline (in this example the model of no association); and, finally, the delta or dissimilarity index (reporting the proportion of cases in the real table that are misclassified by the model).

We can see from the results of this analysis that model 2, which constrains only the association between class origins and nation to be the same in the real and imaginary worlds, provides a poor fit to the data—yielding a G^2 of 349.71, with 21 degrees of freedom, and a 'gap' between the model and real tables that is unlikely—less than one time out of 1,000—to be due merely to sampling error. This model reduces the deviance in the baseline model (of no association) by only a little over 25 per cent, and misclassifies more than 20 per cent of the cases in the cells. Model 3 (which then adds the association between class destinations and nation to model 2) does rather better, reducing both the deviance and the proportion of misclassified cases—but still leaves a statistically significant gap between the imaginary world so created and the real world of the frequencies actually observed.

The fourth model then adds the further constraint that the association between class origins and class destinations be the same in both nations— and so postulates the hypothesis of 'common social fluidity' across the two countries. This now provides an acceptable fit to the data, since the deviance is reduced to only 12.76 with 9 degrees of freedom, a gap between model and real tables that is (as it were) so small that we cannot prove 'beyond reasonable doubt' that it retains statistical significance. (By convention the p-value is usually set at the 95 per cent level; in other words, there is a 5 per cent or greater probability that the remaining deviance could have resulted by chance, so that we cannot reject the null hypothesis that there is 'no difference' between the frequencies expected under the model and those observed in reality.) The deviance in the baseline model has been reduced by more than 97 per cent, and the model now misclassifies fewer than 3 per cent of all cases.

Crucially, therefore, for the particular hypothesis here under test, it is not necessary to saturate the model, by allowing for the possibility of interaction effects (in this case ODN) between the three variables. (In a three-dimensional analysis the interaction model always fits, since it is an exact copy of the data table.) That is to say, we can conclude from these results that the association between origins and destinations does not itself vary by nation; alternatively, that the effect which origins have on destinations is no different among Polish men from the effect among their German counterparts.

Often, the results of a log-linear analysis are set out in such a way that they include only a selection of the possible models; indeed (as will be seen by comparing Tables B.2 and 4.4) we ourselves take the 'conditional independence' model 3 (ON + DN) as our baseline—since we wish specifically to test the CmSF model proposing an identical association between origins and destinations across nations. Note also that in this particular example the three-way effect (were it to be statistically significant) would be easy to interpret. We would conclude that the association between class origins and destinations is somewhat different across the two countries—just how different would depend upon how large or small was the interaction in comparison with the pairwise association model. Three-way (or, where additional variables are involved, higher-order four-way) interaction effects can, however, be difficult to interpret and explain—since one is looking for a variable which has an effect among one group in one (let us say) nation—but a different effect among the corresponding group elsewhere.

Logistic Regression

It should be clear from the previous section that log-linear models are theory driven. They test for the presence or absence of an association in which one has a substantive interest. For example, we might predict an interaction effect between origins, destinations, and birth-cohort (to be expected under the hypothesis that relative mobility chances vary according to age group); or, alternatively (as in the above illustration), investigate the proposition that the association between origins and destinations stays constant across nations (the CmSF hypothesis). However, if one is interested in the *strength* of an association, or in the relative importance of two or more causal influences, regression methodology is more appropriate.

Logistic regression is tailored to the situation in which the dependent variable is dichotomous (or binary). For example, these might include whether or not one is unemployed, receiving higher education, or is/is not a member of the salariat. The results of logistic regression models can be expressed in the form of odds ratios, telling us how much change there is in the probability of being unemployed, receiving higher education, being found in the salariat (or whatever), given a unit change in any other given variable—but holding all other variables in the analysis constant. More simply, the results (as measured by the changed odds on being found in a particular category) tell us how much a hypothesized cause has affected this outcome, taking the role of all other hypothesized causes into account.[4]

Typically we report three statistics in our regression models. The first of these is the beta (parameter estimate or standardized regression coefficient), which is—crudely speaking—a measure of the size of the effect that an independent variable (let us say class of origin) has on a dependent variable (for example the probability of being found in a salariat destination), after the effects of another variable (such as educational attainment) have been taken into account (as in Table 6.8 above). The standard error provides us with a means of judging the accuracy of our predictions about the effect in question. One rule of thumb is that the beta should be at least twice the size of the standard error. Finally, as already noted, we include the odds ratios themselves—which make the relative probabilities being described in the model intuitively easier to grasp.

NOTES

1. Disagreement about the precise significance of the distinction between absolute and relative mobility rates nevertheless remains a feature of the specialized literature on social mobility. See e.g. the exchange between Geoff Payne and John Westergaard in Clark et al. (1990: 277–302). For an earlier 2-volume study which tends to confound changes in the class structure with changes in social fluidity, see Payne (1987a; 1987b). Both the debate and the confusion explain why we have tended to labour the point about the appropriateness of this distinction in the context of debates about equality of opportunity.
2. The controversy between the competing class analysis and status attainment approaches to the study of stratification and social mobility, which sometimes features disputes about the relative merits of log-linear and multiple regression techniques, is largely beyond the concerns of this volume. The nature of these arguments is well represented in the debate between Walter Müller and Jonathan Kelley in Clark et al. (1990: 307–57). See also Appendix I below.
3. The best introduction to the logic of log-linear analysis is probably Gilbert (1981). Knoke and Burke (1980) gives a fuller account of some of the problems and debates surrounding the technique but requires rather more from the reader by way of mathematical skills.
4. For a short introduction to the technique, see Walsh (1990: ch. 15). A more advanced discussion will be found in Aldridge and Nelson (1984).

APPENDIX C
Constructing Goldthorpe Classes

I

Sociologists who do research on social stratification—particularly those involved in cross-national comparative studies—may well feel short-changed by our discussion of social class in Chapter 3. There, we simply observed that our analysis made use of the class categories devised for the Oxford Mobility and CASMIN Projects by John Goldthorpe and his colleagues; explained the underlying logic of the schema itself; and cited evidence that validates the claims made by its authors regarding the class characteristics of the various categories (particularly the idea that there are substantial inequalities of position between the working, intermediate, and service classes). In subsequent chapters the Goldthorpe classification was (more or less) straightforwardly applied to the analysis of our class mobility and other data.

Matters are, of course, not really that simple. Even if one endorses Goldthorpe's general approach, as against that offered by any of the several other class theorists who have devised alternative ways of mapping the class structure, there are still a number of controversial aspects of his schema that are sidestepped by our earlier discussion, and in respect of which specialists may wish to know both where we stand and how (in practice) we resolved the issues.

Three problems in particular deserve mention. All are prominent in the current sociological literature on class stratification. First, there is the charge that Goldthorpe's classification lacks adequate theoretical foundations, a criticism that has generated a debate in which one of us (Marshall) has already been involved. A second line of critique centres on the claim that the Goldthorpe schema is inherently sexist, because it is rooted in a taxonomy of occupations that ignores the personal characteristics of incumbents, most notably their sex. Finally, there are questions of reliability raised by the cross-national coding of occupations, this being a topic about which many previous comparative researchers of class and social mobility have fought the academic equivalent of pitched battles. Let us consider each of these issues in turn.

II

The charge that the Goldthorpe scheme is 'inadequately theorized' or 'merely commonsensical' is long-standing but has as yet to be given a precise formulation. Often it is heard among class analysts whose more abstract theories of class structure and processes have failed to translate into plausible empirical findings. Many of these have a Marxist pedigree and involve detailed elaboration of the principles outlined in *Capital*. Invariably, however, the predictions arrived at by this means have been falsified because the categories devised for the analysis can make only limited sense of class-related phenomena in which researchers are interested. Data concerning shared life-styles or values and collective action simply cannot be made to fit the theories. Some of these critics have subsequently acknowledged that Goldthorpe's approach is empirically the more sound; or, more precisely, that the Goldthorpe categories have greater external (or construct) validity. Against this background, the claim that his classification is nevertheless flawed because 'theoretically underdeveloped' seems—to us at least—to amount to little more than rhetorical flourish.[1]

The most sustained attack along these lines (from, as it happens, a non-Marxist quarter) does little more than assert that the premises underpining Goldthorpe's work somehow represent 'a retreat from class theory'. These allegedly flawed premises include Goldthorpe's insistence that class concepts be as sharply defined as is operationally feasible; his interest in determining which class categorizations are most effective in displaying variation in the dependent variables under examination; and his refusal to make assumptions about the pre-existence of class. Presumably, however, as others have pointed out on Goldthorpe's behalf, his 'open-minded and sensible empirical approach' is to be preferred, if the alternative is 'to prejudge the relevance of class analysis, to disregard effectiveness in explanation, and to adopt woolly and vague concepts'.[2]

Rather than rerun this rather acrimonious debate here, we will attempt instead to justify our counterclaim that the Goldthorpe scheme provides an appropriate basis for our own particular study of class and justice, because it is conceptually well grounded—so that calls for further 'theorization' of its premises are unwarranted.

As the major publication emanating from the CASMIN Project makes clear (Erikson and Goldthorpe 1992*a*: 37–42), its authors propose that employment relations are crucial to delineating the structure of class positions in modern societies, and that the primary distinction is between employers (who buy the labour of others and so assume some degree of control and authority over them), employees (selling their labour to employers and placing themselves under this control and authority), and the self-employed (who do neither). In these societies, the basic structure of class positions is then modified by the transformation of property into corporate forms (such that most major employers are private or public organizations rather than individuals), and by the growth and differentiation of the category of employee within these increasingly bureaucratic enterprises. Individual proprietors are mainly small employers with relatively few employees. The latter clearly occupy a range of work and labour-market situations. In terms of their class positions, the most important distinction stems from the quite different conditions of employment enjoyed by the salariat and the working class, as reflected in the contrasting terms of the service relationship on the one hand and the labour contract on the other.

Erikson and Goldthorpe (1992a: 43–4) describe at some length the conceptual foundations of the distinction they make between the professional, higher technical, administrative, and managerial positions of the salariat, and the wage-earning manual occupations of the working class. In particular, they emphasize the way in which members of the salariat are required to exercise delegated authority or specialized knowledge and expertise on behalf of the employing organization, in return for which they enjoy both the trust of their employers and relatively favourable conditions of employment (see also Goldthorpe 1982). However, since this contrast is of an ideal-typical kind, the classes are further distinguished according to the range of responsibilities and beneficial conditions surrounding the service relationship (classes I and II) and the extent to which the external controls of the money-for-effort exchange are relaxed to allow the exercise of necessary discretion on the part of (mainly skilled) manual workers (classes VI and VII). The routine clerical (class III) and lower-grade technical or supervisory (class V) positions are associated with employment relationships that take a mixed form between the extremes of the service relationship and the pure labour contract. Characteristically, as the authors of the scheme themselves point out, difficulties arising from this intermediate standing frequently surface in employer/employee conflicts over issues such as time-keeping, chances of promotion, and methods of remuneration. Organizations themselves are ambivalent about whether these personnel are 'staff' or 'labour'. The routine non-manual employees comprising class IIIb share conditions of employment that are barely distinguishable from those of non-skilled manual workers in general—so the two can reasonably be considered together in this form of class analysis. Finally, the division between agricultural and other proprietors and workers is justified by distinctive elements of the conditions of employment in the primary sector, arising from the holding of property in land, the organization of production being often family-based, and the substitution of payments in kind for at least part of the monetary wage.

It is difficult to see precisely why the class schema that is derived by this reasoning should be deemed to be a retreat from theory. It articulates the quite specific hypothesis that employment relations are the crucial determinant of the structure of class positions in industrial societies. These positions are identified in a conceptually precise and logically consistent manner. A research programme of class analysis is then pursued that allows one to formulate and evaluate this approach alongside others, in terms of its heuristic and explanatory performance in studying relationships between class structures, class mobility, class-based inequalities, and class-based action.

It is true that, unlike the deterministic class analysis that characterizes Marxist sociology, Erikson and Goldthorpe's strategy entails no theory of history according to which class conflict must serve as the engine of social change, no theory of class exploitation proposing that class relations are necessarily antagonistic, and no theory of class-based collective action suggesting that individuals in similar class positions are automatically predisposed to pursue common class interests. Instead, as has been pointed out elsewhere, these are matters reserved for empirical investigation. As Goldthorpe sees it (rightly in our view), class analysis explores (rather than 'theorizes') the relationships between class structure on the one hand (here defined by employment relations in labour markets and production units in different sectors of national economies), and on the other

the processes through which individuals and families are distributed and redistributed among these positions over time; and the consequences thereof for their life-chances and for the social identities that they adopt and the social values and interests that they pursue.[3]

This is a commitment to a research programme, rather than a declaration of faith in axiomatic propositions about the relationships between structure, consciousness, and action. But it has very clear theoretical foundations in sociology and is not, surely, the exercise of mere commonsense.

III

A second, currently fashionable, criticism of the scheme also raises issues of its reliability with reference to the classification of women's occupations. A long and complex tale about the interaction (or lack of it) between class processes and those associated with gender has been woven around the construction of Goldthorpe's scheme and the results with which it is associated. At least some of the details of this story emerge in the analysis of intergenerational class mobility patterns that is offered in Appendix G below. (See, in particular, the results presented in Table G.1.) All that needs be grasped at this juncture is the fundamental point that the original class categories were designed as part of an investigation into male social mobility patterns. For the largest part the CASMIN Project is itself a study of social mobility among men. Not surprisingly, therefore, a number of critics have suggested that it is male conditions of employment that Goldthorpe has in mind in constructing his classes. This operational logic is said to make the class analysis (and the categories themselves) sex-specific. In particular, critics have pointed to the generally accepted wisdom that the occupational division of labour is sex-segregated, since women are concentrated in some occupations rather than others; that most occupational classifications differentiate poorly between women's jobs; and that, within specific occupational categories, women tend to have inferior conditions of service to corresponding males (see e.g. Crompton and Sanderson 1990: 3–15).

It seems to us that this criticism is less damaging than might at first appear to be the case. It is clear that, because of processes such as sex-typing and patriarchal exclusion, there is indeed a marked vertical and horizontal segregation of occupations in the labour markets of most advanced industrial societies. However, it is then a moot point as to whether the subsequent crowding of women into a relatively small number of occupational categories and statuses is an artefact of supposedly sexist class taxonomies, or merely a reflection of the realities of male power over the world of paid work. Critics of the Goldthorpe scheme seem to want to argue both that sex discrimination in employment constrains women into a limited number of lower-level jobs and that any classificatory device that reflects this is somehow inadequate or sexist.

Attempts to construct non-sexist class taxonomies that might obviate this difficulty have, in any case, proved singularly unsuccessful. These have foundered on the rocks of ad hocery, since the categories that have been devised for women typically embrace such characteristics as the presence of dependent children, stage in family life cycle, educational attainment, and life-style—although it is by no means clear how (if at all) these may be said to be criteria that define *class* positions. Until a scheme is brought forward which not only includes more women on a more finely differentiated basis but also does so in a manner that is consistent with a recognizable theory of the delineation of the structure of class positions within modern society, there would seem to be little to be gained by pursuing this particular line of criticism.[4]

IV

Finally, we must acknowledge that no cross-national comparative study based on survey results in which a social class variable features prominently is complete, without some explicit consideration being given to the problems of measurement incomparability that have characterized many earlier analyses.

These problems are widely recognized among the experts in this field. For example, in the introduction to their cross-national test of the so-called FJH hypothesis (see Appendix H below), Ganzeboom et al. (1989: 4) note:

Despite efforts by most comparative analysts to recode occupational data from different countries into a single classification, so as to effect cross-national comparisons uncontaminated by variations in occupational classification schemes, such comparisons remain vulnerable to errors resulting from imperfect comparability of measurement no matter how carefully they are carried out. For this reason, it is difficult to know to what extent differences (and similarities) observed in the data reflect true variations in mobility patterns and to what extent they merely reflect classification and measurement errors.

In an attempt to transcend this difficulty, Ganzeboom and his colleagues examined multiple mobility tables for each country, giving more weight in their analyses to those studies which—in their judgement—mapped occupational details most precisely into Goldthorpe class categories.

In contrast, the researchers who undertook the CASMIN Project addressed these same issues of data comparability via the alternative strategy of reanalysing existing national mobility studies in their 'raw', rather than their 'processed', form. That is, instead of attempting to correct for the uneven quality of published mobility tables in the analysis, Goldthorpe and his colleagues opted for extensive recoding of the basic occupational information itself—at the unit-record level—into (what were then taken to be) cross-nationally standardized class variables.

Against this background of (still unresolved) dispute about comparability of measurement, experts may wish to be reassured about our own coding procedures, while the uninitiated—but still curious—reader might simply find that a descriptive account of how class researchers actually draw up their various class maps helps to fill in a space that is usually left blank in most published reports on this topic. How, then, was the Goldthorpe scheme operationalized in our own particular study?

The logic of the scheme, as was explained in Chapter 3, is to aggregate occupational groups whose members share similar market and work situations. The resulting class categories are, therefore, supposed to differentiate positions within labour markets and production units in terms of the employment relations and conditions of employment that they entail. These conditions and relations of employment are indicated by an individual's occupational title and employment status. In the British case, the categories and definitions most frequently used are those found in the *Classification of Occupations 1980*, published by the Office of Population Censuses and Surveys. This volume lists some 549 occupational groups, together with nine employment statuses, which for the purposes of generating Goldthorpe classes are collapsed into seven: self-employed with 25 or more employees, self-employed with fewer than 25 employees, and self-employed without employees; managers in establishments with 25 or more employees, and those in establishments with fewer than 25 employees; foremen and supervisors; and, finally, employees (including family workers, apprentices, and trainees). A class position is obtained for each respondent by cross-classifying his or her occupational title and employment status, each possible legitimate combination having previously been allocated a place within one of the eleven Goldthorpe class categories, according to the different conditions of employment experienced by typical individuals so described.

This is a mechanical procedure usually involving the use of a simple look-up table. Thus, for example, the *OPCS-80* occupational code for 'bookbinders and finishers' is 09402. If a respondent has been given that occupational code on the basis of his or her description of their job, and is self-employed with more than 25 employees, then he or she is allocated to Goldthorpe class I. On the other hand, if the employment status is 'self-employed with less than 25 employees', the appropriate Goldthorpe class is IVa. The same occupational code, when combined with the employment status 'self-employed with no employees', points to Goldthorpe class IVb. A manager in an establishment with fewer than 25 employees is given Goldthorpe class II, while a rank-and-file employee, family worker, or apprentice is placed in Goldthorpe class VI—and so on.

The occupational information in all of the British data-sets in our study has been coded in this way—and so provides the basic building-blocks for our Goldthorpe class categories. Since the relevant class algorithm and coding conventions were drawn up by John Goldthorpe himself (sometimes in collaboration with colleagues such as Anthony Heath), these particular occupational data—namely those derived from the Essex Class Project and British General Election Surveys—would seem to be relatively unproblematic, from a data comparability point of view. This is, of course, not the same as saying that the coding of occupational information in these studies is entirely error-free. We would claim only that, to the extent errors have occurred in deriving detailed occupational codes or Goldthorpe class locations for respondents, these will have been random and relatively infrequent—rather than systematic because rooted in arbitrary coding conventions or inconsistent class algorithms.

Unfortunately, the raw survey data of job descriptions provided by interviewees tend to be coded to different classifications of occupation and employment status in different countries, each taxonomy embracing distinct principles and categories. Government departments are fiercely protective of these local standards. More seriously, from our point of view, the individuals within survey agencies or research institutes who code the raw data tend to be familiar only with the logic and details of their own particular national scheme. This makes cross-national comparison of these sorts of data notoriously difficult. For example, in the case of the CASMIN Project, as we have already noted, the researchers had to recode the occupational and employment status information for each of the national studies they explored, in order to obtain comparable class distributions for fathers and sons across countries. In other words, the Goldthorpe class look-up tables had to be created anew for each case, on a time-consuming *ex post facto* basis.

To the extent that our own analysis incorporates the CASMIN Project data-sets, then, we have simply exploited the earlier concern for data quality and comparability shown by Goldthorpe and his colleagues. Consequently, we are grateful for their efforts, and persuaded by the argument that their recoding to Goldthorpe classes of the original occupational data from the mobility studies of the early and mid-1970s justifies the reasonable presumption that cross-national differences in class mobility revealed in these data are real—rather than being mere artefacts of the different coding procedures followed in each country.

The various British and CASMIN data-sets therefore caused us no real difficulties from the point of view of cross-national comparability. Was it also then possible to generate reliable Goldthorpe class positions from the occupational data gathered by the different countries participating in the newer International Social Justice Project? We believe so, and since we ourselves were involved in this project from the outset, we have the advantage of a good deal of insight into the relevant coding procedures.

Anticipating problems of comparability, the teams involved in the ISJP agreed to collect occupational data in a standardized way, and to code the information provided by respondents to both the International Standard Classification of Occupations for 1968 and a modified version of the German employment status (*Berufsstellungen*) typology. The former was chosen because it is the one occupational taxonomy for which a standard codebook exists in all the major languages. It has also been in cross-national use for a quarter of a century, and many national research agencies are therefore familiar with its procedures and principles. Unfortunately, since it tends to group occupations by industrial sector rather than employment status, it is particularly unsuited to the task of generating Goldthorpe class categories. Typically, for example, people involved in (let us say) the manufacture of musical instruments tend to be given the same code—no matter whether they own the factory, are an employee, supervise other employees, or are a self-employed artisan. The German employment status codes, on the other hand, were selected precisely because they are especially sensitive to the distinction between managers, employers, self-employed, and employees that is central to Goldthorpe's approach. We believe that it is possible to combine these variables in specially designed algorithms which are unique to these data but preserve the integrity of the original class scheme.

This particular version of the Goldthorpe class categories was created in the following way. First, we ourselves generated a baseline Goldthorpe class distribution for Britain, coding the occupational data collected by interviewers to the standard OPCS occupational title and employment status categories for all respondents in jobs. In other words, we followed precisely the same procedure as Goldthorpe himself, using the same basic building-blocks and the same look-up file as were used in the Oxford Mobility Project and its allied studies. It was possible to do so because we had our survey agency code this single occupational point twice: once, to the full *OPCS-80* five-digit level; secondly (and quite independently), to the *ISCO-68* three-digit level. The former exercise yields the percentages shown in the column for 1991 in Table C.1. This can be compared with the figures for 1984, as reported in the well-known Essex Class Project, since the procedure used to generate the two sets of results was identical for both studies. It will be seen that the class distributions are not dissimilar. The most obvious difference is the smaller proportion now involved in skilled manual work (classes V and VI), although this is probably to be expected, given the decline of British manufacturing industries during the 1980s. In short, there is no reason to suspect that this baseline coding is seriously unreliable, and good reason to believe it offers a trustworthy point of comparison for distributions derived in other ways.

The next step is to attempt to recreate these baseline classes using an algorithm based on the German *Stellung im Beruf* and the *ISCO-68*. Information regarding *Berufsstellungen* was obtained by placing respondents into one of the categories indicated in Table C.2. The *ISCO-68* codes were

TABLE C.1. *Frequency Distributions for Collapsed Goldthorpe Classes, Essex Class (1984), and British Social Justice (1991) Projects*

Goldthorpe Class (collapsed)	Classes included	1984 (%)	1991 (%)
Salariat	I, II	27.3	30.8
Routine clerical	IIIa	15.1	17.2
Petite bourgeoisie	IVa, IVb	7.9	9.4
Farmers, smallholders	IVc	0.8	1.0
Skilled manual	V, VI	20.6	15.9
Unskilled manual	IIIb, VIIa	27.8	24.4
Agricultural workers	VIIb	0.5	1.3
TOTAL		100.0	100.0
N		1,315	832

TABLE C.2. *ISJP Employment Status Categories*

FILTER

01 Self-employed farmer
02 Self-employed professional
03 Self-employed in business or trade
04 Employee in non-manual occupation
05 Employee in manual occupation
06 On training scheme or volunteer worker
    Country specific codes
97 Other
99 NA
00 Inappropriate

FULL

A. Self-employed farmer

10 small farm (up to 50 acres)
11 medium farm (50–249 acres)
12 large farm (250–749 acres)
13 very large farm (750 acres or more)
14 farmer in agricultural association

B. Self-employed professional

(e.g. a doctor or lawyer in own practice)
20 works alone
21 one other employee
22 2–9 employees
23 10 employees or more

C. Self-employed in business or trade

30 works alone
31 one other employee
32 2–9 employees
33 10–49 employees
34 50 employees or more
36 Other self-employed in business or trade
37 Member of a production association

40 helps out/assists in family business

D1. Employee in non-manual occupation (government)

50 civil servant (*Beamter*) doing routine clerical tasks (e.g. typist, counter clerk, cashier, receptionist, shop assistant)
51 civil servant (*Beamter*) having some self-directed responsibilities (e.g. laboratory technician, draftsman)
52 civil servant (*Beamter*) self-directed, but working under the supervision of others (e.g. research officer, secondary school teacher) or having limited supervisory responsibilities for other white-collar employees (e.g. head clerk, secondary school head of department)

TABLE C.2. Continued

---

53 civil servant (*Beamter*) mainly self-directed or mainly involved in management
and policy-making (e.g. head of department or division, university lecturer,
school principal, diplomat, military officer, judge)

D2. Employee in non-manual occupation (non-government)

60 doing routine clerical tasks (e.g. typist, counter clerk, cashier, receptionist,
shop assistant)
61 having some self-directed responsibilities (e.g. laboratory technician, draughts-
man)
62 self-directed, but working under the supervision of others (e.g. research
officer, secondary school teacher) or having limited supervisory responsibilities for other white-collar employees (e.g. head clerk, secondary school head
of department)
63 mainly self-directed or mainly involved in management and policy-making
(e.g. head of department or division, university lecturer, school principal,
diplomat, military officer, judge)
64 armed forces, non-officer only

E. Employee in manual occupation

70 labourer (e.g. furniture remover)
71 semi-skilled worker (e.g. assembly-line worker)
72 qualified craftsman (e.g. motor mechanic, carpenter)
73 supervisor or foreman of manual workers

---

derived by the professional coders involved in the different national surveys, from open-ended accounts of their occupational roles offered by
respondents, reinforced by interviewer prompts aimed at soliciting exact
occupational titles and detailed descriptions of what particular jobs en-
tailed. (Respondents were also asked to provide information, where appropriate, using the same format but applied to their own previous job and first
ever job, partner's current or previous job, and father's job when the respondent was aged 15.) The version of the *Berufsstellungen* shown in the
table was used in countries such as Germany which make a legalistic distinction between civil servants and other employees. Where this complication
did not arise (in fact in the majority of cases) these codes were simply
omitted.

Applying the suggested algorithm to the data for respondents to the
British project, and cross-tabulating the result against the distribution for
baseline Goldthorpe classes as described above, we find that there is a high
degree of correspondence in the results achieved (Table C.3). Moreover,
the discrepancies are not systematic, and the degree of reliability does not
seem to vary much across the individual classes.[5]

TABLE C.3. *Cross-tabulation of Baseline Goldthorpe Classes against Social Justice Project Goldthorpe Classes for Britain*

Baseline	Justice Project						
	Salariat	Routine clerical	*Petite bourgeoisie*	Farmer	Skilled manual	Unskilled manual	Agricultural worker
Salariat	222	14	6	0	5	9	0
Routine clerical	17	113	0	0	3	11	0
Petite bourgeoisie	9	0	67	0	2	0	0
Farmer	0	0	4	4	1	0	0
Skilled manual	12	4	0	0	100	15	0
Unskilled manual	5	14	1	0	12	164	1
Agricultural worker	0	0	0	0	0	0	11

Note: Classes are salariat (I, II), routine clerical (IIIa), *petite bourgeoisie* (IVa, IVb), farmers and small-holders (IVc), skilled manual employees (V, VI), semi-skilled and unskilled manual employees (IIIb, VIIa), and agricultural workers (VIIb).

A good deal of the necessary taxonomic work is here being done by the *Berufsstellungen* codes. This is perhaps not surprising, since these classify respondents in terms of dimensions which are prominent in the operationalization of the original Goldthorpe classes. However, four *ISCO-68* correctives were generally found to be necessary, in order to reclassify those routine clerical employees who were wrongly placed in the salariat; to distinguish between agricultural labourers and the rest of the working class; to separate skilled manual from semi-skilled and unskilled manual employees; and to standardize the classification of personal-service employees (who were divided as to whether they described their occupations as 'routine non-manual' or 'routine manual' at the initial filter).

Inspection of the off-diagonal cells in the table suggests that a few of the observed discrepancies are due to mechanical punching errors in one or other of the coding exercises. In the majority of cases, however, there is a simple incompatibility between the categories represented in the *OPCS-80* and *ISCO-68* classifications themselves, such that specific job titles under one scheme can only be allocated to alternative categories under the other, and in such a way that different Goldthorpe class positions must result. The cases in the cell defined by row 6, column 2 (N = 14) provide a convenient illustration of this problem. Many of these are individuals who have been coded as 'bookkeepers and cashiers', using the *ISCO-68* listing, and as 'retail shop cashiers, check-out and cash and wrap operators' using *OPCS-80*. The former determines that individuals are placed in Goldthorpe class IIIa (routine clerical), whereas the latter allocates the same people to class IIIb (sales personnel), and therefore to the semi-skilled and unskilled working class. In short, the two coding systems are simply incompatible at the level of specific occupational groups, such that there is no obviously correct way of arbitrating in the matter of disputed cases.

But the degree of mismatch between the class distributions generated by these two rather different approaches to operationalization is in any case rather small. There is no reason to suspect that it seriously compromises the reliability of these particular class data.

Similar algorithms can be applied to the occupational information for the other countries. The results can then be placed alongside those reported by the CASMIN researchers, since several countries happen to appear in both projects, and the comparison used to provide independent confirmation of the plausibility of this approach—for example, by inspection of marginals, and of the parameter estimates obtained by fitting the CASMIN 'core model' (see Appendix H below) to the relevant ISJP data-sets. The newer surveys are based on samples that are too small to permit reliable modelling in these terms—in the sense that few of the eight parameter estimates for the effects in the model reach statistical significance—but one can at least confirm that the estimates have the signs expected under the model.[6]

In short, although our study uses data-sets from twenty different social surveys, which code occupational information for a dozen or so separate countries to a variety of occupational classifications, we are inclined to believe that our class mobility analyses report results that are real rather than merely artefactual—despite the many difficulties (which we ourselves acknowledge) of maintaining cross-national comparability of these sorts of data.

NOTES

1. On this general point, see the exchange between Gordon Marshall and Göran Ahrne in Clark et al. (1990: 47–76). A particularly prominent example of the tendency to try and resolve the sociological issues surrounding social class by reference to theoretical rather than empirical criteria is provided by the so-called boundary debate within Marxism during the 1970s. On this, see Wright (1980) and cf. Marshall and Rose (1990).
2. Cf. Pahl (1989), Marshall (1991), Goldthorpe and Marshall (1992), Pahl (1993), and (the article from which the quotations in the text have been taken) Scott (1994). For a spirited defence of Goldthorpe and Marshall's argument that class analysis is not *a* theory but a research programme which

is concerned with the empirical testing of *rival* class theories, see Breen and Rottman (1995*b*).

3. Goldthorpe and Marshall (1992: 382). Of course, as these authors go on to observe, 'no-one would suppose that the *immediate* causes of, for example, low educational attainment, voting Labour, and suffering from chronic bronchitis are all the same. But, in so far as a linkage can be traced back from each of the different sets of immediate causes involved to the location of individuals or families in (let us say) unskilled working-class positions, then the importance of class is enhanced rather than diminished' (Goldthorpe and Marshall 1992: 386). Unravelling the exact sequences involving these immediate causes is an often difficult task—although Geoffrey Evans (1993) has shown how, in e.g. the case of political preferences, the association between (Goldthorpe) class and vote is primarily attributable to the variation between classes in individuals' perceptions of their career prospects. The connection between the immediate cause and Goldthorpe and Erikson's theory of class is here obvious: '[service class] employees render service to their employing organization in return for "compensation", which takes the form not only of rewards for work done, through a salary and various perquisites, but also comprises important *prospective* elements—for example, salary increments on an established scale, assurances of security in employment and, through pension rights, after retirement, and, above all, well-defined career opportunities' (Erikson and Goldthorpe 1992*a*: 41–2).

4. Cf. e.g. Dale et al. (1985), Murgatroyd (1984), and Roberts and Barker (1986). Roderick Martin and Judith Wallace (1984: 24, 35) state that 'the customary classifications of social class and socio-economic group are not very satisfactory bases for classifying women's jobs because most of the more common women's jobs fall into a limited number of categories', and offer instead a typology of women's occupations 'constructed inductively . . . on the basis of type of occupation', grouping together 'occupations sharing certain characteristics'. Unfortunately, the characteristics in question are never made clear, nor indeed is the relationship between the occupational categories so identified and the concept of social class itself.

   Perhaps it is worth making the further point here that, in so far as the sex of incumbents does affect the typical conditions of employment in what come to be regarded as 'women's occupations', this represents the systematic effect of a shared social *status*—namely, being female rather than male. Crucially, as is shown in Appendix G below, it does not undermine the finding that men and women are affected by *class* processes in more or less equal measure. Failure to make the analytical distinction between social class and social status (in the strong Weberian sense of 'status group') is a commonplace error that has often clouded debates in this area (see e.g. Crompton 1993: 114–19).

5. The one obvious exception, in the table for Britain at least, concerns the farmers constituting class IVc. Our results suggest that there are 9 farmers under the baseline classes, 5 of whom have been allocated to other class

positions, using the ISJP procedure. However, whilst this might seem to constitute a rather low degree of correspondence, there are in fact only 2 individuals differently classified. This seeming anomaly is explained by sample weighting. Like many other similar social surveys, that for the British Social Justice Project carries a weighting factor according to a number of demographic characteristics identified by the survey agency, and in terms of which the sample was checked (and then weighted appropriately) in order to ensure representativeness. One of the misallocated farmers happens to have received a sample weighting of almost 4—hence the apparently substantial degree of mismatch affecting class IVc. Moreover, this female respondent described herself as a self-employed 'schooler' who broke in horses at an equestrian centre, so it is genuinely unclear as to whether she should be classified as *petite bourgeoisie* (as under the ISJP) or a farmer and small-holder (as in Goldthorpe's 'baseline' approach). The other discrepant case is no less ambiguous, since the respondent specifically described himself as supervising 10 employees in an East Anglian agribusiness. One of the coding procedures emphasizes the agricultural element in his description, whereas the other places greater importance on the supervisory aspect. In other words, neither approach is guilty of systematic misclassification. The more important general point to be made here is that we find no evidence of substantial misallocation of farmers and agricultural workers in those countries in which employment in the agricultural sector is much more common (e.g. in Eastern Europe).

6. Thus e.g. if the data for the former FRG and GDR are pooled (in effect creating a data-set for the new unified Germany), and the national variant of the core model proposed by Erikson and Goldthorpe for the FRG is then fitted to these data, all of the parameter estimates have the signs expected under the model, and all but 3 of the effects reach or come close to the level of statistical significance. The actual estimates are shown below (cf. Erikson and Goldthorpe 1992*a*: 147):

hi1	*hi2*	*in1*	*in2*	*in3*	*se*	*af1*	*af2*
ns	− 0.42	0.32	1.25	ns	− 1.1	− 0.39	ns

The fact that these data come close to fitting this complex topological model provides strong circumstantial evidence in favour of their reliability.

APPENDIX D
Coding Educational Attainment

The coding of educational achievement creates measurement problems that are widely recognized by specialists in this field. Performance in examinations is a more nuanced—and probably more valid—indicator of attainment than is the simpler alternative of counting the number of years spent in receipt of formal instruction. However, the list of recognized credentials in any particular country is invariably rather long, so that qualifications usually must be aggregated in order to facilitate analysis. When (as in this volume) a comparison of educational attainment is attempted across several countries, these problems of creating and coding to sociologically meaningful educational categories are simply compounded, given the additional requirement of maintaining cross-national comparability in measurement.

Fortunately for us, researchers involved in the earlier CASMIN Project faced precisely this difficulty, and devoted substantial resources to investigating the educational systems of the different countries in which they were interested. As a result, they were able to devise a manageable schema for the measurement and cross-national analysis of educational attainment, and since this has been tested and refined in several subsequent studies it seems sensible to follow their lead. By adopting this particular approach we can also compare our results with those obtained during the CASMIN and other similar projects.[1]

The coding schema is designed with the role of educational systems as transmitters, consequences, and causes of social inequality in mind. It focuses specifically upon 'the selection effects which the educational system has for children of different social origins and upon the educational system's function in social selection and the allocation of individuals to class positions'.[2] (The schema is, therefore, perfectly suited to the subject-matter of our own particular study.) After reviewing the historical development of education in nine societies, König and his colleagues demonstrate that the variety, differentiation, and dynamics in the various systems make numerical indicators (such as number of years spent in education) an extremely unreliable basis for longitudinal and cross-national comparisons. They propose the alternative criterion of functional equivalence in the creation of educational categories. More specifically, given their theoretical interest in processes of class formation and social mobility, they argue that it is most appropriate to distinguish educational levels according to their selectivity effects. In other words, the different levels should reflect the processes of (more or less) meritocratic selection according to educational performance, as well as 'enabling the appreciation of those differentiations significant for utilization on the labour market'.[3] This broadly functional emphasis on selectivity in the process of occupational allocation leads them to favour a certificate-oriented scale based on two criteria: the differentiation of a hierarchy of educational levels according to investment expenditures and value on the labour market of the certificates achieved, and a further differentiation between 'general' and 'vocationally oriented' education.

The resulting classification is reproduced in Table D.1. Although the countries within the UK have somewhat different educational regimes, in broad terms category 1a corresponds in Britain to persons who report a school-leaving age lower than that which would be expected from legislation on compulsory schooling, whereas those in 1b will have completed such schooling but undertaken no further education. Category 1c identifies individuals who have extended compulsory schooling by means of an apprenticeship or other training up to a basic vocational qualification (but not including a City and Guilds Exam). Categories 2a and 2b mainly cater for people who have completed apprenticeships, passed City and Guilds Examinations up to intermediate or final levels, or hold O-level certificates or more recent equivalents. Category 3a comprises individuals who have completed A-levels but hold no further vocational qualifications; 3b is defined by City and Guilds Full Technological Certificates and Higher National Certificates or Diplomas; and 3c by possession of a university degree or professional equivalent. The educational qualifications of other countries

TABLE D.1. *The CASMIN Project Educational Attainment Classification (Four-Category Collapse)*

Level	CASMIN categories	
1. Low	1a	inadequately completed general elementary education
	1b	general elementary education
	1c	general elementary education and basic vocational training
2. Ordinary	2a	intermediate vocational qualification
	2b	intermediate general qualification
3. Advanced	3a	higher (secondary school) education—maturity examination
	3b	lower tertiary (including vocational) certificates
4. Degree	3c	higher education: upper-level tertiary certificates

are allocated to these categories in a similar way and according to the criteria described above.

Note that, even with the relatively large data-sets that we create for Britain in Chapters 5 and 6 above, it is necessary—in order to avoid problems of sparseness in some of the tables—to use a four-category collapsed version of the scheme throughout our analysis. This does, however, have the virtue of creating an educational attainment variable that is more clearly hierarchical.

NOTES

1. For details of the CASMIN educational categories, and a full account of the logic behind their construction, see König et al. (1988).
2. Ibid. 2. The authors therefore emphasize that the specific selection process taking place *within* schools—'the manner in which selection is realized according to meritocratic or other criteria'—is outside the scope of their analysis.
3. Ibid. 55. It is perhaps worth noting here that we find this functional approach to the creation of an educational scale more satisfactory, and more appropriate to a class analysis, than the alternative strategy of devising a continuous education variable. Earlier attempts at measuring educational achievement in a continuous way reveal some of the many methodological difficulties in this exercise. Most such scales rely heavily on the researcher's subjective assessment of the relative value (often prestige) of different types of certificate and schooling, and therefore upon assumptions and evaluations which are almost inevitably contentious, and certainly open to challenge by other social scientists (see e.g. Hope 1981). Those scales that are empirically grounded (see e.g. Treiman and Terrell 1975) tend towards circular reasoning, determining the value of each educational element by reference to its correlation with a criterion variable such as occupational status or income, thus confounding the subsequent analysis of the impact of educational attainment on (in this case) occupational status and income.

APPENDIX E
Social Justice and Non-vertical
Social Mobility

In Chapter 3 we noted that the Goldthorpe class scheme is not strictly hierarchical. This would seem to raise the question of why somebody concerned specifically with the relation between social mobility and social justice should be interested in movements between class positions that are neither better nor worse than one another. Although our analyses in this book use collapses of the Goldthorpe scheme that do license claims about the vertical nature of the mobility that we identify—and hence our focus is indeed on issues of access to positions characterized by unequal levels of advantage—we think it worth pointing out that non-vertical mobility may itself be relevant to issues of social justice.

To see why, it will be necessary to recall our earlier discussion (in Chapter 2) of the different conceptions of social justice identified by political theorists. On that occasion, we considered an argument for equality of opportunity and meritocracy that appealed to notions of societal efficiency, rather than those of individual desert. The reasoning was that justice implies a concern for the well-being of the least advantaged members of society. This well-being is maximized when a society is allocating its resources, human and non-human, efficiently. What matters about access and opportunity on this account is not that it enables individuals to get what they deserve but rather that it indicates an absence of barriers to the efficient allocation of individuals to occupational roles. Nothing in this line of reasoning presupposes or implies anything about those occupational roles forming a hierarchy or being in any way unequally rewarded. It is true, as we have seen, that functional considerations may serve to justify inequality. But it is also true that we could have functional reasons for valuing equality of opportunity to achieve positions that were not unequal. We would care, on functional grounds, if it were harder for people from some backgrounds to get certain kinds of job even if we did not regard those jobs and backgrounds as better or worse than one another.

This is one reason for thinking that non-vertical mobility might be relevant to considerations of social justice: that the least advantaged in any society will tend to benefit where there is equality of opportunity, in the sense that there are no obstacles getting in the way of people finding the kinds of jobs to which their abilities are most appropriately suited. Another reason for thinking that movement between positions that are not unequal could matter to social justice appeals not to considerations of efficiency but to the value of individual self-realization. Here, equality of opportunity is valued neither on desert-based nor on functional grounds, but because it is implied by the idea that each member of society should have the same chances for self-fulfilment.

Again, the work of John Rawls may be helpful at this point. We have already seen that Rawls rejects conventional desert claims, and that he believes inequalities are justified only if they serve the advantage of the worst-off group in society. However, he also argues that all members of society should enjoy fair equality of opportunity, and on grounds quite independent of both these considerations (Rawls 1971: 84). His argument for equality of opportunity (or 'open positions') is rooted neither in desert nor in efficiency but in the value of self-realization, which he calls 'one of the main forms of human good'. This justification for valuing equality of opportunity does not presuppose that the positions that people should have equal opportunity to achieve are themselves unequal in the sense that their possessors enjoy different amounts of advantage. If there were barriers to my becoming a doctor, yet doctoring is that activity the pursuit of which would realize my self most fully, this would be objectionable irrespective of the distributive advantage accruing to the position of doctor. Imagine a society in which those born into certain kinds of background were prevented (perhaps for reasons of caste, for example) from taking up certain kinds of job. We could judge that this violated the value of equal opportunity for self-realization even if we knew nothing about the rewards attached to the jobs in question.

We can, then, distinguish three distinct grounds for valuing equality of opportunity. One involves claims about individuals deserving a fair chance to achieve the rewards that their abilities merit. The second points to the functional value in having an efficient allocation of people to jobs. The third derives from a quite distinct interest in people having equal chances of self-realization. All of these can sensibly be regarded as relevant to considerations of social justice, although, as we have seen, they of course appeal to different conceptions of that idea. Only the first presupposes that the positions between which people should have equal opportunity to move are themselves unequal. A popular version of the second does involve claims about inequality, in so far as it argues that people need incentives, in the form of unequal rewards, to exercise their abilities optimally. While this is undoubtedly the version that is politically most relevant, we have seen that it is perfectly possible to value the efficient allocation of individuals to occupations without presupposing that those positions are unequally rewarded. Like the second, the third also does not necessarily assume a context of inequality. While part of the value of equality of opportunity for self-realization might involve the idea that people should have a fair chance of achieving positions that are better than others, there are kinds of self-realization that do not involve any such claim.

In short, and to the (as we have seen) limited extent that movement between particular Goldthorpe classes is not clearly advantageous or disadvantageous (in terms of the rewards and privileges accruing to particular class positions), it is entirely reasonable to defend even non-vertical mobility as being relevant to considerations of social justice. None the less, as we have said, our concern in this book is solely with movement as between classes that can be regarded as hierarchically ordered. Our discussion of the justice of the patterns of movement that we identify is accordingly concerned specifically with the principles that might legitimate the distributive phenomena—inequalities of access to positions of unequal advantage—that those movements indicate.

APPENDIX F
The Ideology of Meritocratic Socialism

All communist regimes have experimented with a variety of systems of remuneration and distribution in the attempt to reduce inequalities of outcome or condition in the lives of their citizens. One thinks here, for example, of early Russian drives towards the levelling of wages and benefits; of the short-lived hopes of substituting moral for material incentives in post-revolutionary Cuba; and of the periodic and catastrophic attempts in China to restructure the allocation of rewards without inducing either economic stagnation or administrative chaos. The long-term consequences of these and other initiatives have been debated at considerable length. There is some evidence—though keenly disputed—that communist redistribution may have diminished inequalities of outcome, as these have historically been evident in the disposition of wealth, health care, housing, and the like. However, the jury of international scholarship is still out on this issue, and we do not intend here to anticipate any decisions at which it may yet arrive.[1]

But the communists themselves never mistook egalitarianism for socialism. No less an authority than Stalin insisted:

Equalitarianism owes its origin to the individual peasant type of mentality, the psychology of share and share alike, the psychology of primitive 'communism'. Equalitarianism has nothing in common with Marxist socialism. Only people who are unacquainted with Marxism can have the primitive notion that the Russian Bolsheviks want to pool all wealth and then share it out equally.[2]

In this respect, Stalin and the many others who wrote in similar vein were simply rehearsing the tenets formulated by Marx himself, who (as was noted in Chapter 2) considered the desert-oriented principle of rewarding each 'according to his labour contribution' to be entirely appropriate to the first or lower (and present) stage of socialism. This second-best criterion was to be superseded by the maxim 'to each according to his needs' only in a subsequent (and, in the event, never realized) higher stage.[3]

Perhaps ironically, therefore, appeals to social justice in later communist writings typically took the form of the liberal principle of increasing equality of opportunity to earn rewards proportionate to merit. Having conceded that inequalities of outcome, although arguably somewhat diminished, would continue to be a necessary feature of socialist societies for the fore-seeable future (at least if economic growth were to be secured), élites then offered the alternative argument that socialism nevertheless promoted dis-tributive justice by giving people more equal access to unequally rewarded positions, in a society still (temporarily) characterized by a hierarchy of offices carrying with them significantly different levels of material advan-tage. From this point of view, a competition with unequal outcomes is fair as long as people have equal chances to win, and as long as the outcomes reflect the differing abilities of those taking part. Individuals get what they deserve, and the socialist society, though unequal, is nevertheless just—certainly more so than its capitalist equivalent.[4]

As Walter Connor has observed, most socialist societies were therefore characterized by an unresolved conflict between different conceptions of justice, evident in the policy disputes that separated those whom he de-scribes as 'ideological egalitarians' from their 'pragmatic reformist' oppo-nents. Examples abound, but one obvious illustration is provided by Soviet policy towards entry into higher education, which alternated between com-peting egalitarian and meritocratic initiatives. What we now call positive (or reverse) discrimination was often practised in the attempt to guarantee equal outcomes in the distribution of university places. Children of workers and peasants were compensated for cultural and other disadvantages by being awarded studentships irrespective of their educational achievements. At other times, performance in competitive examinations was the principal criterion of admission, and the concerns of individual merit were given priority over those of class preference. In this particular instance, as in other attempts to resolve the possible tensions between equality of outcome and equality of opportunity, most socialist governments pursued a middle course—'retaining the promise of greater equality in the future, and claim-ing that much of it has been achieved, while citing the socialist performance principle as a contemporary guide to reward'.[5]

This tension, and the dispute between egalitarians and pragmatists in general, is sometimes presented as a contrast between two rather different types of mobility that are said to characterize actually existing socialism: collective (or class) mobility and individual (or social) mobility. The former pursues what Włodzimierz Wesołowski and Bogdan Mach (1986: 25, 27) describe as 'the collective mobility of the unprivileged classes'; that is, greater 'equality of conditions', the principle supposedly governing state intervention in the process of distributing goods. Individual mobility, on the other hand, refers to 'mobility through qualifications and occupations [and] posits the creation of similar opportunities for achieving unequally re-warded positions. It derives from the pragmatic and reformist version of socialism or its meritocratic version.' As Wesołowski and Mach concede, Marxist sociologists have historically been somewhat reticent in discussions about equality of opportunity, on the grounds that Marx himself regarded this as a bourgeois ideal that was largely irrelevant to the classless communist societies of the future. However, as they also acknowledge, parity in the chances for individual social mobility was 'an important problematic' in the real socialist societies of Eastern Europe, since 'propaganda suggests that there has been a close approximation to the ideal of equal opportunities'.[6]

The broadly meritocratic defence of social inequality under socialism is also a prominent theme in the sociological literature on stratification. For example, in their review of the history and functions of social mobility under real socialism, Wesołowski and Mach observe:

During the first stage of a socialist regime, a stress on equality of positions as the main characteristic of the new order is of strategic importance for those in authority. Later a new problem confronts this type of regime. It consists in associating egalitarian promise with mobility through qualifications, in order to foster societal support for an inegalitarian, but meritocratic, system generating achievement motivation and capable of growing and innovating. To this end, steps must be taken mainly to ensure equality of access to qualifications . . . Furthermore, social norms must operate so that competence and qualifications are the grounds on which important posts are allocated and that their lack cannot be compensated for by social origin or by other group affiliation (e.g. party membership and social ties).[7]

Like Connor, Wesołowski and Mach can see 'some unclarity' in the relationship between these two principles, since equality of opportunity points to individual occupational mobility (mainly through qualifications) while equality of conditions seems to call for collective mobility (secured by state intervention to redistribute resources).

Soviet and other socialist scholars of the post-Stalinist period therefore employed the language of class (or strata) and of class inequality (or differentiation) readily enough. But they steadfastly maintained that there were important differences in the degree of openness in class structures East and West. In particular, the former offered far greater equality of opportunity than did the latter.[8] In the late 1960s, for example, Rutkevitch and Filippov (1973: 235) concluded that 'in a socialist society, as a result of fundamental changes in the social class structure, most of the real barriers to social mobility disappear', although this judgement appears to have been reached more through Marxist theory than sociological research.[9] Similarly, in the mid-1980s, Aitov (1986: 256, 270) conceded that 'socialist society does not yet enjoy full social equality', but concluded from his study of social mobility in the Russian city of Magnitogorsk that 'socialist society is far more "open" than its capitalist counterpart'.[10]

These assessments are based mainly on the evidence provided by some methodologically suspect studies of social mobility in particular industrial enterprises, towns, or regions within the former Soviet Union. We have reviewed this rather disparate material elsewhere (see Marshall, Sydorenko, and Roberts 1995). It will be clear, not only from the new data on cross-national rates of social mobility reported in Chapter 4 but also from other reliable studies (many of which are mentioned in Appendix H), that these claims greatly exaggerate the differences between mobility regimes in democratic capitalist and state socialist societies. However, from the point of view of the present study, the significance of this literature lies less in its assertions about enhanced mobility than in the distinction that was made by apologists for communism, almost from the outset, between equality of condition ('collective mobility') and equality of opportunity ('individual mobility')—and the emphasis that was placed upon the latter under (what soon came to be) the prevailing ideology of meritocratic socialism. The unwarranted claims that were then made for equality of opportunity in the Soviet East precisely parallel those made by liberal theorists in the capitalist West.

NOTES

1. In any case, it seems highly unlikely that this complex question will have a simple answer. After reviewing the evidence, we are inclined to agree with the authors of one study who concluded that 'in sum it appears a valid generalization that, if private ownership of the means of production is replaced by collective ownership, some types of inequality are eliminated, some others remain, and some new sorts of inequalities emerge in social life' (Kolosi and Wnuk-Lipiński 1983: 3). The evidence relating to the Soviet Union is reviewed in Lane (1982: ch. 3). That for socialist East-Central Europe more generally is reported in the chapters on incomes, consumption and housing, in Kende and Strmiska (1987). On Cuba, see the essays collected in Mesa-Lago (1971). The Chinese experience is summarized by Parish (1981).
2. Stalin (1955: 120–1). On this issue critical Marxists tend to share in the view of the orthodoxy; e.g. Zsuzsa Ferge (1979: 40–1) insists that socialism and communism should not be defined in terms of equality, although 'the reduction of existing inequalities' is a realistic objective of socialist social policy.
3. This hierarchical interpretation of Marx's theory of justice is stated concisely in Elster (1985: 229–30). Later Marxist thinking on the issue of social justice is usefully summarized in Lukes (1985: ch. 4). For overviews of the wider literatures, see Cohen (1986) and Scherer (1992). According to many observers, the distributive inequalities of condition found under real socialism were the result not only of rewarding 'each according to his work' but also of giving unequal rewards for equal work. For example, Włodzimierz Wesołowski (1988: 3–7) has argued that because of the widespread tendency to discriminate against women, and to favour

members of the Party in general and workers in the so-called productive sectors of the economy in particular, under state socialism the 'gender, sector and nomenklatura principles undermine the model assumption of equal pay for equal work'.

4. V. Z. Rogovin (1989: 137) summarizes the official view in these terms: 'The concepts of social justice and social equality are not identical . . . equality in, say, material status of members of society may be unjust, especially when it is due to wage equalization although the respective work done may be unequal in quality and quantity. The principal form of a just distribution in the position of individuals and social groups under socialism is a differentiation based on the consistent observation of the principle of distribution according to work performed.' Here too it is hard to distinguish critical from orthodox Marxist commentators. For example, in her review of the Hungarian experience, Ferge (1979: 305–6) argues: 'The most pressing needs in Hungary have by and large been covered by now. Hunger, mass squalor, precarious living conditions, general scarcity are problems of the past, and have hopefully been wiped out for ever . . . How should the new prosperity be used? What aims should be served by the new products? Up to now only one "model of prosperity" has found answers to these questions—that of the advanced capitalist economies . . . But it is clear by now that the modern capitalist system does not correspond to a socialist ideal . . . In 1969 the Hungarian Commission for Perspective Planning on Manpower and Standard of Living published its hypotheses concerning the orientation of social development for the next fifteen years . . . The final version of the long-term plan later emphasized certain elements which undoubtedly overstep the traditional boundaries of a "bourgeois way of life". Its principal ideas were—besides material progress—to assure a secure and stable life for everybody; to strengthen the open character of society by maintaining mobility at a high level; to enhance the socialist character of income distribution, implying the reduction of the distance between extremes . . .'

5. Connor (1979: 25). See also Meier (1989: 169–70), who notes: 'The educational system in all socialist societies has to fulfill at least two universal functions: to provide as much social equality . . . as seems necessary for the stability and legitimation of the socialist order, and to produce an educated labour force . . . both a pool of highly trained and selected talents and a specialized, educated "normal" labour force . . . Educational systems in both the Soviet Union and the GDR have experienced situations in which the egalitarian principle of guaranteeing equal educational rights and chances to students from all classes and strata in practice came into conflict with the meritocratic principle by which recruitment for the different trades and professions is managed. The twofold universal use of education periodically creates tensions that hardly can be ignored. Educational planning from above tries to orchestrate the conflicting purposes in such situations by giving priority to one or the other goal and reversing the rank order of functions from time to time.'

6. Wesołowski (1988: 17) later argued explicitly that *both* 'the reduction of social differences' and 'processes of intergenerational mobility' should be taken as 'indicators and elements of socialist changes' in any study of stratification under real socialism. See also Ferge (1979: 42–4).

7. Wesołowski and Mach (1986: 30). David Lane (1976: 178) has rightly noted that the Soviet ideology of meritocracy also embodied strongly functionalist overtones: 'State-socialist societies *aspire* to communism and therefore to an equalitarian form of society. But in their present arrangements all state-socialist societies manifest distinct patterns of inequality. How do they justify these inequalities? Paradoxically, the argument put forward by the élites of state-socialist societies, which is now inherent in their central value systems, is essentially a functionalist one. It derives from Stalin's statement that under socialism men give according to their ability and receive according to their *work*. According to Stalin, some work contributes more to the national income than other work, and requires greater training and more skill; another fact is that some workers perform more efficiently than others. These differences in skill and effort (in input) justify differential rewards, and in practice workers are paid according to the amount of work done, the level of skill and the efficiency in applying their skill.' Wesołowski's (1988: 11–12) own restatement of the normative theory of stratification under socialism is a good example of how the meritocratic and functionalist defences of inequality became intertwined. In his account, socialism 'is based on the assumption that the division of labour is an inseparable feature of every modern society and that this is linked with two of its correlates: the unequal distribution of power and the unequal distribution of material goods. The division of labour manifests itself, among other things, in a multiplicity of specific jobs, some of which require greater qualifications, or expert knowledge, and others—lesser qualifications ... One may say that jobs which differ as regards qualifications and knowledge give unequal inputs to the well being of society. Likewise, the differentiation between managerial and non-managerial positions gives unequal inputs to the progress and welfare of society as a whole. The principle of socialist justice calls for higher remuneration of both jobs with higher qualifications and positions of power. In this model not only the actual results of different jobs and actions are taken into consideration. But also the effort made to become better qualified likewise counts ... Jobs and functions that require greater preparations should be more highly evaluated ... In this way the model postulates: (1) that there are "more valuable" jobs and functions; (2) that these deserve higher rewards.'

8. This was, of course, not the only alleged difference between classes in the West and stratification under real socialism. An earlier (now unfashionable) argument was that status inconsistency (the correlation between education, occupation, income, housing conditions, cultural consumption, and suchlike) was lower under state socialism than democratic capitalism (see e.g. Alestalo et al. 1980). For a discussion of the similarities between this view and the theory of 'complex equality' proposed by Michael Walzer, see

Swift (1995). The Soviet literature also offers extensive discussion about such issues as cross-class cooperation, intra-class differentiation or class fractions, and the relationship with the Party. These are not really germane to the issue of social justice and need not be considered here. A good summary of the various official theories of class under state socialism will be found in Matthews (1972). The more recent views of critical socialists are outlined in Borocz (1989).

9. No substantiating evidence is cited, the authors merely insisting that 'there is no doubt that only Marxist dialectics and the materialist conception of history can provide a genuinely scientific basis for understanding the social structure of any society and all the processes of its change, including social mobility' (Rutkevich and Filippov 1973: 229).

10. See also Hegedüs (1977: 59, 71), and Charvát et al. (1978: 162), who offer the same argument in almost the same terms. Reviewing this field a decade or so later, Wesołowski and Mach (1986: 27) observed that, in real socialist societies, 'those in power appear to have adopted a convenient stance. According to them, so much has been done to equalize opportunities and the process of levelling the social position of classes is proceeding so rapidly that there is no need to query how the equality of opportunities should be implemented in practice. To a certain extent thought has leapt into a world better than the one which has been created in reality. However, questions about the degree to which opportunities have been made equal cannot be avoided.'

APPENDIX G
The Class and Gender Debate

The problem of describing the relationship between class and gender has been prominent in recent sociological discussion of social inequality in advanced societies. Early in the 1970s, feminists began to mount a sustained challenge against the orthodox view that social classes comprised households centred on a male 'head', whose formal employment (whether conceptualized in terms of occupational prestige, socio-economic standing, or labour-market situation) was a valid indicator of the class location of all household members. These critics argued that the conventional approach to class analysis was naïve, since large and growing numbers of married women were not only in full-time jobs but also concentrated in particular parts of the occupational structure, so that the male and female class distributions for any society were invariably rather different.

Moreover, official statistics showed that households quite commonly were headed by single females, and sociological research seemed to suggest that the division of resources within households generally favoured men over women. Finally, it was widely argued that there was strong evidence of a growing mood of self-awareness and confidence among females (because of the influence of feminism and the women's movement), so that it was no longer plausible to attribute class and other identities to married women simply on the basis of their husbands' class positions. The last of these claims, in particular, addressed the problem that we think is central to this whole debate (although of marginal significance as regards issues of class and justice): that of specifying the appropriate unit of class composition.[1]

Against this background, orthodox class analysis was increasingly accused of (at worst) intellectual sexism or (at best) the barely less damaging charge of tunnel vision. Some critics took the view that the individual was now the unit of class composition. Class locations and other class characteristics were therefore attributed to individuals within households on the basis of their own employment. Others favoured the adoption of some kind of joint classification of husbands and wives. Here, the unit of class composition remained the household, but class membership was assigned via a composite measure of the occupations or employment status of both partners.[2]

The most sustained defence of the conventional approach was mounted by John Goldthorpe and his colleagues in the context of the CASMIN project. In a series of publications spanning a decade or so, Goldthorpe in particular attempted to show that the increased participation of women in paid labour carried fewer implications for studying class than critics supposed, and that the unit of class composition remained the household—as characterized by the class standing of its putative head.[3]

Goldthorpe claims there are good theoretical as well as empirical grounds for supposing this still to be the case. The thesis of class unity in the family does not preclude inequalities of power or economic condition within households, but merely insists that intrafamilial differentiation and conflicts must be viewed as attributes of sex (or, where generations are concerned, of age), rather than of class. Similarly, where two married women in identical jobs (say, routine clerical work) are married to an unskilled manual worker and skilled professional respectively, he cannot imagine how those who favour an individualistic approach propose satisfactorily to conceptualize the differences in the living standards and economic prospects of the two women in question: if they are not differences of class, then precisely how are they to be understood?

Moreover, the argument continues, heads of household tend to be men. In support of this position Goldthorpe cites evidence from a number of studies which show that women's paid participation in employment is typically more intermittent and limited than that of men (since it is often interrupted by childbirth), so that even today it is still the case that husbands rather than wives have the major attachment to the labour market, at least in terms of the continuity of their work histories or the contribution they are able to make to family incomes. Indeed, it has been argued further that proponents of the individualist approach actually do their feminist colleagues a disservice, by seeming to argue that the twin ills of sexual discrimination in the labour market and the patriarchal norms of family life within nuclear households both oppress women—yet this oppression is somehow insufficient to support the logic of an orthodox class analysis. An individualistic approach would appear to deny the very subordination of women to men, in both the labour market and household, that is insisted upon by conventionalists.[4]

Furthermore, those large-scale surveys which have compared typical occupational histories for both sexes (attributing a social-class location to each individual by reference to his or her own employment) commonly suggest that the pattern of relative mobility rates (or social fluidity) underlying women's intergenerational mobility is virtually the same as that which characterizes men's mobility. In other words, while the standard origins-to-destinations mobility matrices do indeed confirm that the position of women within the class structure is different from (and less favourable than) that of men, these differences in absolute rates are almost entirely attributable to differences in the marginal (destination) distributions in the table. That is, *sex* segregation in the occupational structure means that men and women are likely to end up in different destinations, but *class* mobility inequalities scarcely vary by sex. This suggests that class background and sex do not interact, as critics of the conventional view have often claimed, since the same set of class-linked processes is evident among males and females alike. The social practices that generate sex segregation in employment (hence women's restricted opportunities) are therefore of a different order from those that form the subject-matter of class analysis.

Finally, according to Goldthorpe and Erikson, empirical studies consistently show an asymmetrical pattern of association by sex between class self-identity and a respondent's social class, on the one hand, and the class position of his or her partner on the other. More specifically, where both a respondent and spouse in a dual-earner conjugal family are assigned a class position individually (by reference to their own employment), not only (as one would expect) is there a tendency to class homogamy, but there is also a strong association between the husband's class position and his own (subjective) class identification. However, when both associations are controlled for, there is typically little or no association between the husband's class identity and the wife's class position, although the obverse is not also true. Thus, not only is a woman's class identification only weakly associated with the class position indicated by her own employment, but it is invariably also the case that a further significant (and usually stronger) association exists between a wife's class identification and the social-class standing of her husband or partner. This pattern is also found when political partisanship, rather than class identity, is investigated. In short, as Goldthorpe puts it, not only 'sexist' sociologists but also married women themselves seem to view their class position as one which, at least in these particular socio-political aspects, is derived largely from the employment of their husbands. Among advocates of the conventional approach, therefore, the household remains the unit of class fate, class formation, and class action—in short, of class composition.[5]

This debate rumbles on. At the time of writing, the evidence seems to suggest that, in advanced capitalist societies (though not necessarily those of post-communism), married women continue to see their class interests and affiliations as being more importantly determined by their husbands' employment than by their own. We ourselves have elsewhere—and at some length—pursued this issue in attempting to identify the unit of class composition. In particular, we test the so-called asymmetry hypothesis, concerning the pattern of relationships among the class positions of spouses and the attributes that are said to comprise socio-political class formation.[6] This aspect of the debate is, however, largely tangential to the concerns of the present volume. Of greater moment would seem to be the issue of intergenerational social mobility itself. Is the picture for Britain still as the conventionalists paint it—one of differences between the sexes in absolute mobility rates but of similar mobility chances—or have matters changed in recent years?

We can see, by looking back at Tables 4.1 and 4.2, that the absolute mobility rates for the two sexes in each nation are indeed different. Consider the case of Britain. It is clear that women in this country tend to find employment disproportionately in particular locations in the class structure. Almost a third of females are in routine clerical jobs. Another quarter or so are in unskilled manual work. Only 10 per cent are to be found in skilled manual positions. By comparison, only 5 per cent of males are in routine clerical positions, while approximately one-fifth are in each of the two manual classes. Clearly, therefore, absolute rates for the sexes will be governed by the realities of this gendered labour market.

How, if at all, do these labour-market processes affect relative class mobility chances? The evidence shown in Table G.1 suggests that they do not. Here we investigate the issue of a sex differential in the origins-to-destinations trajectories of respondents to the surveys included within the ISJP. The results, not only for Britain but also for all other countries, confirm the patterns identified in the previous paragraph. There is indeed a strong association between an individual's class destination and his or her sex (DS). A person's class destination is further distinguished according to his or her class of origin (OD). Most importantly however, from our point of view, the pattern of association between origins and destinations is the same across the sexes. A satisfactory fit to the data is obtained, in all cases, by the model of common social fluidity. There is, therefore, no significant interaction (the ODS term in the model) between a person's class origins, class destination, and his or her sex.[7]

Furthermore, this conclusion is not undermined by the more stringent requirements of the uniform difference test, which returns no significant improvement on the simpler model of common social fluidity. Relative class mobility rates are, in other words, the same for each sex; class standing is to a considerable degree intergenerationally transmitted; men and women are to some extent distributed to different classes; but the association between class origins and class destinations does not itself vary significantly by sex.[8]

These findings may be of some assistance in resolving disputes about the relationship between class and gender. They suggest that, in the case of Britain (as in the other industrial societies also here examined), sex differences in intergenerational occupational mobility processes are precisely that: they are differences attributable to one's social status (as a male or female) in the labour market. Women are distributed to different destinations because they are women—not because their *class* mobility chances are in any sense distinct.

TABLE G.1. *Results of Testing the Model of Common Social Fluidity against Data on Intergenerational Mobility for the Sexes in Eight Countries (Women's Class Determined by Reference to Own Employment)*

	Model	G^2	df	p	delta	beta
GBR	Independence	189.39	72	0.000	18.30	
	CmSF	33.02	36	0.611	5.31	
	UNIDIFF	33.00	35	0.565	5.22	− 0.0236 (ns)
FRG	Independence	203.67	72	0.000	17.75	
	CmSF	37.62	36	0.395	6.63	
	UNIDIFF	34.67	35	0.484	6.05	− 0.3448 (ns)
BUL	Independence	202.35	72	0.000	16.98	
	CmSF	37.23	36	0.412	6.11	
	UNIDIFF	34.15	35	0.509	5.59	0.3369 (ns)
SLO	Independence	189.77	72	0.000	16.48	
	CmSF	36.52	36	0.445	7.05	
	UNIDIFF	34.85	35	0.476	6.42	0.2465 (ns)
GDR	Independence	97.11	72	0.026	12.82	
	CmSF	30.20	36	0.741	5.94	
	UNIDIFF	29.29	35	0.740	6.10	− 0.2850 (ns)
CZA	Independence	127.11	72	0.000	15.51	
	CmSF	26.10	36	0.888	6.59	
	UNIDIFF	25.61	35	0.877	6.44	− 0.1636 (ns)
POL	Independence	324.59	72	0.000	23.59	
	CmSF	36.16	36	0.461	5.75	
	UNIDIFF	35.59	35	0.441	5.65	− 0.1081 (ns)
USA	Independence	150.41	72	0.000	15.07	
	CmSF	38.66	36	0.351	5.53	
	UNIDIFF	37.57	35	0.352	5.29	− 0.2079 (ns)

Notes
1. Class origin (O) and class destination (D) each have 7 levels, as in Table 4.1.
2. S = Sex.
3. Nations are Great Britain (GBR), Bulgaria (BUL), Czechoslovakia (CZA), East Germany (GDR), Poland (POL), Slovenia (SLO), the United States (USA), and West Germany (FRG).
3. Independence model = OS + DS.
4. Common social fluidity model = OS + DS + OD.
5. G^2 = log-likelihood ratio; delta = proportion of misclassified cases.
6. beta − UNIDIFF parameter estimate; males set at zero; ns = not significant.

On the other hand, since class background and sex do not in this sense interact, much of the debate about class and gender is simply rendered irrelevant from the point of view of assessing the implications for social justice of social class. The forces that shape the association between origins and destination among men would, after all, seem to be sex-blind—operating in much the same way among women.

234 APPENDIX G

NOTES

1. Overviews of the debate (of which there have been many) include Payne and Abbott (1990), Crompton and Mann (1986), Sørensen (1994), and (perhaps most useful of all) the exchange between Susan McRae and Shirley Dex on 'Class and Gender' in Clark et al. (1990).
2. The conventional, individual, and joint-classification approaches to class assignment are summarized in Bonney (1988) and Duke and Edgell (1987).
3. See Goldthorpe (1983; 1984; 1980, 2nd edn.: ch. 10), Erikson (1984), Erikson and Goldthorpe (1992a: ch. 7; 1992b).
4. The joint-classification approach raises other difficulties. This attempted solution to the problem of class assignment generates rates of class mobility that are spuriously high (since every movement in or out of the labour market by the wife alters the class standing of the family), and also confounds class effects with those of household composition. Indeed, joint classification so accentuates the problems of identifying class boundaries that the whole rationale of class analysis is undermined, which is presumably not what its proponents intended. Perhaps in recognition of these problems, Anthony Heath—probably the most noted proponent of this strategy—has revised his initial position, on the basis of an investigation of the impact of respondent's and spouse's class on voting behaviour in Britain over the period 1974–87. Heath now maintains that 'the search for a single simple rule for the classification of families, such as the conventional procedure or the individual procedure, may be fruitless'. His analysis suggests complex interaction effects, which result in women in service-class and blue-collar occupations taking more account of their own class than of their partner's, whereas women in the *petite bourgeoisie* and routine non-manual class take relatively little account of their own class position (see De Graaf and Heath 1992). It is not clear what kind of strategy this implies for class assignment—although the unit of class composition would still seem to be the household.
5. Goldthorpe has more recently argued that the principle of 'dominance' offers an alternative operational solution to the problem of attributing heads to households. This is a variant of the conventional approach that was initially developed by Robert Erikson. The dominance criterion for determining the class of the conjugal family locates class in the employment of either husband or wife by giving priority to the partner whose labour-market participation may be regarded as dominant in terms of employment status and level of employment. In practice, this means that employment takes priority over non-employment, full-time employment over part-time, and higher-level employment (judged according to the criterion of an appropriate class schema) dominates lower-level employment. Empirically, of course, these criteria suggest that most heads of household (at least in Britain) continue to be males.
6. See Marshall, Roberts et al. (1995) and Roberts and Marshall (1995).

7. The distribution of cases across cells is such that the data for Russia, Estonia, and Japan cannot be modelled at the level of the seven-category (CASMIN) version of the Goldthorpe class scheme. Four-category collapses (salariat, intermediate, working, agricultural) confirm that the CmSF model provides a good fit to the data in each case, and one which is not improved upon significantly by the UNIDIFF test. The Russian results are discussed at length in Marshall, Sydorenko, and Roberts (1995).

8. For an earlier 5-nation comparison which arrives at the same conclusion, see Erikson and Goldthorpe (1992a: 246).

APPENDIX H
The Featherman–Jones–Hauser Hypothesis

Systematic cross-national comparative research on social mobility was focused initially on Martin Lipset and Hans Zetterburg's (1959) hypothesis that, since industrial societies tend to experience similar changes in their economic and occupational structures, they should have similar overall patterns of intergenerational social mobility—or, as we now say, similar absolute mobility rates. Our own data confirm that this is patently not the case (see especially Tables 4.1 and 4.2). However, as the Lipset–Zetterburg thesis is already widely discredited, our results are on this point entirely unremarkable. Since the mid-1970s, debate has centred instead upon the argument about relative rates advanced by David Featherman, Frank Lancaster Jones, and Robert Hauser. The implications of our findings for the contemporary controversy surrounding the so-called 'FJH hypothesis' are less clear and more limited.

Featherman and his colleagues argued that observed differences in absolute rates of social mobility are due to variables extraneous to the processes transmitting class privilege across generations. If these variables are controlled—for example by distinguishing between absolute rates and relative chances—then a basic cross-national similarity does in fact become apparent. In other words, the FJH hypothesis proposes that if mobility is considered *net* of the influence exerted by the various economic, technological, and demographic factors that are known to vary greatly across countries, then underlying mobility (or the pattern of relative chances) 'in industrial societies with a market economy and a nuclear family system is basically the same' (Featherman et al. 1975: 340).

The manner in which this thesis is expressed raises at least two obvious problems for the researcher intent upon subjecting it to empirical scrutiny. The first is the gap between the loose verbal formulation of the argument and the strict common social fluidity model against which it is conventionally tested. The former refers to a basic similarity across nations, whereas the latter postulates an identical cross-national association between origins and destinations. The second problem is to determine whether or not the thesis is intended to apply to societies without a market economy—such as the former communist states of Central and Eastern Europe.

The latter issue is the more easily resolved. Featherman and his colleagues themselves raise the possibility that their arguments also apply in non-capitalist countries. In any case, whatever the original intentions of its authors, it is certainly possible to test the hypothesis in this way. Subsequent researchers have therefore extended the original formulation so that data for communist (and formerly communist) countries are now routinely included in the relevant investigations (see e.g. Grusky and Hauser 1984).

However, the terminological inexactitude of the hypothesis itself continues to cause difficulties, so that debate about its empirical standing remains lively and unresolved.[1]

On the one hand, there are those such as Erikson and Goldthorpe who argue that the weaker (verbal) formulation is essentially sound, and that the key features of cross-national common fluidity patterns can be represented in a so-called 'core model'. This is a complex topological (or levels) model that seeks to capture a series of specific effects that are exerted on the pattern of relative rates. Rather than postulate common (i.e. identical) social fluidity, Erikson and Goldthorpe proposed a multi-matrix model embracing four effects that are predicted from sociological theory: those of hierarchy, inheritance, sector, and affinity. These anticipate respectively a reduced probability of social mobility (*ceteris paribus*) where inter-generational crossing of lines of hierarchical division is involved (*hierarchy 1*); that long-range vertical mobility will be especially low (*hierarchy 2*); a generally increased propensity for individuals to be found in their class of origin rather than any other (*inheritance 1*); a distinctively high degree of immobility within classes IVa + IVb (the *petite bourgeoisie*), IVc (farmers and smallholders), and I + II (the salariat) (*inheritance 2*); an especially high propensity towards father–son succession in farming (*inheritance 3*); the enhanced probability of movements of an intrasectoral as against an intersectoral kind—especially in relation to the distinction between agricultural and non-agricultural class positions (*sector*); a disaffinity between the salariat and the class of agricultural workers (*affinity 1*); and a series of affinities that derive from specific continuities between classes—specifically the salariat and routine clerical classes, the two agricultural classes, and those where there is the greatest possibility of transferring capital between generations (*affinity 2*).

Although the CASMIN data for fifteen countries show that there are still cross-national variations in relative rates that are not captured by this model, these are relatively minor, and (more importantly) cannot be explained systematically in terms of any macro-sociological variables that are obvious to Erikson and Goldthorpe. These authors conclude, therefore, that their particular interpretation of what would count as a 'basic' cross-national similarity of relative mobility rates in the modern world is clearly vindicated: that 'a particular pattern of such rates is identifiable, to which the patterns actually found in different national societies will all approximate even though any, or indeed all, of these societies may show some amount of deviation' (Erikson and Goldthorpe 1992*a*: 117).

On the other hand, Ganzeboom et al. (1989: 3–4, 47–8) have argued that analysis of 149 intergenerational class mobility tables from thirty-five countries 'suggests that the hypothesis of common social fluidity is simply incorrect'. Their results seem to show both that 'the between-country variance accounts for about one third of the total variance in the mobility parameters, indicating that there are significant between-country differences' and that 'within countries the extent of inequality in mobility chances is on average decreasing at about one percent per year, in the long run a substantial rate'. The authors concede that there may be a basic similarity in mobility patterns, but insist that there are substantial cross-national and cross-temporal differences in the extent (or rates) of mobility, especially with respect to both the degree of immobility and the equality of mobility chances among those who do not remain in their social classes of origin. These results would seem to count against the FJH hypothesis—at least as Ganzeboom and his colleagues understand the original claim.

It is difficult to arbitrate between these and other similarly competing accounts, not only because they tend to adopt different criteria as to what constitutes mobility rates that are 'basically the same', but also because they have invariably been arrived at from an analysis of alternative data-sets, coded to class schemes (including Goldthorpe class schemes) of varying complexity and reliability, and conducted on the basis of competing statistical tools.[2]

Against this particular background, the empirical results presented in Chapter 4 above are clearly of limited significance, although they do extend the range of countries and data-sets that can be included in the discussion. Nevertheless, and with due acknowledgement having been made to the limitations inherent in our small sample sizes and crude global models, there are two conclusions that do seem to us to emerge from our own data and which have some bearing on the unresolved matter of the FJH hypothesis.

The first is that the degree of commonality in social fluidity across nations is undeniably substantial. The common social fluidity model (see Table 4.4) in fact accounts for more than 92 per cent of the total association in our three-way origin by destination by nation table for men—or, alternatively, more than 80 per cent of the variation in the independence model (which posits different origin and destination distributions in each country but no common pattern of association between origins and destinations across countries). The corresponding figures for females are 89 per cent and 73 per cent. These are impressively high—and researchers having access to larger data-sets have found the associations to be higher still. Even critics have conceded that this is a substantial common core of relative mobility rates. Grusky and Hauser (1984: 26), for example, accept that their results 'make it quite clear that the cross-nationally common element heavily predominates over the cross-nationally variable one'. Erikson and Goldthorpe's (1992a: 389) overall assessment is therefore quite widely shared: that 'the total amount of the association between class origins and destinations that is cross-nationally variable is, in any event, only very small relative to the amount that is cross-nationally common'.

Second, whether or not we think of the FJH hypothesis in its strict sense as being vindicated by this degree of correspondence, our results certainly falsify the claims made by liberal theorists of industrial society and by those who would argue that there are major or systematic differences in class mobility according to (say) type of political regime or national culture. Supporters of the FJH hypothesis generally do not deny that there are *some* variations in social fluidity across nations. Rather, they argue that such differences as are apparent cannot be explained systematically in terms of macro-sociological variables, but only by reference to historical particulars within each society.[3] Our own results tend to confirm this interpretation: the model of common social fluidity does not quite fit the data, but the residuals and UNIDIFF parameter estimates show no obvious pattern in terms of political regime, level of economic development, or some similar such generalized explanation.

In summary then, our results would lead us to conclude that, although all industrialized societies do not appear to have identical mobility regimes, together with many previous researchers we would surmise that the degree of social fluidity within industrialized nations is indeed 'basically similar'.

NOTES

1. Subsequent restatements of the thesis by its authors have not really addressed this particular problem. For example, in a recent study that is claimed to 'confirm the FJH hypothesis about the fundamental invariance of mobility regimes in industrial societies', Jones and his colleagues conclude that data pertaining to trends in social mobility in Japan and Australia show a 'substantial invariance' in the mobility regimes of these nations—'a largely common' pattern that has not changed over time in Japan and has changed 'only marginally' in Australia over the past 30 years or so (see Jones et al. 1994).
2. The latter set of problems is well illustrated by the special issue of the *European Sociological Review* (vol. 8, no. 3, 1992) that was devoted to an assessment of the CASMIN Project. See esp. e.g. the papers by Hout and

Hauser (1992) and Sørensen (1992). Erikson and Goldthorpe's (1992c) reply is given in the same issue.
3. See e.g. Erikson (1990), who argues that the relatively high Swedish fluidity rate may, at least in part, be related to government policies aimed at equalizing educational opportunities and income.

APPENDIX I
Status Attainment and Meritocracy

Studies within the earlier status attainment tradition of research into social mobility regularly reported that the socio-economic status and prestige scores of occupations were associated not only with the educational achievement of individuals but also with their social origins.

For example, in the original Blau–Duncan model for the U.S. in 1962, the total correlation between son's current occupation and father's occupation was 0.405. This could be decomposed into an indirect effect via education of 0.227 (57 per cent) and an effect net of education (direct or through the son's first job) of 0.178 (43 per cent). In this same study, the ratio of the effect of education on current occupation to the direct effect of father's occupation on current occupation was calculated to be 2.9 to 1, a finding which led Blau and Duncan to conclude that achievement was more important than ascription in determining occupational status in mid-twentieth-century America.

The later so-called Wisconsin Model, developed by William H. Sewell and his associates, continued in the Blau–Duncan mould by relating the family background and ascribed characteristics of students to their occupational status via the mediation of ability and educational achievement. Various Wisconsin studies showed that socio-economic status affected educational and occupational outcomes through its effects on parental and peer influences and on the shaping of educational aspirations. Academic ability was also found to have a strong effect on educational attainment (independently of socio-economic status) and an effect on occupational attainment through its impact on educational and occupational aspirations. In other words, both schooling and family background affected status attainment, mainly through effects transmitted by social psychological processes.[1]

The implications of these findings for arguments about equality of opportunity and meritocracy soon became a matter of controversy. Some observers (such as Robert Hauser) took them to mean that status attainment in the US was mainly a meritocratic process since the effects of family background could (apparently) be overcome by those attributable to schooling. Others (including Christopher Jencks) argued that such results undermined meritocratic interpretations of the status-attainment process because both ascription and achievement continued to exert a substantial influence on mobility outcomes. Moreover, Jencks and his colleagues maintained that the importance of family background was underestimated in the Wisconsin model, and that of aptitude and aspirations overestimated, because of measurement errors in the original studies.[2]

Issues of equality of opportunity and meritocracy continue, if only implicitly, to inform much of the research within the status attainment paradigm. For example, in an article on stratification and meritocracy in the US (published in 1981), Larry Griffin and Arne Kalleberg conclude that '(white) men in that country 'are not generally sorted into class positions on the basis of "meritocratic" criteria'. Their results seem to show, instead, that 'educational credentials only minimally affect recruitment of the . . . men into class positions' (Griffin and Kalleberg 1981: 1, 15).

Many of these studies are, however, something of a hybrid between the status attainment and class analysis traditions. Griffin and Kalleberg, for example, include father's *socio-economic status* (measured in terms of O. D. Duncan's scale) as an independent variable in a regression analysis of the determinants of placement into *social classes* (categorized in terms of a scheme which attempts to operationalize the class theory of Erik Olin Wright). Other predictor variables tested in the regression include father's and mother's education, parental income, a thirteen-item factor-weighted acquisition index of possessions in the respondent's high-school household (all aspects of 'social origins'), and years both of work experience and in present job—these last two, together with years of schooling completed and educational certificates obtained, being taken as indicators of the respondent's 'achieved skills'.

This blend explains Griffin and Kalleberg's (otherwise perhaps puzzling) observation, in response to the question of whether or not 'achievement processes' in the US are meritocratic: 'There is no *one* answer to this question because the structure of positional inequality in the U.S. is multidimensional.' 'We have', they continue,

identified two of these stratification systems. One is based on occupational position . . . an indicator of the technical division of labour, and the evidence— especially on the very powerful role of schooling—suggests that achievement in this system is largely meritocratic. The other stratification system is based on ownership and control relations, and achievement in this system is but modestly susceptible to meritocratic influences . . . Hence, in our view, we should be quite cautious about accepting an *overall* meritocratic interpretation of achievement and inequality in contemporary American society. Despite the popular appeal of such a view . . . it does not appear to be the basis upon which men are sorted and selected into the American *class* structure. (Griffin and Kalleberg 1981: 31)

Similarly, in his recent study of the transition to adulthood in Great Britain, Alan Kerckhoff shows that (as expected) both social origins and educational experience have some association with the (Treiman-scored) *prestige* level of first job and current job—where social origins is indicated by the Registrar General's social *class* standing of fathers. Kerckhoff (1990: 182) therefore arrives at the conclusion that

the level of a man's father's occupation had a persistent effect on his outcomes. Net of all other variables included in the analysis, men whose fathers had higher-class occupations obtained higher-level qualifications by the time they entered the labour force, they received greater occupational prestige returns to those qualifications, and they obtained greater occupational prestige returns to qualifications they added after labour-force entry.

In other words, someone's social class of origin has a substantial direct effect on the prestige score of his or her occupation, even after educational qualifications and ability have been taken into account.

These studies are good illustrations of the shift that was made in the status-attainment tradition, during the 1980s, towards the study of structural limitations and selection criteria as well as socialization processes: that is, away from the question of how socio-economic status and educational attainment affects occupational placement, towards analysis of the impact on occupational outcomes of variation in class origins and in labour-market structures. This change of emphasis probably represents an attempt to overcome the perceived failure of status-attainment research to consider the impact of structural effects upon educational and occupational attainment. The earlier themes of equality of opportunity and meritocracy tend, therefore, to be somewhat less prominent in these studies.[3]

NOTES

1. For an overview of these and later findings in relation to status attainment, see Treiman and Ganzeboom (1990), and, more generally, Hallinan (1988).
2. See e.g. the exchange between Jencks et al. (1983), Hauser et al. (1983), and Campbell (1983).
3. For a review of this later literature, see Kalleberg (1988).

APPENDIX J
Popular Beliefs about Meritocracy

In his review of empirical work on people's beliefs about distributive justice, David Miller observes that the general principle of 'reward according to contribution' receives a good deal of popular support, both in experimental work, by which small groups have to arrive at a just allocation of scarce goods, and in surveys of attitudes towards fairness about society-wide distributions of resources.[1]

In fact, as Miller himself advises, both bodies of evidence should be treated with due caution. Laboratory studies tend to involve a narrow range of participants (college students) and to report upon artificial situations and tasks. Surveys mainly tap broad beliefs, support for which may be arrived at via several distinct lines of reasoning, so that (for example) researchers usually cannot determine whether assent to an item favouring the idea that 'people with more ability should earn higher salaries' indicates support for the principle of justice as desert or is merely a claim about the necessity of having incentives. In both micro- and macro-studies, where desert does seem to emerge as a preferred criterion of fairness, its precise basis is usually unclear; for example, as between rewarding people according to ability, effort expended, or performance and achievement. Moreover, most of this empirical material originates in the US, and it is only recently that researchers have begun to explore systematically the similarities and differences across countries.[2]

One such study is the International Social Justice Project (ISJP), a cross-national comparative survey of popular beliefs about distributive justice in selected democratic capitalist and former state socialist societies, upon which we have already drawn in assembling our data on social mobility.[3] It is interesting to consider the evidence that has emerged from this project regarding the views about social justice held by ordinary citizens, specifically with respect to the issues of equality, opportunity, and merit, particularly in the light of Miller's (1992b: 588) own speculation—made admittedly on the basis of the scanty evidence available at the time—that 'the preeminence of desert criteria, which was a major theme running through our analysis of studies undertaken in Western societies, may be radically weakened if we look elsewhere'.

Consider, therefore, the proportion of respondents, within each country studied as part of the ISJP, who agreed or disagreed with the various statements shown in Table J.1. The columns in the table report the percentage of those interviewed in each of the nationally representative sample surveys who agreed with the items, minus the percentage who disagreed, together with the separate averages for the four democratic capitalist and seven former state socialist societies (and the resulting difference between the two).[4]

It is clear from the first item that there is little support for equality of outcome in the distribution of income and wealth in any of the countries studied—capitalist and post-communist alike. The percentage of respondents who disagree with the proposition that 'the fairest way of distributing wealth and income would be to give everyone equal shares' is so much larger than the proportion who endorse this idea that a substantial negative figure will be found in every column of the table. The average for the two types of society is similar, at minus 40 and minus 45 for capitalist and socialist regimes respectively, so that the difference is a relatively small 5 percentage points.

The pattern of responses to the next four questions suggests that, by contrast, a substantial majority in all countries think that inequalities of outcome can be justified as long as all have equality of opportunity, that people are entitled to keep what they have earned even if this results in inequalities of wealth, and that people who work hard deserve to earn more than those who do not. They also reject the Rawlsian view that differences in skill and intelligence are a matter of luck and so not deserving of reward. Again, the degree of similarity across countries far exceeds any difference between them, and the averages for the two types of regime (democratic capitalist and former state socialist) are very similar—indeed, in the case of all but one item, nearly identical.

Of course, these are very broad attitudes, in respect of which Miller's earlier observations about survey evidence are entirely apposite. For example, it is not clear how people would weigh up the balance between rewarding skill or effort (items 4 and 5), as a basis for desert in any particular context.[5] However, the degree of support for what can reasonably be described as broadly meritocratic principles applied to a competition in which all have equal chances to win is impressive, and apparently similar among citizens in different types of society—as the column reporting the difference between the average for advanced capitalist and post-communist nations makes clear.

However, when we turn from the realm of moral principles to that of beliefs about the extent to which the existing distribution of rewards is in accordance with those principles, the differences between the two types of society become much more pronounced. Each of the four advanced

TABLE J.1. *Support for Distribution Principles, and Perceptions of Inequality, in Eleven Nations (Percentages)*

Item	BUL	CZA	GDR	EST	POL	RUS	SLO	GBR	JAP	USA	FRG	AS	AC	Dif
1	−42	−50	−42	−68	−51	−29	−31	−32	−39	−51	−37	−45	−40	5
2	68	54	70	47	50	70	69	71	40	74	72	61	64	3
3	66	80	91	92	49	90	83	72	56	88	83	79	75	4
4	97	88	96	96	87	93	87	93	86	89	89	92	89	3
5	−29	−64	−35	−5	−14	−58	−32	−56	−37	−66	−27	−34	−47	13
6	−55	−7	−35	−48	−35	−45	−5	−6	10	37	21	−33	16	49
7	−62	−53	1	−43	−51	−44	−3	10	25	49	56	−37	35	72
8	−67	−49	27	−70	−42	−49	−5	27	51	56	66	−36	50	86
9	−83	−74	−80	−72	−79	−76	−70	−51	−48	−55	−45	−76	−50	26

Notes

1. Nations are as in Table 4.1, n. 2.

2. AS = average % for all former state socialist nations.

3. AC = average % for all democratic capitalist nations.

4. Dif = difference between averages for state socialist and democratic capitalist nations.

5. Attitudinal items are: (1) The fairest way of distributing wealth and income would be to give everyone equal shares; (2) It's fair if people have more money or wealth, but only if there are equal opportunities; (3) People are entitled to keep what they have earned—even if this means some people will be wealthier than others; (4) People who work hard deserve to earn more than those who do not; (5) It is just luck if some people are more intelligent or skilful than others, so they don't deserve to earn more money; (6) In (COUNTRY) people have equal opportunities to get ahead; (7) In (COUNTRY) people get rewarded for their intelligence and skills; (9) Do you think you are paid much less than you deserve, somewhat less than you deserve, about what you deserve, somewhat more than you deserve, or much more than you deserve?

6. For item (9), % is of those who felt they were paid less than they deserved minus those who felt they were paid more; in other words they record a perceived 'desert deficit'.

capitalist states was perceived, in the main, to be broadly meritocratic in practice. By comparison, respondents in the formerly socialist countries were markedly more likely to characterize their societies as being ones in which people did not have equal opportunities to get ahead, were not rewarded for their efforts or talents, and earned much less than they deserved. (It should be remembered here that the surveys were conducted in 1991, so respondents in the Central and Eastern European states were commenting on societies which had only recently emerged from communism, mainly since 1989.) In other words, it is people's perceptions of the prevailing situation that are here cross-nationally divergent, rather than their support for broadly meritocratic principles of social justice.

Perhaps this disjuncture is not surprising. We have already observed (see Appendix F) that communist ideology reinforced the principle of increasing equality of opportunity to earn rewards proportionate to merit. Inequalities of outcome were accepted as a necessary feature of socialism, which nevertheless promoted distributive justice by giving people equal access to unequally rewarded positions, or at least more equal access than was to be found under the alternative of advanced capitalism. Such an ideology seems to have reinforced popular support for broadly meritocratic principles, as applied to a competition in which all have equal opportunities for advancement, and so created expectations which were at odds with the reality of everyday life under actually existing socialism.[6]

It is not, then, difficult to imagine why the popularly perceived gap between principle and practice became so pronounced. Meritocratic aspirations will have been raised to a high level by the rhetoric of enhanced social fluidity under communism. Yet, at the same time, meritocratic principles were widely flouted—for example in policies enacting positive discrimination on behalf of workers and peasants. There was also widespread public awareness of the covert and overt discrimination that was practised in favour of men, productive workers, and members of the Party. Be that as it may, it seems certain that in the context of state socialism the perceived failure of the Party to deliver on its promise of creating an open society will have exacerbated the already considerable problems of regime legitimation, since it was the state itself that took responsibility for distributive outcomes and for effecting social change.

This conclusion is implicit in Wesołowski and Mach's (1986: 25) commentary on the functions of social mobility under state socialism. 'In socialist systems', they observe, 'state intervention takes the form of reorganizing social life'. Furthermore,

since the state authorities in 'reorganizing society' intervene strongly in all macro-structures, the problem of legitimation becomes global as a result. The authorities which feel qualified to recreate reality are perceived by the population as responsible for everything . . . In revolutionary systems, which initially derived their legitimacy, at least in part, from promising extensive social change, the issue of maintaining and of widening the legitimacy resting on such foundations is crucial.

The meritocratic aspirations of West Germans, Americans, the Japanese, and British, and their perception of advanced capitalist nations as societies in which people (in broad terms) obtained their due deserts, are consistent with the earlier evidence summarized by Miller. In these countries, the popular belief that inequality results from equal opportunities and reflects meritocratic reward serves to legitimate market outcomes, since success and failure are routinely attributed to individual talents and effort (or their absence).[7]

However, under real socialism, the potential for legitimation inherent in meritocratic beliefs was undermined by the supreme power claimed by (and attributed to) the state. Eastern Europeans seem to have endorsed meritocratic principles as strongly as those living in the West (the ideology of meritocratic socialism serving to reinforce these aspirations); but, at the same time, they also held expectations about the role of government (and its responsibility for delivering on policy promises) which were consistent with living in a centrally planned society. When these expectations were not fulfilled (at least with regard to equality of opportunity) then the state was the obvious culprit.[8]

From the point of view of regime legitimation, therefore, the most important point about meritocratic beliefs in general, and the notion of equality of opportunity in particular, might seem to be that these individualize the causes of success and failure. By claiming all responsibility for distributive outcomes in the name of socialism, the Party effectively denied that possibility, and ensured instead that these causes were identified within the state itself. For this reason, popular discontent could easily be focused upon the central authorities, rather than internalized by attributing failure to individual responsibility.

NOTES

1. Miller (1992*b*). Earlier accounts along similar lines include Soltan (1982) and Cook and Hegtvedt (1983).
2. The experimental work (mainly undertaken by social psychologists) is fully described in Walster et al. (1978). The (mostly sociological) survey material is documented in Kluegel and Smith (1986).
3. The methodology of the project is fully explained in Kluegel et al. (1995).
4. Responses to the questions were precoded, typically on a 5-point Likert scale, ranging from strongly agree and agree through a neutral category to disagree and strongly disagree.

5. Furthermore, since item 5 contains 2 distinct propositions, it is impossible to tell whether these responses indicate that respondents do not accept that intelligence and skill are a matter of luck—perhaps believing that a person's skill at least is a result of their efforts in developing their natural abilities— or that they do regard them as chance attributes but think them deserving of reward none the less. Similarly, with respect to item 4, it may be that respondents understand the claim that people who work hard deserve to earn more than those who do not to be a claim about legitimate expectations, given current institutions and practices, rather than a claim about desert in the stronger pre-institutional sense. Our attempts to ask more specific questions were rejected by our colleagues in the ISJP, on the grounds that such questions were inappropriately abstract, and too complicated for a questionnaire of the kind that we were constructing. If our colleagues were right, then this suggests that the survey method cannot be used to tap people's beliefs about justice with the level of precision necessary to identify their positions on issues that arise in the philosophical literature.

6. See also e.g. the arguments of Jadwiga Koralewicz-Zebik (1984: 225) in relation to Poland under rule of communism. She maintains that 'changes in the perception of inequalities in Poland . . . show that . . . greatest frustration was due to a decomposition of the system of meritocratic justice, accepted by the majority of Poles, combined with the expansion of other, unaccepted, criteria for rewards. Thus the growth of increasing inequalities was accompanied by a total withdrawal of the legitimization of inequalities.'

7. See e.g. the literature on attributions for poverty and wealth summarized in Kluegel and Smith (1981).

8. This interpretation is consistent with other recent evidence regarding the popular culture of at least some of the formerly state socialist societies. See e.g. the findings reported for East Germany by Edeltraud Roller (1994: 115), who concludes from survey evidence gathered in late 1990 that 'East Germans supported the achievement principle of the market economy to the same degree as the West Germans. At the same time, they harboured higher expectations regarding the role of government, expectations that are more congruent with a planned economy.'

REFERENCES

AITOV, N. A. (1986), 'The Dynamics of Social Mobility in the Soviet Union', in M. Yanowitch (ed.), *The Social Structure of the USSR: Recent Soviet Studies* (Armonk, NY: M. E. Sharpe), 254–70.

ALDRIDGE, J., and NELSON, F. (1984), *Linear Probability, Logit, and Probit Models* (London: Sage).

ALESTALO, M., SŁOMCZYŃSKI, K. M., and WESOŁOWSKI, W. (1980), 'Patterns of Stratification', in E. Allardt and W. Wesołowski (eds.), *Social Structure and Social Change: Finland and Poland Comparative Perspective* (Warsaw: Polish Scientific Publishers), 117–46.

ANASTASI, A. (1988), *Psychological Testing* (London: Macmillan).

ARNESON, R. (1990), 'Is Work Special? Justice and the Distribution of Employment', *American Political Science Review* **84**: 1121–41.

ATKINSON, A. B. (ed.) (1980), *Wealth, Income and Inequality* (Oxford: Oxford University Press).

——and MICKLEWRIGHT, J. (1992), *Economic Transformation in Eastern Europe and the Distribution of Income* (Cambridge: Cambridge University Press).

BALL, S. J. (1986), *Education* (London: Longman).

BARTLEY, M., CARPENTER, L., DUNNELL, K., and FITZPATRICK, R. (1996), 'Measuring Inequalities in Health: An Analysis of Mortality Patterns Using Two Social Classifications', *Sociology of Health and Illness* **8**: 455–74.

BAXTER, J., EMMISON, M., WESTERN, J., and WESTERN, M. (eds.) (1991), *Class Analysis and Contemporary Australia* (Melbourne: Macmillan).

BELL, D. (1976), *The Coming of Post-Industrial Society* (Harmondsworth: Penguin).

BERG, I. (1971), *Education and Jobs: The Great Training Robbery* (Boston: Beacon Press).

BILLS, D. B. (1988), 'Educational Credentials and Promotions: Does Schooling Do More than Get You in the Door?', *Sociology of Education* **61**: 52–60.

BLACKBURN, R. M., and MARSH, C. (1991), 'Education and Social Class: Revisiting the 1944 Education Act with Fixed Marginals', *British Journal of Sociology* **42**: 507–36.

BLAU, P. M., and DUNCAN, O. D. (1967), *The American Occupational Structure* (New York: Wiley).

BOGUSZAK, M. (1990), 'Transition to Socialism and Intergenerational Class Mobility', in M. Haller (ed.), *Class Structure in Europe* (London: M. E. Sharpe), 233–60.

BONNEY, N. (1988), 'Gender, Household and Social Class', *British Journal of Sociology* **39**: 28–46.

BOROCZ, J. (1989), 'Mapping the Class Structures of State Socialism in East-Central Europe', *Research in Social Stratification and Mobility* **8**: 279–309.

BOUDON, R. (1974), *Education, Opportunity and Social Inequality* (New York: Wiley).

BRAHAM, P., RHODES, E., and PEARN, M. (eds.) (1981), *Discrimination and Disadvantage in Employment* (London: Harper & Row).

BREEN, R., and ROTTMAN, D. B. (1995*a*), *Class Stratification* (London: Harvester Wheatsheaf).

———— (1995*b*), 'Class Analysis and Class Theory', *Sociology* **29**: 453–73.

——and WHELAN, C. T. (1993), 'From Ascription to Achievement? Origins, Education and Entry to the Labour Force in the Republic of Ireland during the Twentieth Century, *Acta Sociologica* **36**: 3–17.

———— (1994), 'Modelling Trends in Social Fluidity: The Core Model and a Measured-Variable Approach Compared', *European Sociological Review* **10**: 259–72.

BRODY, N. (1992), *Intelligence* (London: Academic Press).

BROWN, P., and SCASE, R. (1994), *Higher Education and Corporate Realities* (London: UCL Press).

CAMPBELL, R. T. (1983), 'Status Attainment Research: End of the Beginning or Beginning of the End?', *Sociology of Education* **56**: 47–62.

CAMPBELL, T. (1988), *Justice* (London: Macmillan).

CHARVÁT, F., LINHART, J., and VEČERNIK, J. (1978), 'Some Remarks on the Application of Mobility Approach in a Socialist Society', in W. Wesołowski, K. M. Słomczyński, and B. W. Mach (eds.), *Social Mobility in Comparative Perspective* (Warsaw: Polish Academy of Sciences Press), 159–71.

CLARK, J., MODGIL, C., and MODGIL, S. (eds.) (1990), *John Goldthorpe: Consensus and Controversy* (London: Falmer).

COHEN, G. A. (1989), 'On the Currency of Egalitarian Justice', *Ethics* **99**: 906–44.

——(1995), 'Incentives, Inequality and Community', in S. Darwall (ed.), *Equal Freedom* (Ann Arbor: University of Michigan Press), 331–97.

COHEN, R. L. (ed.) (1986), *Justice: Views from the Social Sciences* (New York: Plenum).

COLLINS, R. (1979), *The Credential Society* (New York: Academic Press).

Commission on Social Justice (1993), *Social Justice in a Changing World* (London: Institute for Public Policy Research).

——(1994), *Social Justice: Strategies for National Renewal* (London: Vintage).

CONNOR, W. D. (1979), *Socialism, Politics and Equality* (New York: Columbia University Press).

COOK, K. S., and HEGTVEDT, K. A. (1983), 'Distributive Justice, Equity, and Equality', *Annual Review of Sociology* **9**: 217–41.

COULTER, P. B. (1989), *Measuring Inequality* (Boulder, Colo.: Westview Press).

CROMPTON, R. (1993), *Class and Stratification* (Cambridge: Polity).

CROMPTON, R., and MANN, M. (eds.) (1986), *Gender and Stratification* (Cambridge: Polity Press).

——and SANDERSON, K. (1990), *Gendered Jobs and Social Change* (London: Unwin Hyman).

DALE, A., GILBERT, N. G., and ARBER, S. (1985), 'Integrating Women into Class Theory', *Sociology* **19**: 384–409.

DANIELS, N. (1978), 'Merit and Meritocracy', *Philosophy and Public Affairs* **7**: 206–23.

DAVIES, S. (1995), 'Leaps of Faith: Shifting Currents in Critical Sociology of Education', *American Journal of Sociology* **100**: 1148–78.

DAVIS, K., and MOORE, W. E. (1945), 'Some Principles of Stratification', *American Sociological Review* **10**: 242–9.

DE GRAAF, N. D., and HEATH, A. (1992), 'Husbands' and Wives' Voting Behaviour in Britain: Class-Dependent Mutual Influence of Spouses', *Acta Sociologica* **35**: 311–22.

DEX, S., and SHAW, L. B. (1986), *British and American Women at Work* (Basingstoke: Macmillan).

DORE, R. (1982), *The Diploma Disease: Education, Qualification and Development* (London: Allen & Unwin).

DRONKERS, J. (1993), 'Educational Reform in the Netherlands: Did It Change the Impact of Parental Occupation and Education?', *Sociology of Education* **66**: 262–77.

DUKE, V., and EDGELL, S. (1987), 'The Operationalisation of Class in British Sociology: Theoretical and Empirical Considerations', *British Journal of Sociology* **38**: 445–63.

DUNCAN, O. D. (1961), 'A Socioeconomic Index for All Occupations', in A. Reiss (ed.), *Occupations and Social Status* (New York: Free Press), 109–38.

DWORKIN, R. (1981*a*), 'What is Equality? Part 1: Equality of Welfare', *Philosophy and Public Affairs* **10**: 185–246.

——(1981*b*), 'What is Equality? Part 2: Equality of Resources', *Philosophy and Public Affairs* **10**: 283–345.

EDGELL, S. (1993), *Class* (New York: Routledge).

ELSTER, J. (1985), *Making Sense of Marx* (Cambridge: Cambridge University Press).

——(1988), 'Is There (or Should There Be) a Right to Work?', in A. Guttmann (ed.), *Democracy and the Welfare State* (Princeton, NJ: Princeton University Press), 53–78.

ERIKSON, R. (1984), 'Social Class of Men, Women and Families', *Sociology* **18**: 500–14.

——(1990), 'Politics and Class Mobility: Does Politics Influence Rates of Social Mobility?', in I. Persson, (ed.), *Generating Equality in the Welfare State: The Swedish Experience* (Oslo: Norwegian University Press), 247–65.

——and Goldthorpe, J. H. (1992*a*), *The Constant Flux* (Oxford: Clarendon Press).

————(1992*b*), 'Individual or Family? Results from Two Approaches to Class Assignment', *Acta Sociologica* **35**: 95–105.

————— (1992c), 'The CASMIN Project and the American Dream', *European Sociological Review* **8**: 283–305.

————— and JONSSON, J. O. (1996), 'Explaining Class Inequality in Education: The Swedish Test Case', in Erikson and Jonsson (eds.), *Can Education Be Equalized? The Swedish Case in Comparative Perspective* (Oxford: Westview Press), 1–63.

EVANS, G. (1992), 'Testing the Validity of the Goldthorpe Class Schema', *European Sociological Review* **8**: 211–32.

————— (1993), 'Class, Prospects and the Life-Cycle: Explaining the Association between Class Position and Political Preferences', *Acta Sociologica* **26**: 263–76.

————— (1996), 'Putting Men and Women into Classes: An Assessment of the Cross-Sex Validity of the Goldthorpe Schema', *Sociology* **30**: 209–34.

FEATHERMAN, D. L. (1981), 'Social Stratification and Mobility: Two Decades of Cumulative Social Science', *American Behavioural Scientist* **24**: 364–85.

————— and HAUSER, R. M. (1978), *Opportunity and Change* (New York: Academic Press).

————— JONES, F. L., and HAUSER, R. M. (1975), 'Assumptions of Social Mobility Research in the US: The Case of Occupational Status', *Social Science Research* **4**: 329–60.

FEINBERG, J. (1980), 'Noncomparative Justice', in *Rights, Justice and the Bounds of Liberty* (Princeton, NJ: Princeton University Press), 265–306.

FERGE, Z. (1979), *A Society in the Making* (White Plains, NY: M. E. Sharpe).

FISHKIN, J. (1983), *Justice, Equal Opportunity and the Family* (New Haven, Conn.: Yale University Press).

FOGELMAN, K. et al. (1983), 'Social Factors Associated with Changes in Educational Attainment Between 7 and 11 Years of Age', and 'Patterns of Attainment', in Fogelman (ed.), *Growing Up in Great Britain: Papers from the National Child Development Study* (London: Macmillan), 27–45.

GAMBETTA, D. (1987), *Were They Pushed or Did They Jump? Individual Decision Mechanisms in Education* (Cambridge: Cambridge University Press).

GAMBLE, A. (1988), *The Free Economy and the Strong State* (London: Macmillan).

GANZEBOOM, H. B. G., LUIJKX, R., and TREIMAN, D. J. (1989), 'Intergenerational Class Mobility in Comparative Perspective', *Research in Social Stratification and Mobility* **8**: 3–84.

————— TREIMAN, D. J., and ULTEE, W. (1991), 'Comparative Intergenerational Stratification Research: Three Generations and Beyond', *Annual Review of Sociology* **17**: 277–302.

GARDNER, H. (1995), 'Cracking Open the IQ Box', in S. Fraser (ed.), *The Bell Curve Wars: Race, Intelligence, and the Future of America* (New York: Basic Books), 23–35.

GILBERT, G. N. (1981), *Modelling Society* (London: Allen & Unwin).

GINTIS, H. (1980), 'The American Occupational Structure Eleven Years Later', *Contemporary Sociology* **9**: 12–16.

GOLDTHORPE, J. H. (1982), 'On the Service Class: Its Formation and Future', in

A. Giddens and G. Mackenzie (eds.), *Social Class and the Division of Labour* (Cambridge: Cambridge University Press), 162–85.

——(1983), 'Women and Class Analysis: In Defence of the Conventional View', *Sociology* **17**: 465–88.

——(1984), 'Women and Class Analysis: Reply to the Replies', *Sociology* **18**: 491–9.

——(1990), 'A Response', in J. Clark, C. Modgil, and S. Modgil (eds.), *John Goldthorpe: Consensus and Controversy* (London: Falmer), 399–438.

——(1991), 'Employment, Class and Mobility: A Critique of Liberal and Marx-ist Theories of Long-Term Change', in H. Haferkamp and N. J. Smelser (eds.), *Modernity and Social Change* (Berkeley: University of California Press), 122–46.

——(1995a), 'The Service Class Revisited', in M. Savage and T. Butler (eds.), *Social Change and the Middle Classes* (London: UCL Press), 313–29.

——(1995b), 'Le "noyau dur": fluidité sociale en Angleterre et en France dans les années 70 et 80', *Revue française de sociologie* **36**: 61–79.

——(1996a), 'Problems of "Meritocracy"', in R. Erikson and J. O. Jonsson (eds.), *Can Education Be Equalized? The Swedish Case in Comparative Perspective* (Oxford: Westview Press), 255–87.

——(1996b), 'Class Analysis and the Reorientation of Class Theory: The Case of Persisting Differentials in Educational Attainment', *British Journal of Sociology* **47**: 481–505.

——and MARSHALL, G. (1992), 'The Promising Future of Class Analysis: A Response to Recent Critiques', *Sociology* **26**: 381–400.

——and PAYNE, C. (1986), 'Trends in Intergenerational Class Mobility in England and Wales, 1972–1983', *Sociology* **20**: 1–24.

——with LLEWELLYN, C., and PAYNE, C. (1980, 2nd edn. 1988), *Social Mobility and Class Structure in Modern Britain* (Oxford: Clarendon Press).

GOODWIN, B. (1987), *Using Political Ideas* (Chichester: Wiley).

GOULD, S. J. (1995), 'Curveball', in S. Fraser (ed.), *The Bell Curve Wars: Race, Intelligence, and the Future of America* (New York: Basic Books), 11–22.

GREEN, D. G. (1990), *Equalizing People* (London: Institute of Economic Affairs).

GREEN, S. J. D. (1988), 'Is Equality of Opportunity a False Ideal for Society?', *British Journal of Sociology* **39**: 1–27.

GRIFFIN, L., and KALLEBERG, A. (1981), 'Stratification and Meritocracy in the United States: Class and Occupational Recruitment Patterns', *British Journal of Sociology* **32**: 1–38.

GRUSKY, D. B., and HAUSER, R. M. (1984), 'Comparative Social Mobility Revisited: Models of Convergence and Divergence in 16 Countries', *American Sociological Review* **49**: 19–38.

HALABY, C. N. (1994), 'Overeducation and Skill Mismatch', *Sociology of Education* **67**: 47–59.

HALLINAN, M. T. (1988), 'Equality of Educational Opportunity', *Annual Review of Sociology* **14**: 249–68.

HALSEY, A. H. (1977), 'Towards Meritocracy? The Case of Britain', in

J. Karabel and A. H. Halsey (eds.), *Power and Ideology in Education* (New York: Oxford University Press), 173–86.

HASLETT, D. W. (1994), *Capitalism With Morality* (Oxford: Clarendon Press).

HAUSER, R. M., TSAI, S.-L., and SEWELL, W. H. (1983), 'A Model of Stratification with Response Error in Social and Psychological Variables', *Sociology of Education* **56**: 20–46.

HAYEK, F. A. (1974), *The Mirage of Social Justice* (London: Routledge & Kegan Paul).

——(1978*a*), 'The Atavism of Social Justice', in *New Studies in Philosophy, Politics, Economics and the History of Ideas* (London: Routledge & Kegan Paul), 57–68.

——(1978*b*), 'Competition as a Discovery Procedure', in *New Studies in Philosophy, Politics, Economics and the History of Ideas* (London: Routledge & Kegan Paul), 179–90.

HEATH, A. (1981), *Social Mobility* (London: Fontana).

——JOWELL, R., and CURTICE, J. (1985), *How Britain Votes* (Oxford: Pergamon).

————————(1994), *Labour's Last Chance? The 1992 Election and Beyond* (Aldershot: Dartmouth).

HEATH, A., MILLS, C., and ROBERTS, J. (1992), 'Towards Meritocracy? Recent Evidence on an Old Problem', in C. Crouch and A. Heath (eds.), *Social Research and Social Reform* (Oxford: Clarendon Press), 217–43.

HEGEDÜS, A. (1977 [1970]), *The Structure of Socialist Society* (London: Constable).

HERRNSTEIN, R. J., and MURRAY, C. (1994), *The Bell Curve: Intelligence and Class Structure in American Life* (New York: Free Press).

HOCHSCHILD, A. R. (1983), *The Managed Heart: Commercialization of Human Feeling* (Berkeley: University of California Press).

HOPE, K. (1981), 'Constancies in the Analysis of Social Stratification: A Replication Study', *Quality and Quantity* **15**: 481–503.

HOUT, M., and HAUSER, R. M. (1992), 'Symmetry and Hierarchy in Social Mobility: A Methodological Analysis of the CASMIN Model of Class Mobility', *European Sociological Review* **8**: 239–66.

——RAFTERY, A. E., and BELL, E. O. (1993), 'Making the Grade: Educational Stratification in the United States, 1925–1989', in Y. Shavit and H.-P. Blossfeld (eds.), *Persistent Inequality: Changing Educational Attainment in Thirteen Countries* (Boulder, Colo.: Westview Press), 25–49.

HUDSON, R., and WILLIAMS, A. M. (1989), *Divided Britain* (London: Pinter).

HURLEY, S. (1993), 'Justice Without Constitutive Luck', *Ethics, Royal Institute of Philosophy Supplement* **35** (ed. A. Phillips Griffiths), 179–212.

ISHIDA, H., MÜLLER, W., and RIDGE, J. (1995), 'Class Origin, Class Destination, and Education: A Cross-National Study of Ten Industrial Nations', *American Journal of Sociology* **101**: 145–93.

JENCKS, C., CROUSE, J., and MUESER, P. (1983), 'The Wisconsin Model of Status Attainment: A National Replication with Improved Measures of Ability and Aspiration', *Sociology of Education* **56**: 3–19.

JENCKS, C. et al. (1975), *Inequality* (Harmondsworth: Penguin).
——et al. (1979), *Who Gets Ahead?* (New York: Basic Books).
JONES, F. L., KOJIMA, H., and MARKS, G. (1994), 'Comparative Social Fluidity: Trends over Time in Father-to-Son Mobility in Japan and Australia, 1965–1985', *Social Forces* **72**: 775–98.
JONSSON, J. O. (1991), *Towards the Merit-Selective Society?* (University of Stockholm: Swedish Institute for Social Research).
——(1993*a*), 'Education, Social Mobility, and Social Reproduction in Sweden: Patterns and Changes', in E. J. Hansen et al. (eds.), *Welfare Trends in the Scandinavian Countries* (Armonk, NY: M. E. Sharpe), 91–118.
——(1993*b*), 'Persisting Inequalities in Sweden', in Y. Shavit and H.-P. Blossfeld (eds.), *Persistent Inequality: Changing Educational Attainment in Thirteen Countries* (Boulder, Colo.: Westview Press), 101–32.
——and MILLS, C. (1993), 'Social Class and Educational Attainment in Historical Perspective: A Swedish–English Comparison, Parts I and II', *British Journal of Sociology* **44**: 213–47, 403–28.
JOSEPH, K., and SUMPTION, J. (1979), *Equality* (London: John Murray).
KALLEBERG, A. L. (1988), 'Comparative Perspectives on Work Structures and Inequality', *Annual Review of Sociology* **14**: 203–25.
KELLEY, J., and EVANS, M. D. R. (1993), 'The Legitimation of Inequality: Occupational Earnings in Nine Nations', *American Journal of Sociology* **99**: 75–125.
KENDE, P., and STRMISKA, Z. (eds.) (1987), *Equality and Inequality in Eastern Europe* (Leamington Spa: Berg).
KERCKHOFF, A. C. (1990), *Getting Started* (Oxford: Westview Press).
——and TROTT, J. M. (1993), 'Educational Attainment in a Changing Educational System: The Case of England and Wales', in Y. Shavit and H.-P. Blossfeld (eds.), *Persistent Inequality: Changing Educational Attainment in Thirteen Countries* (Boulder, Colo.: Westview Press), 133–53.
KING, D. S. (1987), *The New Right* (London: Macmillan).
KLEIN, M. (1990), *Determinism, Blameworthiness, and Deprivation* (Oxford: Clarendon Press).
KLUEGEL, J. R., and SMITH, E. R. (1981), 'Beliefs About Stratification', *Annual Review of Sociology* **7**: 29–56.
————(1986), *Beliefs About Inequality: American's Views of What Is and What Ought to Be* (New York: Aldine de Gruyter).
——MASON, D. S., and WEGENER, B. (eds.) (1995), *Social Justice and Political Change* (New York: Aldine de Gruyter).
KNOKE, D., and BURKE, P. J. (1980), *Log-Linear Models* (London: Sage).
KOLOSI, T., and WNUK-LIPIŃSKI, E. (1983), *Equality and Inequality under Socialism* (London: Sage).
KÖNIG, W., LÜTTINGER, P., and MÜLLER, W. (1988), 'A Comparative Analysis of the Development and Structure of Educational Systems', CASMIN Working Paper **12**: University of Mannheim.
KORALEWICZ-ZEBIK, J. (1984), 'The Perception of Inequality in Poland 1956–1980', *Sociology* **18**: 225–38.

KURZ, K., and MÜLLER, W. (1987), 'Class Mobility in the Industrial World', *Annual Review of Sociology* **13**: 417–42.

LAMONT, J. (1994), 'The Concept of Desert in Distributive Justice', *Philosophical Quarterly* **44**: 45–64.

LAMPARD, R. (1996), 'Might Britain Be a Meritocracy? A Comment on Saunders', *Sociology* **30**: 387–93.

LANE, D. (1976), *The Socialist Industrial State* (London: Allen & Unwin).

——(1982), *The End of Social Inequality?* (London: Allen & Unwin).

LEE, D., MARSDEN, D., RICKMAN, P., and DUNCOMBE, J. (1990), *Scheming for Youth: A Study of YTS in the Enterprise Culture*, (Milton Keynes: Open University Press).

LIPSET, S. M., and ZETTERBERG, H. L. (1959), 'Social Mobility in Industrial Societies', in S. M. Lipset and R. Bendix (eds.), *Social Mobility in Industrial Society* (Berkeley: University of California Press), 11–75.

LOGAN, J. A. (1983), 'A Multivariate Model for Mobility Tables', *American Journal of Sociology* **89**: 324–49.

LUKES, S. (1985), *Marxism and Morality* (Oxford: Clarendon Press).

MAHLER, V. A. (1989), 'Income Distribution Within Nations: Problems of Cross-National Comparison', *Comparative Political Studies* **22**: 3–32.

MARSHALL, G. (1986), 'The Workplace Culture of a Licensed Restaurant', *Theory, Culture and Society* **3**: 33–47.

——(1988), 'Classes in Britain: Official and Marxist', *European Sociological Review* **4**: 141–54.

——(1990), *In Praise of Sociology* (London: Unwin Hyman).

——(1991), 'In Defence of Class Analysis: A Comment on R. E. Pahl', *International Journal of Urban and Regional Research* **15**: 114–18.

——(1996), 'Was Communism Good for Social Justice? A Comparison of the Two Germanies', *British Journal of Sociology* **47**: 397–420.

——ROBERTS, S., and BURGOYNE, C. (1996), 'Social Class and Underclass in Britain and the USA', *British Journal of Sociology* **47**: 22–44.

————BURGOYNE, C., SWIFT, A., and ROUTH, D. (1995), 'Class, Gender, and the Asymmetry Hypothesis', *European Sociological Review* **11**: 1–15.

——and ROSE, D. (1990), 'Out-classed by Our Critics?', *Sociology* **24**: 255–67.

——ROSE, D., NEWBY, H., and VOGLER, C. (1988), *Social Class in Modern Britain* (London: Hutchinson).

——and SWIFT, A. (1993), 'Social Class and Social Justice', *British Journal of Sociology* **44**: 187–211.

————(1996), 'Merit and Mobility: A Reply to Peter Saunders', *Sociology* **30**: 375–86.

——SYDORENKO, S., and ROBERTS, S. (1995), 'Intergenerational Social Mobility in Communist Russia', *Work, Employment and Society* **9**: 1–27.

MARTIN, R., and WALLACE, J. (1984), *Working Women in Recession* (Oxford: Oxford University Press).

MATTHEWS, M. (1972), *Class and Society in Soviet Russia* (London: Allen Lane).

MEIER, A. (1989), 'Universals and Particularities of Socialist Educational Systems: The Transition from School to Work in the German Democratic

Republic and the Soviet Union', in M. Kohn (ed.), *Cross-National Research in Sociology* (Newbury Park: Sage), 167–84.

MESA-LAGO, C. (ed.) (1971), *Revolutionary Change in Cuba* (Pittsburgh: University of Pittsburgh Press).

MILES, A. (1993), 'How Open Was Nineteenth-century British Society? Social Mobility and Equality of Opportunity, 1839–1914', in A. Miles and D. Vincent (eds.), *Building European Society* (Manchester: Manchester University Press), 18–39.

MILLER, D. (1989), *Market, State and Community* (Oxford: Oxford University Press).

——(1991), 'Review Article: Recent Theories of Social Justice', *British Journal of Political Science* 21: 371–91.

——(1992a), 'Deserving Jobs', *Philosophical Quarterly* 42: 161–81.

——(1992b), 'Distributive Justice: What the People Think', *Ethics* 102: 555–93.

——(1996), 'Two Cheers for Meritocracy', *Journal of Political Philosophy* 4: 277–301.

——and WALZER, M. (eds.) (1995), *Justice, Pluralism and Equality* (Oxford: Oxford University Press).

MINER, J. B. (1957), *Intelligence in the United States* (New York: Springer).

MÜLLER, W., and KARLE, W. (1993), 'Social Selection in Educational Systems in Europe', *European Sociological Review* 9: 1–23.

——LÜTTINGER, P., KÖNIG, W., and KARLE, W. (1990), 'Class and Education in Industrial Nations', in M. Haller (ed.), *Class Structure in Europe* (Armonk, NY: M. E. Sharpe), 61–91.

MURGATROYD, L. (1984), 'Women, Men and the Social Grading of Occupations', *British Journal of Sociology* 35: 473–97.

MURPHY, J. (1981), 'Class Inequality in Education: Two Justifications, One Evaluation, but No Hard Evidence', *British Journal of Sociology* 32: 182–201.

——(1990), 'A Most Respectable Prejudice: Inequality in Educational Research and Policy', *British Journal of Sociology* 41: 29–54.

MURRAY, C. (1990) *The Emerging British Underclass* (London: Institute of Economic Affairs).

NAGEL, T. (1991), *Equality and Partiality* (Oxford: Oxford University Press).

NEWBY, H. (1977), *The Deferential Worker* (Harmondsworth: Penguin).

NICHOLAS MASCIE-TAYLOR, C. G. (1990), 'The Biology of Social Class', in Nicholas Mascie-Taylor (ed.), *Biosocial Aspects of Social Class* (Oxford: Oxford University Press), 117–42.

NOZICK, R. (1974), *Anarchy, State and Utopia* (Oxford: Blackwell).

PAHL, R. E. (1989), 'Is the Emperor Naked? Some Questions on the Adequacy of Sociological Theory in Urban and Regional Research', *International Journal of Urban and Regional Research* 13: 709–20.

——(1993), 'Does Class Analysis Without Class Theory Have a Promising Future? A Reply to Goldthorpe and Marshall', *Sociology* 27: 253–8.

PARISH, W. L. (1981), 'Egalitarianism in Chinese Society', *Problems of Communism* 30: 37–53.

PARSONS, T. (1940), 'An Analytical Approach to the Theory of Social Stratification', repr. in Parsons, *Essays in Sociological Theory* (New York: Free Press, 1954), 69–88.

——(1953), 'A Revised Analytical Approach to the Theory of Social Stratification', in Parsons, *Essays in Sociological Theory* (New York: Free Press, 1954), 386–439.

——(1961), 'The School Class as a Social System: Some of Its Functions in American Society', in A. H. Halsey, J. Floud, and C. A. Anderson (eds.), *Education, Economy and Society* (New York: Free Press), 434–55.

——(1971), *The System of Modern Societies* (Englewood Cliffs, NJ: Prentice-Hall).

PAYNE, G. (1987a), *Mobility and Change in Modern Society* (London: Macmillan).

——(1987b), *Employment and Opportunity* (London: Macmillan).

——and ABBOTT, P. (eds.) (1990), *The Social Mobility of Women* (Bristol, Pa.: Falmer).

PENN, R. (1981), 'The Nuffield Class Categorization', *Sociology* **15**: 265–71.

PHELPS BROWN, H. (1988), *Egalitarianism and the Generation of Inequality* (Oxford: Clarendon Press).

RAWLS, J. (1971), *A Theory of Justice* (Cambridge, Mass.: Harvard University Press).

REHBERG, R. A., and ROSENTHAL, E. R. (1978), *Class and Merit in the American High School* (New York: Longman).

REID, I. (1989), *Social Class Differences in Britain* (London: Fontana).

RILEY, J. G. (1976), 'Information, Screening and Human Capital', *American Economic Review* **66**: 254–60.

ROBERTS, H., and BARKER, R. (1986), *The Social Classification of Women* (London: Social Statistics Research Unit, City University).

ROBERTS, S., and MARSHALL, G. (1995), 'Intergenerational Class Processes and the Asymmetry Hypothesis', *Sociology* **29**: 43–58.

ROGOVIN, V. Z. (1989 [1986]), 'Social Justice and the Socialist Distribution of Vital Goods', in M. Yanowitch (ed.), *New Directions in Soviet Social Thought* (London: M. E. Sharpe), 133–54.

ROLLER, E. (1994), 'Ideological Basis of the Market Economy: Attitudes Toward Distribution Principles and the Role of Government in Western and Eastern Germany', *European Sociological Review* **10**: 105–17.

ROSE, M. (1985), *Re-working the Work Ethic* (London: Batsford).

——(1988), 'Attachment to Work and Social Values', in D. Gallie (ed.), *Employment in Britain* (Oxford: Basil Blackwell), 128–56.

RUBINSTEIN, W. D. (1986), *Wealth and Inequality in Britain* (London: Faber & Faber).

RUTKEVICH, M. N., and FILIPPOV, F. R. (1973), 'Principles of the Marxist Approach to Social Structure and Social Mobility', in M. Yanowitch and W. A. Fisher (eds.), *Social Stratification and Mobility in the USSR* (White Plains, NY: International Arts & Sciences Press), 229–40.

SADURSKI, W. (1985), *Giving Desert Its Due* (Dordrecht: Reidel).

SAUNDERS, P. (1989), 'Left Write in Sociology', *Network* **44**: 3–4.

SAUNDERS, P. (1990), *Social Class and Stratification* (London: Routledge).
——(1994), 'Is Britain a Meritocracy?', in R. M. Blackburn (ed.), *Social Inequality in a Changing World* (Cambridge: Faculty of Social and Political Sciences).
——(1995), 'Might Britain Be a Meritocracy?', *Sociology* **29**: 23–41.
SAVAGE, M., BARLOW, J., DICKENS, P., and FIELDING, T. (1992), *Property, Bureaucracy and Culture* (London: Routledge).
SCANLON, T. (1995), 'The Significance of Choice', in S. Darwall (ed.), *Equal Freedom* (Ann Arbor: University of Michigan Press), 39–104.
SCASE, R. (1992), *Class* (Buckingham: Open University Press).
SCHEFFLER, S. (1992), 'Responsibility, Reactive Attitudes and Liberalism in Philosophy and Politics', *Philosophy and Public Affairs* **21**: 299–323.
SCHERER, K. S. (ed.) (1992), *Justice: Interdisciplinary Perspectives* (Cambridge: Cambridge University Press).
SCOTT, J. (1982), *The Upper Classes* (London: Macmillan).
——(1991), *Who Rules Britain?* (Cambridge: Polity).
——(1994), 'Class Analysis: Back to the Future', *Sociology* **28**: 933–42.
SEN, A. (1995), 'Equality of What?', in S. Darwall (ed.), *Equal Freedom* (Ann Arbor: University of Michigan Press), 307–30.
SHAVIT, Y., and KRAUS, V. (1990), 'Educational Transitions in Israel: A Test of the Industrialization and Credentialism Hypotheses', *Sociology of Education* **63**: 133–41.
SHER, G. (1987), *Desert* (Princeton: Princeton University Press).
SOLTAN, K. E. (1982), 'Empirical Studies of Distributive Justice', *Ethics* **92**: 673–91.
SØRENSEN, A. (1994), 'Women, Family and Class', *Annual Review of Sociology* **20**: 27–47.
SØRENSEN, J. B. (1992), 'Locating Class Cleavages in Inter-generational Mobility: Cross-national Commonalities and Variations in Mobility Patterns', *European Sociological Review* **8**: 267–81.
SPENCE, M. (1973), 'Job Market Signalling', *Quarterly Journal of Economics* **87**: 355–74.
STALIN, I. V. (1955), 'Talk with Emil Ludwig', in *Collected Works*, xiii (Moscow: Foreign Languages Publishing House).
SUTHERLAND, G. (1984), *Ability, Merit and Measurement: Mental Testing and English Education 1880–1940* (Oxford: Clarendon Press).
SVALLFORS, S. (1995), 'Institutions and the Comparative Study of Beliefs and Justice', in Svallfors (ed.), *In the Eye of the Beholder* (Umeå: Impello Saljsupport), 116–26.
SWIFT, A. (1995), 'The Sociology of Complex Equality', in D. Miller and M. Walzer (eds.), *Pluralism, Justice and Equality* (Oxford: Oxford University Press), 253–80.
——MARSHALL, G., BURGOYNE, C., and ROUTH, D. (1995), 'Distributive Justice: Does it Matter What the People Think?', in J. R. Kluegel, D. S. Mason, and B. Wegener (eds.), *Social Justice and Political Change* (New York: Aldine de Gruyter), 15–47.

TREIMAN, D. J. (1970), 'Industrialisation and Social Stratification', in E. O. Laumann (ed.), *Social Stratification: Research and Theory for the 1970s* (Indianapolis: Bobbs Merrill), 207–34.

——and GANZEBOOM, H. B. G. (1990), 'Cross-National Comparative Status-Attainment Research', *Research in Social Stratification and Mobility* **9**: 105–27.

——and TERRELL, K. (1975), 'The Process of Status Attainment in the United States and Great Britain', *American Journal of Sociology* **81**: 563–83.

——and YIP, K.-B. (1989), 'Educational and Occupational Attainment in 21 Countries', in M. L. Kohn (ed.), *Cross-National Research in Sociology* (London: Sage), 373–94.

TURNER, B. S. (1986), *Equality* (London: Tavistock).

VALENTINE, C. (1968), *Culture and Poverty* (Chicago: University of Chicago Press).

VAN PARIJS, P. (1993), 'Rawlsians, Christians and Patriots: Maximin Justice and Individual Ethics', *European Journal of Philosophy* **1**: 309–42.

WADSWORTH, M. E. J. (1991), *The Imprint of Time* (Oxford: Clarendon Press).

WALLACE, R. J. (1994), *Responsibility and the Moral Sentiments* (London: Harvard University Press).

WALSH, A. (1990), *Statistics for the Social Sciences* (New York: Harper & Row).

WALSTER, E., WALSTER, G. W., and BERSCHEID, E. (1978), *Equity: Theory and Research* (Boston: Allyn & Bacon).

WALZER, M. (1983), *Spheres of Justice* (Oxford: Martin Robertson).

WEAKLIEM, D., McQUILLAN, J., and SCHAUER, T. (1995), 'Toward Meritocracy? Changing Social-Class Differences in Intellectual Ability', *Sociology of Education* **68**: 271–86.

WEBER, M. (1968 [1922]), *Economy and Society* (New York: Bedminster Press).

WERTHEIMER, A. (1983), 'Jobs, Qualifications and Preferences', *Ethics* **94**: 99–112.

WESOŁOWSKI, W. (1988), 'Does Socialist Stratification Exist?', The Fifth Fuller Bequest Lecture (Colchester: University of Essex).

——and MACH, B. W. (1986), 'Unfulfilled Systemic Functions of Social Mobility, 1: A Theoretical Scheme', *International Sociology* **1**: 19–35.

WESTERGAARD, J. (1995), *Who Gets What? The Hardening of Class Inequality in the Late Twentieth Century* (Cambridge: Polity Press).

WITTE, J. C., and KALLEBERG, A. (1995), 'Matching Training and Jobs: The Fit Between Vocational Education and Employment in the German Labour Market', *European Sociological Review* **11**: 293–17.

WONG, R. S.-K., (1992), 'Vertical and Nonvertical Effects in Class Mobility: Cross-National Variations', *American Sociological Review* **57**: 396–410.

WOOLDRIDGE, A. (1994), *Measuring the Mind: Education and Psychology in England, c.1860–c.1990* (Cambridge: Cambridge University Press).

——(1995), *Meritocracy and the 'Classless Society'* (London: Social Market Foundation).

WRIGHT, E. O. (1980), 'Varieties of Marxist Conceptions of Class Structure', *Politics and Society* **9**: 299–322.

XIE, Y. (1992), 'The Log-Multiplicative Layer Effect Model for Comparing Mobility Tables', *American Sociological Review* **57**: 380–95.

YAMAGUCHI, K. (1982), 'The Structure of Intergenerational Occupational Mobility. Generality and Specificity in Resources, Channels, and Barriers', *American Journal of Sociology* **88**: 718–45.

YOUNG, M. (1958), *The Rise of the Meritocracy 1870–2033* (Harmondsworth: Penguin).

ZAITCHIK, A. (1977), 'On Deserving to Deserve', *Philosophy and Public Affairs* **6**: 370–88.

INDEX